The Tiwanaku: Portrait of an Andean Civilization

The Peoples of America

General editors
Alan Kolata and Dean Snow

This series is about the native peoples and civilizations of the Americas, from their origins in ancient times to the present day. Drawing on archaeological, historical, and anthropological evidence, each volume presents a fresh and absorbing account of a group's culture, society, and history.

Accessible and scholarly, and well illustrated with maps and photographs, the volumes of *The Peoples of America* will together provide a comprehensive and vivid picture of the character and variety of the societies of the American past.

Published

The Tiwanaku: Portrait of an Andean Civilization
Alan Kolata

In preparation

The Aztecs
Michael E. Smith

The Cheyenne
John Moore

The Incas
Terence N. D'Altroy

The Iroquois
Dean Snow

The Moche
Garth Bawden

The Nascas
D. M. Brown and Helaine Silverman

The Navajo
Alan Downer

The Timucua
Jerald T. Milanich and Kathleen A. Deagan

The Tiwanaku: Portrait of an Andean Civilization

Alan Kolata

BLACKWELL

Cambridge MA & Oxford UK

First published 1993

Blackwell Publishers
238 Main Street
Cambridge, Massachusetts 02142,
USA

108 Cowley Road
Oxford OX4 1JF,
UK

Library of Congress Cataloging-in-Publication Data

Kolata, Alan L.
    The Tiwanaku: portrait of an Andean civilization / Alan Kolata.
            p.   cm. — (The Peoples of America)
    Includes bibliographical references and index.
            ISBN 1–55786–183–8
    1. Tiahuanaco culture. 2. Indians of South America—Andes Region—
History. 3. Indians of South America—Andes Region—Antiquities. 4. Andes
        Region—Antiquities. I. Title. II. Series.
            F3319.1.T55K64   1993
                984'.12—dc20   92–39248
                                                                                CIP

British Library Cataloguing in Publication Data

A CIP catalogue record for this book is available from the British Library.

Typeset in 10 on 12 pt Sabon
by Graphicraft Typesetters Ltd., Hong Kong
Printed in the United States of America

This book is printed on acid-free paper

Contents

List of Figures vii

Acknowledgments xv

1 The Myth of Tiwanaku 1

The Native Myths 1
The Modern Mythographers 10
Myth, History, and the People of Tiwanaku 18

2 The Sources 21

The Ethnohistoric Evidence 22
The Archaeological Evidence 27
The Linguistic and Ethnographic Evidence 32
The Paleoecological Evidence 36

3 The Natural and Social Setting 38

Ecology and Economy 51

4 Tiwanaku Emergence 56

Tiwanaku Precursors 59
Tiwanaku Emergence 81

5 Taypikala: The City at the Center 87

Sacred Geography and Urban Design 90
Tiwanaku's Civic-Ceremonial Core 103
Tiwanaku's Social Map 172

6   Metropole and Hinterland   177

    Local Environment   179
    Tiwanaku's Local Economy   181
    The Technology of Raised Field Agriculture   183
    Carrying Capacity, Population, and Food Supply   199
    The Social Organization of Agricultural Production   205
    Herders and Fishers   231
    Political Economy and the Social Nature of Tiwanaku   240

7   The Empire Expands   243

    Ideology and Imperialism in the Titicaca Basin   246
    The *Yungas* Zones: Colonial Agricultural Provinces   250
    Caravans, Clients, and the Far Periphery   272

8   The Decline and Fall of Tiwanaku   282

    Climate and Collapse   284
    Vulnerability of Tiwanaku Agricultural Systems   291
    The Evidence of Changing Settlement Patterns   295
    The Aftermath of Collapse   298

Bibliography   303
Index   313

List of Figures and Tables

Figures

Figure 1.1   The four quarters of the Inca empire: Cuntisuyu, Chinchaysuyu, Antisuyu, and Collasuyu.   2

Figure 1.2   The two conceptual halves of the sixteenth-century Aymara world: *Urcosuyu* to the west of Lake Titicaca and *Umasuyu* to the east.   9

Figure 1.3   The diffusion of Tiwanaku civilization throughout the Americas according to Arthur Posnansky.   14

Figure 1.4   The "Gateway of the Sun" at Tiwanaku.   17

Figure 2.1   The Lupaqa Kingdom and its seven principal towns, or *cabeceras*, located along the western shore of Lake Titicaca.   24

Figure 2.2   Dual political organization of the Lupaqa Kingdom.   25

Figure 2.3   Late nineteenth-century map of Tiwanaku's ruins by Ephraim Squier.   28

Figure 2.4   Chronological chart for the south-central Andes, from the Initial Period to the Late Horizon [Inca conquest].   31

Figure 2.5   Approximate geographic distribution of Aymara and Quechua languages in the south-central Andes (ca. 1532).   35

Figure 3.1   Cross-section illustrating the five principal physiographic divisions of the Andean world: desert coast, *sierra*, *altiplano*, *yungas*, and *selva* (or tropical forest).   40

Figure 3.2   A schematic cross-section of the Pacific coast's physiography and ocean current system.   42

Figure 3.3   The Bolivian *altiplano*, from Lake Titicaca to Lake Poopó.   44

Figure 4.1   The distribution of Wankarani sites north and northeast of Lake Poopó.   60

Figure 4.2   An example of a Wankarani stone effigy llama head.   61

Figure 4.3   Reconstruction of a Wankarani village.   62

Figure 4.4a   A map of structures excavated at Chiripa.   64

Figure 4.4b   Plan of House 2 at Chiripa.   65

Figure 4.5   An idealized reconstruction of the Chiripa Mound.   66

Figure 4.6   Representative pottery of Chiripa.   67

Figure 4.7a–b   Two examples of Chiripa stone sculpture executed in the Yaya-Mama style.   68

Figure 4.8   A plan of Enclosure 2 at Pukara.   71

Figure 4.9   Front and back views of a fragment of a Pukara-style stela, from Wiraqocha Orqo.   72

Figure 4.10   Three faces of the upper portion of a Pukara-style stela, from Wiraqocha Orqo.   72

Figure 4.11   A fragment from a Pukara incised ceramic bowl.   73

Figure 4.12   Two polychrome incised ceramic trumpets from Pukara.   74

Figure 4.13   Fragments from three Pukara ceramic vessels.   75

Figure 4.14   Pukara-style textile with frog iconography from the site of Alto Ramirez in the Azapa Valley, Chile.   77

Figure 4.15   Rollout drawing of the Yaya-Mama stela from Taraco, Peru.   80

Figure 5.1   Oblique, low altitude aerial photograph of the central civic-ceremonial precinct at Tiwanaku, looking east.   91

Figure 5.2   High altitude aerial photograph of Tiwanaku.   94

Figure 5.3   A map of Tiwanaku's central ceremonial
architecture.   96

Figure 5.4   The distribution of Tiwanaku regional
centers around the southern shore of Lake Titicaca.   103

Figure 5.5a   Map of the Akapana pyramid according to
Posnansky.   105

Figure 5.5b   Idealized reconstruction of the Akapana
pyramid, as it would have been viewed from the north-east.   106

Figure 5.6   A section of the first terrace on the east
side of Akapana, exposed during the 1976 excavations
directed by Gregorio Cordero Miranda (INAR).   107

Figure 5.7   Upper terraces on the west side of Akapana.   107

Figure 5.8   Carved stone panel with a front-faced puma
design from Tiwanaku.   108

Figure 5.9   A view of the Quimsachata mountain range,
looking southward.   110

Figure 5.10   One of the stone-lined subterranean drains
located on the summit of Akapana.   112

Figure 5.11   *In-situ* copper clamp, joining individual stone
blocks of Akapana's drainage network.   113

Figure 5.12   Exterior stone drain tenoned into the vertical
face of an upper terrace at Akapana.   114

Figure 5.13   A drainage tunnel located in the basal terrace
of Akapana.   115

Figure 5.14a   A plan of the residences located on the
summit of Akapana (north-east sector).   118

Figure 5.14b   Six of the Akapana summit structures
exposed during 1988 and 1989 excavations.   119

Figure 5.15a–b   Side and front views of a Tiwanaku
incensario, or incense burner, in the form of a puma,
recovered during 1987 excavations at Lukurmata.   120

Figure 5.16   Miniature copper fox figurine found in
an offering in Room 11, on the summit of Akapana.   121

Figure 5.17   One of the human dedicatory burials
uncovered at the base of Akapana.   122

Figure 5.18   The remains of an infant, approximately two years old, buried face down at the base of Akapana.   123

Figure 5.19   A small section of the spectacular ceramic offering on a lower terrace of the Akapana.   124

Figure 5.20   An example of an intact *kero*, one of the vessel forms most frequently encountered in the Akapana ceramic offering.   125

Figure 5.21   A *kero* illustrating a stylized human trophy head.   126

Figure 5.22   A carved stone *chachapuma* holding a trophy head.   127

Figure 5.23   The basalt sculpture of a *chachapuma*, as it was being uncovered at the base of Akapana's western staircase during 1989 excavations.   128

Figure 5.24   Three views of the basalt *chachapuma* found at the base of the Akapana.   129

Figure 5.25   The Puma Punku temple at Tiwanaku, exposed in 1978 by the Bolivian archaeologist Gregorio Cordero Miranda (INAR).   130

Figure 5.26   View of the civic-ceremonial sector at Lukurmata, a Tiwanaku regional center located on the shores of Lake Titicaca.   131

Figure 5.27   Map of Lukurmata illustrating the civic-ceremonial, residential, and agricultural sectors of the city.   132

Figure 5.28   Dog burial found *in-situ* in front of a drainage tunnel at the base of Akapana, during 1988 excavations.   133

Figure 5.29   A view of the Semi-subterranean Temple and the Kalasasaya, looking north from the top of Akapana.   136

Figure 5.30   The west wall of the Semi-subterranean Temple (foreground), and the monolithic eastern staircase of the Kalasasaya framing a monumental stone sculpture, the Ponce Monolith.   137

Figure 5.31   One of the carved stone tenon-heads flanking the interior of the Semi-subterranean Temple.   138

Figure 5.32   The Bennett Stela as it was being moved
from Tiwanaku to the Miraflores Museum in La Paz.   139

Figure 5.33a   A rollout drawing of the iconography on all
four sides of the Bennett Stela.   140

Figure 5.33b   Detail of a llama image carved on the
Bennett Stela.   140

Figure 5.34   The Ponce Stela, located in the central sunken
court of Kalasasaya.   144

Figure 5.35a–b   Two sculptured stone portrait heads of the
Tiwanaku elite, depicted chewing coca.   146

Figure 5.36a   Map of the Putuni complex.   150

Figure 5.36b   Map of the Palace of the Multicolored
Rooms within the Putuni complex.   151

Figure 5.37   A stone architrave, with opposed pumas
carved in low relief.   153

Figure 5.38   A ceramic representation of a Tiwanaku house.   154

Figure 5.39   Monumental sandstone and andesite drainage
canals underneath the Putuni complex.   155

Figure 5.40   Repoussé miniature gold mask from the
Putuni shaft-and-chamber tomb.   157

Figure 5.41   Copper disc mirror with a lead flask adhered
to its surface, and various metal implements from the
Putuni shaft-and-chamber tomb.   158

Figure 5.42   One of the room-like niches located on the
perimeter of the Putuni platform.   161

Figure 5.43   Stone foundations of a Tiwanaku V period
residence in the Akapana East sector, outside of Tiwanaku's
civic-ceremonial core.   165

Figure 5.44   A pyroengraved llama bone recovered during
the excavation of a domestic structure in the Akapana
East sector of Tiwanaku.   167

Figure 5.45   Terracotta signet ring from one of
Tiwanaku's residential structures in the Akapana East
sector of Tiwanaku.   168

Figure 5.46   View of excavations in a midden associated
with the massive Chijijawira ceramic workshop on the far
eastern periphery of Tiwanaku.   171

Figure 6.1   Map of known raised field distribution around
Lake Titicaca.   178

Figure 6.2   Map of Tiwanaku and adjacent valleys.   179

Figure 6.3   A plan of a representative segment of a raised
field system from the Lakaya sector of the Pampa Koani.   184

Figure 6.4   Internal structure of a raised field.   184

Figure 6.5   Native farmers using the *chakitaklla*, or
traditional Andean foot plow.   186

Figure 6.6   Vectors of heat storage and transfer in
Tiwanaku raised fields in the Titicaca Basin.   189

Figure 6.7   Raised planting platforms at Lakaya, with
water-filled canals on either side.   190

Figure 6.8   Aerial photograph of the southern portions of
the Pampa Koani raised field study area.   191

Figure 6.9   Experimental raised fields in full bloom at
Lakaya in 1988.   192

Figure 6.10   Map of Tiwanaku administrative and ritual
platform mound clusters on the Pampa Koani.   220

Figure 6.11   Graphic representation of Tiwanaku's
hierarchical settlement network in the Pampa Koani region
during Tiwanaku IV-V times.   223

Figure 6.12   The remains of a massive earthen levee along
the Río Catari.   225

Figure 6.13   Map of the investigated portions of the
Tiwanaku Valley canal.   226

Figure 6.14   Cobblestone exterior retaining wall from an
aqueduct at Lukurmata.   227

Figure 6.15   One of the aqueducts at Pajchiri.   229

Figure 6.16   Herd of llamas grazing near the shore of
Lake Titicaca.   236

Figure 7.1   Map of the southern Andean highlands.   244

Figure 7.2   The "Thunderbolt Stela," part of a larger stela
originally from the Pukara site of Arapa near Puno on the
northern shore of Lake Titicaca.   249

Figure 7.3   Topographic map of the Moquegua Valley in
southern Peru.   253

Figure 7.4   Map of the Tiwanaku site group at Omo,
located along the Osmore River in the Moquegua Valley.   254

Figure 7.5   Aerial photograph of the extensive M10
settlement at Omo.   257

Figure 7.6   Plan of the Tiwanaku ceremonial complex at
the Omo site of M10, composed of three plaza groups.   258

Figure 7.7   An example of a ceramic vessel produced as a
portrait head of a Tiwanaku elite chewing coca.   260

Figure 7.8   Reconstruction of a large fermentation
vessel recovered at Omo that was probably used to brew
alcoholic beverages, such as maize beer.   261

Figures 7.9a–b   Two examples of fine ceramic portrait
vessels from Tiwanaku that were used for consuming
alcohol.   262

Figure 7.10   Fragment of a fine Tiwanaku tapestry,
probably from the north coast of Chile.   264

Figure 7.11   An example of the distinctive four-pointed
Tiwanaku hats, which are usually recovered from tombs
of local elites on the Peruvian and Chilean coast.   265

Figure 7.12   Reconstruction of the administrative and
ceremonial complex from the M10 site at Omo.   266

Figure 7.13   Map of key areas of Tiwanaku exchange and
interaction in the south-central Andes.   273

Figure 7.14   Map indicating the location of the Coyo
cemetery within the San Pedro Atacama oasis.   276

Figure 7.15a   Tiwanaku tapestry tunic from the Coyo
Oriental cemetary, San Pedro de Atacama, Chile.   278

Figure 7.15b   Detail of tunic illustrating repeated motif
of running birdheaded figures arranged in geometric panels.   278

Figure 8.1   Map of the south-central Andes.   286

Figures 8.2a–c   Three graphs illustrating the cumulative
annual snow layer deposits on the Quelccaya ice cap from
A.D. 800 to 1410.   288

Figure 8.3a   Time-dependent graph of changes in snow
layer accumulation on the Quelccaya ice cap.   289

Figure 8.3b   Nine-year moving average of ice cap
thickness values, illustrating the dramatic post-A.D. 1000
decline in mean rainfall levels in the south-central Andes.   290

Figure 8.4   Pollen percentage diagram for a Lake Titicaca
sediment core taken near the site of Lukurmata.   291

Tables

Table 3.1   Temperature, precipitation, and altitude ranges
for the principal native Andean crops.   52

Table 6.1   Potato yield of rehabilitated raised fields in the
Pampa Koani.   193

Table 6.2   Potato yield of traditional agriculture lacking
commercial fertilizers.   195

Table 6.3   Potato yield of improved agriculture with
commercial fertilizers (N, P, K).   196

Table 6.4   Potato yields on rehabilitated raised fields in
Huatta, Peru.   197

Table 6.5   Carrying capacity estimates for Tiwanaku
sustaining area assuming 100 percent use of raised fields.   202

Table 6.6   Carrying capacity estimates for Tiwanaku
sustaining area assuming 75 percent use of raised fields.   203

Acknowledgments

I have many special debts, personal and professional, that I must acknowledge here. The first of these is to my wife, Anna, who tolerated endless, difficult separations while the research described in this book was in progress. Without her forbearance and humor, many key discoveries would have remained interred deep in the ground of Tiwanaku. First Alice Kehoe, and later Michael Moseley, opened up the world of anthropology for me and provided invaluable basic training. In Bolivia, Carlos Ponce Sanginés invited me to begin work at Tiwanaku, never imagining, I am sure, to what lengths this would lead. He has been a constant source of support and intellectual encouragement. To him, I owe my entrée into Bolivian science and society, and I acknowledge him with gratitude for his interest in me and with deep admiration for his contributions to Andean archaeology. Lupe Andrade and her entire family adopted this wayward *gringo* from the first day he spilled out onto the frigid tarmac of La Paz's astonishing airport in 1978. They have been hosts, political consultants, teachers, saviors (on more than one occasion), but, most of all, the truest friends one could ever have. During his tenure as U.S. ambassador to Boliva, Robert Gelbard and his family fanatically encouraged and, at times, participated in the research at many critical junctures. When the project was imperiled by dwindling funds, Bob Gelbard came to the rescue, ferreting out funding for the 1991 field season.

I must, of course, acknowledge the financial sources that underwrote, and continues to underwrite, the research program. I have received generous grants in support of the research from the National Endowment for the Humanities, the National Science Foundation, the Inter-American Foundation, the Heinz Charitable Trust, the

University of Chicago, Tesoro Petroleum Corporation, Compañía Minera del Sur (Bolivia), and Occidental Petroleum Corporation. In particular, Dr. Robert V. West, Jr., former chairman and CEO of Tesoro Petroleum Corporation has supported the project financially from its modest inception in 1978. Kevin Healy of the Inter-American Foundation likewise stands as one of our staunchest supporters in Bolivia and Washington. To all of these institutions and individuals, I owe a deep debt of gratitude for their tangible support and confidence in the research program at Tiwanaku and in its hinterland.

First-class graduate students are the life's blood of any major archaeological project. I have been blessed with my share of them at the University of Chicago, and from other splendid institutions as well. Their dedicated work underlies most of my interpretations and speculations regarding the people of Tiwanaku in this book. I am sure they will vehemently disagree with some, if not all of what I have claimed about Tiwanaku. I hope this book will stimulate them to go out and prove me wrong! In particular, I wish to mention my two dedicated assistants, Nicole Couture and Michele Warren who researched and edited this manuscript with consummate artistry, care, and compassion for its author. Senior staff members of the research team, Charles Ortloff, Michael Binford, Mark Brenner, Barbara Leyden, Philip Moore, and Charles Stanish contributed their expertise to the design and execution of the work, and our results are a testament to their scientific integrity and formidable analytical skills.

A North American anthropologist in a native society is not always a welcome visitor. The anthropological literature prior to the 1960s consistently emphasized the Aymara's hostility to foreigners: there, they are routinely portrayed as violent, irresponsible, treacherous, and ill-humored. These are not the Aymara I know. After some 15 years of living in their villages, and learning of their lives, I have felt warmly welcomed and accepted among their families. Above all, I feel privileged to have been given permission to sleep in their farm houses, to work side-by-side in their fields, and to venture out to the sacred *huacas* with my Aymara friends. This book is about their history and their culture. Without their active collaboration and intense interest in their own cultural heritage, this book would never have been written. My most profound debt is to the many Aymara with whom I have worked. I cannot name them all here individually, but the people of the villages of Tiwanaku, Lukurmata, Chojasivi, Lakaya, Lillimani, Quiripujo, Chokara, Korila, Huacullani, Khonko Wankané, Chambi Grande, Chambi Chico, Wankollo, Huaraya, Achuta Grande, Kasa Achuta, Pillapi, Guaqui, Yanarico, Patarani, Andamarca, Yanamani, Pircuta, Corpa, Sullcata, Lacuyo, Kusijata and Copajira are all involved, to various degrees, in the work and life of the research. I thank them all.

Finally, I must acknowledge my profound debt and deepest appreciation for my two *compadres*, Oswaldo Rivera of La Paz and Cesar Callisaya of Tiwanaku. Oswaldo has been my *compañero* in the field from the first day I came to Bolivia (he, quite literally, met me at the airport). Co-director of every project I have undertaken in Bolivia, he has been guiding me ever since I came to his beautiful country. I cannot express all of the personal and professional debts I have accrued with Oswaldo over the past years of intense companionship: Suffice it to say that they can never be adequately repaid. Cesar acts as the foreman and leader of all our skilled Aymara workmen. The respect for him within his community is palpable, impressive, and true. Anything I have learned about his remarkable people, has come through Cesar and his family. Without him the research could not function, but, more importantly, the transformations in my life wrought by living in Cesar's house in Tiwanaku, celebrating births, commemorating deaths, and praying to the mountain gods would never have happened. And I would be a much poorer soul for that. Both Oswaldo and Cesar were present as key actors in one of the most significant events in the lives of myself and my wife: the baptism of our daughter Justine on August 18, 1990, in the colonial church of Tiwanaku and at the ancient, sacred springs of Choquepajcha. Padre Claudio Patty, Catholic priest and an Aymara from the community of Achuta Grande, officiated at the service and gave Justine her Aymara name, Wara. I hope that Wara, too, will have the same intense privilege that my wife and I have had of living in Bolivia and knowing the joy of sharing her life with the Aymara. I know that her godparents are anxiously waiting for her return to Tiwanaku, her second home.

For Anna

1

The Myth of Tiwanaku

The Native Myths

In the year 1549, Pedro de Cieza de León, Spanish conquistador and self-acclaimed "first chronicler of the Indies," journeyed from the newly founded city of Lima on the Pacific coast of Peru into the rugged, mountainous landscapes of the Andean highlands. That year he followed the tortuous Huarochirí road eastward into some of the richest provinces of what was only 20 years before the heartland of the Inca empire, the most powerful native state ever to emerge in the Western Hemisphere. Cieza de León hurried through the shattered, desolate ruins of towns destroyed by the recently ended wars of conquest, and depopulated by foreign pandemic diseases and the ceaseless demands for labor that was to be the legacy of the new European conquerors. His quest now was not to organize new military ventures, but to continue work on a laboriously compiled chronicle of the history of Peru begun some 15 years before upon his arrival in the New World.

It was Cieza's intent to travel southward from Cuzco, the old capital of the Inca empire, into that area of the Inca's domain that was called Collasuyu (Figure 1.1). Collasuyu contained some of the most dramatic and economically productive landscapes in the Andes, and, as Cieza commented, encompassed an area so large that it supported the densest native populations in the "Indies." In this quarter of the realm lay the great lake of Chucuito, or Titicaca as it is called today, the largest body of water in the South American highlands. Here too, near the small village of Tiwanaku on the southern shores of this enormous lake were the ruins of a once magnificent city that even then was attracting the intense interest and admiration of the new conquerors from Spain. Cieza de León was the first of these to incorporate his impressions of this city in ruins into his chronicle of the Indies,

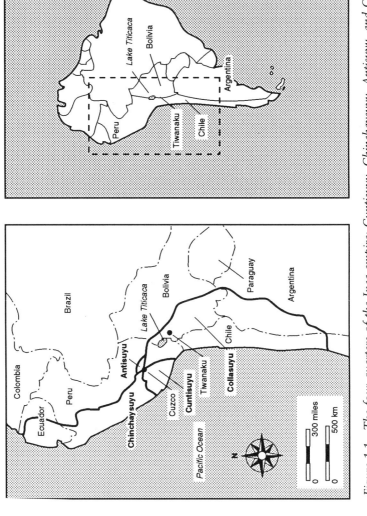

Figure 1.1　The four quarters of the Inca empire: Cuntisuyu, Chinchaysuyu, Antisuyu, and Collasuyu. The site of Tiwanaku is located in Collasuyu, the largest and southernmost quarter of the Inca realm. (Based on Moseley 1992: Figure 10).

bringing the settlement, for the first time, into written human history. But Tiwanaku had long been an important element of indigenous mythology and historical consciousness.

Cieza's observations convey a palpable sense of mystery and of puzzlement concerning the nature and historical role of the ruins that were to be recapitulated in the observations of many subsequent visitors to Tiwanaku.

Tihuanacu . . . is famous for its great buildings which, without question, are a remarkable thing to behold. Near the main dwellings is a man-made hill, built on great stone foundations. Beyond this hill are two stone idols of human size and shape, with the features beautifully carved, so much so that they seem the work of great artists or masters. They are so large that they seem small giants, and they are wearing long robes, different from the attire of the natives of these provinces. They seem to have an ornament on their heads.

Close by these stone statues there is another building, whose antiquity and this people's lack of writing is the reason there is no knowledge of who the people that built these great foundations and strongholds were, or how much time has gone by since then, for at present all one sees is a finely built wall which must have been constructed many ages ago. Some of these stones are very worn and wasted, and there are others so large that one wonders how human hands could have brought them to where they now stand . . . When one considers the work, I cannot understand or fathom what kind of instruments or tools were used to work them, for it is evident that before these huge stones were dressed and brought to perfection, they must have been much larger to have been left as we see them . . . A great stone idol, which they probably worshipped, stands a short distance away in a small recess. It is even said that beside this idol a quantity of gold was found, and around this shrine there were a number of other stones, large and small, dressed and carved . . . I would say that I consider this the oldest antiquity in all of Peru. It is believed that before the Incas reigned, long before, certain of these buildings existed, and I have heard Indians say that the Incas built their great edifices of Cuzco along the lines of the wall to be seen in this place. They go even further and say that the first Incas talked of setting up their court and capital here in Tihuanacu. . . . I asked the natives in the presence of Juan Vargas (who holds an encomienda over them) if these buildings had been built in the time of the Incas, and they laughed at the question, repeating what I have said, that they were built before they reigned, but that they could not state or affirm who built them. However, they had heard from their forefathers that all that are there appeared overnight. Because of this and because they also say that bearded men were seen on the island of Titicaca and that these people constructed the building of Viñaque, I say that it might have been before the Incas ruled, there were people

of parts in these kingdoms, come from no one knows where, who did
these things, and who, being few and the natives many, perished in the
wars. (Cieza de León [1553] 1959:282–3)

Cieza de León's account of Tiwanaku, despite its tantalizing brevity,
foreshadows many of the most important themes concerning native
constructions of the mythic-history of Tiwanaku that are elaborated
in later colonial period texts. Cieza, with remarkable prescience, considered Tiwanaku to be the "oldest antiquity in all Peru," constructed
and occupied well before the still-remembered Inca occupation of
Collasuyu. He based this conclusion on his own careful observations
of the state of ruination of the city's principal structures and the
accounts of the Indians themselves, who, as Cieza tells it, laughed at
the notion that these structures could have been built by the Inca.

But, more significantly, he recounts indigenous claims that the originators of the Inca dynasty first considered establishing their court
at Tiwanaku, and that subsequent Inca kings constructed the dynastic
capital of Cuzco according to an architectural model drawn from the
ancient ruins. These apparently simple assertions carry fundamental
implications regarding the ideological and historical place of Tiwanaku
in the development of native Andean civilizations. In constructing this
mythological association, the Inca lords of Cuzco were tracing their
dynastic heritage to a more ancient line of imperial rule. They were
claiming descent from the ancient kings of Tiwanaku and consciously
emulating the physical symbols of power vested in the monumental
architecture of that ancient city.

Cieza recapitulates a core element of this Inca mythography by
reporting that among the ruins of Tiwanaku "are the lodgings of the
Incas and the house where Manco Inca II, son of Huayna Capac [the
last independent ruler of the Incas], was born, and near them are two
tombs of native lords of this town, as tall as [they are] broad, square-
cornered towers, with their doorways to the rising sun" (Cieza de
León [1553] 1959:284). Here the Inca claim of dynastic association
with Tiwanaku is made most explicit: An heir to the *mascapaycha*,
the scarlet fringe symbolic of kingly office, was born at the site of
the ancient capital alongside the monumental burial mounds of the
Tiwanaku kings. In one symbolic master stroke, Manco Inca II, and
by extension the Inca imperial household, appropriated the majesty
and political legitimacy of a more ancient dynastic line, and established
his right to the mandate of empire by constructing a (presumptively
fictive) royal birthright.

But this passage also subtly implies that the royal mythographers
of the Inca attempted to evoke a more deeply nuanced and profoundly

meaningful association of their specific dynastic line with Tiwanaku than by asserting a simple historical fact: the birth of an heir apparent in that sacred city. Cieza, in a most casual fashion, notes that the native Tiwanaku lords' sepulchral towers possessed doorways that face the rising sun. This seemingly prosaic reference to the spatial orientation of mortuary architecture symbolically associates the Tiwanaku dynasty directly with the forces of nature, specifically with the apparent cyclical passage of the sun through the heavens. This symbolism links the human social order of ancient Tiwanaku, and most explicitly the ruling hierarchy, with the natural order of the cosmos. Tiwanaku's coveted legitimating power resided as much in its perceived status as a principal contact point with the sacred as in its historical role as the seat of a royal dynasty and the capital city of a culturally influential empire.

The source of Tiwanaku's sacredness stemmed from its legendary role as a place of genesis in the ancient Andean world. Several myths salvaged by Spanish chroniclers from the cultural wreckage wrought by the traumatic wars of European conquest graphically describe the creation of the world at Tiwanaku. These myths share the classic thematic progression from cosmological chaos and worldly destruction through the agency of natural catastrophy, archetypically a universal flood or fire, to the subsequent establishment of natural and social order at a sacred point of origin.

One such myth of origins was recorded by Antonio de la Calancha ([1638] 1939) in the latter half of the sixteenth century. This myth recounts the destruction of an ancient, prehuman world by the creator, Pachayachachic, the "Invisible Lord," first by fire, and then again by flood. The fury of Pachayachachic, creator and destroyer of worlds, was visited upon the inhabitants of this world when they began to worship the forces of nature, water and springs, mountains and rocks, rather than the creator himself. Only a few who had not given themselves over to the ecstatic worship of natural forces escaped Pachayachachic's wrath by retreating to protected redoubts on the highest mountain peaks. After the waters receded these survivors were charged with repopulating the land. In time these too lapsed into animistic worship and the creator responded by turning them into stone. Finally, according to Calancha's version of the myth, "it is said that until now Pachayachachic had not created the sun, nor the moon, nor the stars but that he made them now in Tiahuanaco and in the Lake of Titicaca" (Calancha [1638] 1939).

After two abortive attempts subverted by the infidelity of his subjects, the creator at last establishes permanent cosmological order in Tiwanaku. From chaos and rebellion, the natural and social orders are reintegrated. The sun, moon, and constellations are created at the place of origins and the time of mankind begins. The regular passage of these celestial bodies through the heavens now provided a mechanism by which humans could mark the annual cycle of the seasons, thereby enabling them to conceptually merge the rythyms of the natural world with their own patterns of social reproduction.

Remarkable variants of the myth of genesis at Tiwanaku recorded by Juan de Betanzos [1551], Crístobal de Molina [1553], and Pedro Sarmiento de Gamboa [1572] recapitulate the theme of rebellion and subsequent restoration of cosmic order, but extend Calancha's account in a fascinating direction, describing directly the creation and partition of social groups at Tiwanaku. In the version given by Betanzos ([1551] 1987:11), the world creator, called Contiti Viracocha, emerges from the sacred Lake Titicaca and at Tiwanaku begins to fashion "the sun and the day," and orders "the sun to move in its path." After calling out people from caves, rivers, and springs scattered through the mythical landscape of the creation time, Viracocha furiously turns some into stone for sacriligeous behavior. As in Calancha's account, this "original sin" was lack of obeisance to the creator. Later, two survivors who remain with Viracocha in Tiwanaku are sent out to call forth a new race of people on behalf of the creator. Viracocha divides the responsibility of these two sacred messengers: "one he sent to the part and province of Condesuyu, that is, to the left hand side standing in Tihuanacu with one's back to where the sun rises" [west]; "the other he sent to the part and province of Andesuyo, that is, to the right hand side standing in the manner indicated, with the back to where the sun rises" [east] (Betanzos [1551] 1987:13).

Sarmiento, adding substantial texture to the story, and using language evocative of the Christian biblical tale of genesis, recounts a similar legend of creation, destruction, and subsequent partition of the world by two culture heroes created by Viracocha:

> Leaving the island [on Lake Titicaca] [Viracocha] passed by the lake to the mainland taking with him the two servants who survived. He went to a place now called Tiahuanacu in the province of Collasuyu, and in this place he sculptured and designed on a great piece of stone all the nations that he intended to create. This done, he ordered his two servants to charge their memories with the names of all the tribes that he had depicted, and of the valleys and provinces where they were to come forth, which were those of the whole land. He ordered that each one should go by a different road, naming the tribes, and compelling them all to go forth and people the country. His servants, obeying the command of Viracocha, set out on their journey and work. One went by the mountain range which they call the heights over the

plains on the South Sea. The other went by the highlands which over-look the mountain ranges that we call the Andes, situated to the east of the said sea. By these roads they went, saying with a loud voice, "oh you tribes and nations, hear and obey the order of Tici Viracocha Pachayachachi, which commands you to go forth and multiply and settle the land." Viracocha himself did the same along the road be-tween those taken by his two servants, naming all the tribes and places by which he passed. At the sound of his voice every place obeyed, and people came forth, some from lakes, others from springs, valleys, caves, trees, rocks and hills, spreading over the land and multiplying to form the nations which are today Peru. (Sarmiento [1572] 1948:33–34)

In Crístobal de Molina's ([1553] 1916:5–6) version of the same myth, the two culture heroes are the primeval male-female pair, and the children of Viracocha. Like the other variants on the theme of genesis, the events of the myth begin after a universal flood: "all the created things perished through him [Viracocha] except for a man and a woman, who remained in a box, and when the waters receded, the wind carried them to tierra Guanaco [Tiwanaku]." Viracocha orders the pair to remain in Tiwanaku, and gives them, as surrogates of the creator, political dominion over the people that they are charged with calling forth from the sacred landscape. The female of the ori-ginal couple, named Ymay Mama Viracocha, is given domain over the mountainous lands, while the male, Tocapa Viracocha, in contrast, receives the mandate over the peoples of the plains and lowlands.

The three variations of the genesis myth recorded by Betanzos, Molina, and Sarmiento not only identify Tiwanaku as the sacred place of origin for the physical universe, but also as the central point of partition of the social world into two complementary halves. The concept of the bipartition of social space was one deeply embedded in the worldview of Andean peoples. Not surprisingly, the theme of duality, in social, political, economic, and religious spheres of action will reoccur throughout this analysis of the people of Tiwanaku.

For the moment, however, what is of most significance in under-standing the penumbra of the sacred with which Tiwanaku was im-bued is to appreciate the religious and mythic role that this legendary place played as the exemplary center of the ancient Andean world. In symbolic terms, Tiwanaku represented the recognized boundary marker that delineated the fault line, or point of cleavage between two archetypal social groups. Simultaneously, Tiwanaku was the revered center where these complementary, but potentially competitive, so-cial groups merged in a shared cultural identity: a point of partici-pation, commonality, and mediation.

The great Spanish cleric Bernabé Cobo [1653], informs us that before Collasuyu was conquered by the Inca, the autochthonous name of Tiwanaku, was Taypikala, a term taken from the language of the Aymara Indians who inhabited the area at least as early as the fourteenth century, and who remain the principal contemporary inhabitants of the region. As Cobo ([1653] 1939:30) explains it, Taypikala meant "the stone in the center," and the natives ascribed this name to the site because they considered the city to be in "the center of the world, and that from there the world was repopulated after the flood." According to our earliest dictionary of the Aymara language, compiled by the Italian Jesuit Ludovico Bertonio in 1612 (1984:340), *taypi* refers to that which is situated in the middle: and so, *taypi lukana* means "dedo del medio," [middle finger]; *taypi huahua* means "hijo del medio, o segundo cuando tres," [middle child, or the second of three]. But the term *taypi* does not simply denote central location in space and time. Within the more subtle textures of meaning, *taypi* refers to a point, zone, or quality of necessary convergence.

For instance, during the sixteenth century, we know that the Aymara organized their social and physical landscape in a sacred geography redolent with symbolic associations. According to Aymara modes of thought, their world was divided into two halves: *Urcosuyu* and *Umasuyu* (Figure 1.2). *Urcosuyu* referred to the dwellers of the mountain peaks, the high, cold, rolling lands to the west of Lake Titicaca, who specialized in highly mobile pastoral pursuits. The concept of *urco* was associated with the celestial sphere, with the male principle and with qualities of aggressiveness, dryness, and solidity. *Umasuyu*, on the other hand, referred to the inhabitants and the landscapes of the regions to the east of Lake Titicaca, including the zones from the lake edge eastward into the Cordillera Real and the spectacular, incised gorges and lush, subtropical valleys of the Amazonian watershed beyond. The people of *Umasuyu* were conceptually associated with a sedentary, agricultural life style, and with fishing and aquatic hunting. *Uma* conveyed notions of wetness, fertility, passivity, and the female principle (Bouysse-Cassagne 1986:205–9; Saignes 1986:42). Between these two ecological and conceptual zones was the *taypi*, the necessary zone of convergence and mediation, formed by Lake Titicaca itself. As Bouysse-Cassagne (1986:209) aptly comments, "as an element of Aymara thought, Lake Titicaca is not merely a specific geographical location: it is at once a centrifugal force that permits the differentiation of the two terms in opposition and a centripetal force that ensures their mediation. In the symbolic architecture, the *taypi* ... is crucial to the equilibrium of the system."

From the local perspective, *taypi*, as an Aymara geographic ethnocategory, also referred specifically to the zone of convergence between

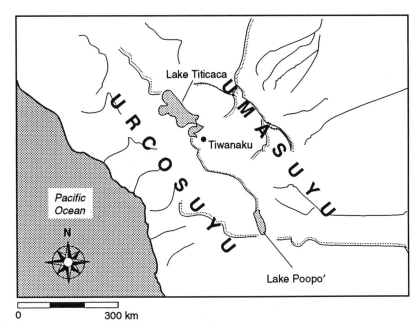

Figure 1.2 The two conceptual halves of the sixteenth-century Aymara world:
Urcosuyu *to the west of Lake Titicaca and* Umasuyu *to the east. (Based on*
Bouysse-Cassagne 1986: Figure 12.5).

maize and tuber agriculture (Saignes 1986:314). This was an important
production zone defined by stratification along the axis of altitude:
ranging variously from about 1,800–3,000 meters above sea level
(masl). This sense of *taypi* emphasizes the quality of the melding of
opposites to form a necessary productive whole.

Many of these associations of *urco*, *uma* and *taypi* are embedded,
in compressed fashion, in the origin myths collected by Betanzos,
Molina, and Sarmiento. The twin culture heroes, Ymay Mama
Viracocha and Tocapa Viracocha, are the primeval female-male
couple, associated with west and east, mountains and plains. In the
act of creation, they journey along diametrically opposed paths (east
versus west) defined by the cosmological axis of the sun's daily points
of rising and setting. The divine force of creation, Viracocha, walks
the intermediate path, the *taypi*, and all set out from Tiwanaku, the
essential point of origin, partition, and convergence.

Tiwanaku, then, and the lake beside which it was founded, were
invested with a powerful and perduring symbolism that crosscut and

conceptually unified religious, social, economic, and political categories. This symbolism even bridged the chasm of linguistic and ethnic divisions, being shared by both the autochthonous Aymara populations, and by their Quechua-speaking Inca overlords during the late fifteenth and early sixteenth centuries.

The indigenous mystique of Tiwanaku grew from its cultural prestige as the capital of a vital and long-lived civilization. Inca elite borrowed liberally from that mystique to justify their assumption of the imperial mandate, and to express the legitimacy of their dynastic pretensions through an audacious claim of royal filiation. But the more fundamental element of the Tiwanaku mystique was its symbolic encapsulation and legitimation of a pre–Inca social order. We can extract much of this from careful interpretation of native myths. However, these myths come down to us through a dual filter, transformed by the self-interest and misunderstanding of at least two dominant colonial powers: first, the Inca, and later the Spanish. The interpretation of myth recorded through such transformative filters is always an ambiguous proposition.

The extent to which these interpretations inform us about the historical place of Tiwanaku in Andean civilization is uncertain. Most of our new information on the political and economic organization of Tiwanaku and its historical meaning in the ancient Andean world will come to us through painstaking, primary archaeological research, and the recent results of this research are the fundamental source material for this book. Nevertheless, the indigenous myths that remain to us offer provocative insights concerning the ideological role of Tiwanaku in the prehispanic cultural landscape. The myth of Tiwanaku is the myth of the *urkultur,* the place and people of origins and creation. It is also the myth of the exemplary center of civilization where social order was ordained by the divine and made to reflect the necessary architecture of the cosmos. The idea of Tiwanaku was a powerful presence in the mind of the native, encoded in the language of myth. It performed a political function of dynastic legitimation for the Inca elite, and perhaps a more deeply rooted, fundamental role as the symbolic distillation of the necessary structure of society, the pre-eminent emblem of native social order.

The Modern Mythographers

The wars of conquest waged by the Spanish against the natives of the high plateau, and subsequently the internecine conflict among the Spaniards themselves, wrought havoc in the land. Colonial censuses preserve the sobering realities of the biological disaster of contact between Old and New Worlds: some provinces of modern Bolivia near the Tiwanaku region lost nearly 80 percent of their native population within the first 50 traumatic years of conquest and European domination (Sánchez-Albornoz 1978). Thousands of Indians perished in the wars, countless others succumbed to the silent terror of pandemic diseases like measles and smallpox carried by the Europeans to the New World. Forced labor in the nightmarish silver mines of Potosí exacted an awful toll on tribute-paying natives. Death by starvation, physical exhaustion, mine shaft collapses, and the insidious effects of mercury poisoning devasted families and entire ethnic groups who were transplanted to Potosí as cheap labor. Before the close of the seventeenth century, enormous tracts of the once densely populated lands of the Collasuyu were reduced to virtual ghost territories whose people had died, been forcibly relocated to the mines, or had fled to wilder lands to escape the tribute assessments which were, in effect, death warrants.

One result of this demographic collapse of unprecedented proportions was an inevitable weakening of social identity as autochthonous and previously self-sufficient communities disappeared suddenly from the landscape. The indigenous memory of the native lords who shaped states and empires, and controlled rich, distant provinces faded rapidly under the yoke of European domination. There were new, equally demanding foreign lords to serve, and fragments of remembered glory gave little comfort. In the wake of the Spanish conquest, the image of historic Tiwanaku was lost. The city was sacked for precious metals and for hard building stones. It lapsed inevitably into lichen encrusted ruins, to become the source for a new phase of mythography that was unfettered by the chain of oral traditions linking the native peoples of the region to their cultural origins.

If the conceptual and physical image of Tiwanaku constituted a significant nexus of historical, religious, and political significance in indigenous thought, its remarkable power to evoke myth-making remains vital today. Unlike the native associations, however, these latter-day myths have little connection with the historical reality of what was Tiwanaku. After the original accounts of the city recorded in the chronicles of the early Spanish conquistadors, clerics, and explorers like Bernabé Cobo, Pedro de Cieza de León, Juan de Betanzos, and Antonio de la Calancha, we hear little about the ruins and their significance until the mid-nineteenth century, a decade or two after the wars of independence from Spain. From that point on, a new wave of European explorers and naturalists have left us their impressions of the ruins.

A unifying theme that runs through these adventurers' accounts is the notion that the once splendid city of Tiwanaku could not possibly have been built by the local natives of the region, who they viewed as "miserable Indians," incapable of the technological and organizational skills that were evidently required to design and construct the great edifices and monumental stone sculptures that graced the metropolis. Speculating on the exotic origins and peoples responsible for the Tiwanaku civilization became a favored intellectual pastime of the generally well-heeled, socially elite European travelers who made the arduous trip to the shores of Lake Titicaca to gaze upon the ruins for themselves. The French count Francis de Castelnau, for instance, comments that:

> they say these monuments [Tiwanaku] were constructed by the Aymara Indians, whose civilization must then have been much more advanced than even that of the Incas. However the buildings of Tihuanacu do not seem to have been finished; they probably pertain to a civilization that has left no traces and disappeared suddenly by some great event whose memory has not been retained in the imbecilic race that inhabits the country today. (Castelnau [1850–1] 1939:56) [my translation]

Castelnau, in fact, seems to have favored the hypothesis that the advanced civilizations of Egypt were responsible for Tiwanaku, not the "imbecilic race" of the Aymara, implying that the monolithic sculptures in the ruins reflect a transplanted cult of Osiris.

Pablo Chalon (1882 and 1884) later concurred with Castelaun's conclusions concerning Tiwanaku origins, pointing out as well that the "edifices and sculptures are not completed," although "they are the most perfect to be found in all Peru." Chalon goes on to suggest that we

> must suppose that the builders [of Tiwanaku] arrived suddenly in that place from some region that was already civilized by the influence of the Old World, only to disappear after a short residence without leaving descendants and without having transmitted to their succesors the secret of their prodigious capabilities . . . traditions tell us little of these people other than that they were white men and bearded, and that having been expulsed from the land, they were forced to take refuge on the islands of the lake where they were exterminated. (Chalon [1882–4] 1939:87) [my translation]

Unlike Castelnau, Chalon was content with the general conclusion that it was some unspecified peoples "civilized by the influence of the Old World" who were responsible for Tiwanaku, although one imagines he would not have been shocked by Castelnau's attribution of an Egyptian source.

The quest for exotic origins led others to putative cultural sources closer to the Andean heartland of Tiwanaku, but nevertheless virtually as improbable as the Egyptian connection proposed by the good count. Some 30 years after Castelnau's account, the Marquise de Nadaillac ([1883] 1939:75) accepted Castelnau's opinion of exotic origins for Tiwanaku, writing that "what is certain is that these monuments could not be the vestiges of an autochthonous civilization" that developed in the cold, high plains of the Andes. Unlike Castelnau, however, the Marquise suggested an origin somewhat closer to home, positing that it was the "Nahua race" (that is, the Mexica-Aztecs of central Mexico) who were the founders of the ancient city on the Bolivian high plateau.

By the early decades of the new century, a peripatetic German adventurer and entrepreneur was to turn the assumption of an exotic, foreign origin of Tiwanaku on its head, and, in the process, craft one of the most exuberant, if ultimately bizarre, portraits of the people of Tiwanaku. After a number of dramatic exploits in the jungles of the Amazon where he engaged in the commercialization of rubber, the young Arthur Posnansky made his way overland into the mountainous heartland of Bolivia, passing through Tiwanaku from the Lake Titicaca port of Guaqui in 1903. Posnansky mapped the ruins in 1904, launching his curious career as the self-styled premier authority on the civilization of Tiwanaku in Bolivia.

Posnansky first systematically outlined his conclusions on what he believed to be the transcendental significance of Tiwanaku in the history of the Americas in 1914, in a book entitled *Una Metrópoli Prehistorica en la América del Sur*. However, his monumental and rare two-volume work *Tihuanacu: The Cradle of American Man* (1945) stands as the principal testament to Posnansky's magnificent obsession with Tiwanaku. Here, as succinctly captured in the title of the work, Posnansky asserted that Tiwanaku was the preeminent and most ancient metropolis of the ancient Americas, and that the intellectually advanced milieu that Tiwanaku engendered was ultimately responsible for every sophisticated civilization that appeared in the Western Hemisphere. A glance at a reproduction of one of Posnansky's maps shows the audacity of his conceptions: here he traces a farflung network of Tiwanaku's putative "influences" on the art styles of the great American civilizations (Figure 1.3). For Posnansky, Tiwanaku was not the product of a more advanced foreign civilization as Castelnau and others believed, but rather a true origin point for humanity, entirely independent of the Old World. He explicitly envisioned peoples from throughout the New World traveling immense distances in pilgrimage to Tiwanaku to have disputes adjudicated by the priests of the city, according to the "moral codes" developed there.

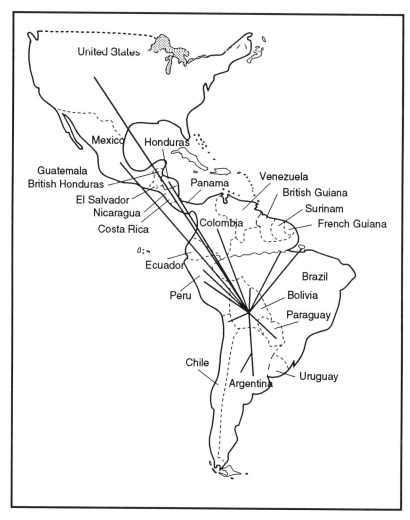

Figure 1.3   The diffusion of Tiwanaku civilization throughout the Americas according to Arthur Posnansky. (1945, vol. 3: Plate 2).

Posnansky attributed the subsequent decline and wide diffusion of Tiwanaku civilization to "malign climatic conditions." As he phrased it:

> Climatic aggression put a walking staff into the hands of the dwellers on the Altiplano, forcing them to go on and on, until they found suitable locations where they could again establish themselves and enjoy

the fruits of their labors. These emigrants then, carrying with them their cultural baggage, spread throughout all those parts of the hemisphere which still remained unaffected by the climatic aggression, disseminating as they went their enlightenment and beliefs. Thus, one of the two races that had formed the most important prehistoric centers of the world at that time, and which had developed in a hidden corner of the Andes, in the heart of the Americas migrated in part to Brazil, in part to Argentina, Chile, Peru, Ecuador, and Colombia, and from there to Central America, Mexico, and even Northern Arizona. (Posnansky 1945:2)

Although coming to an entirely different conclusion regarding the origins of Tiwanaku civilization than that reached by the elite dilletante travelers of the nineteenth century, Posnansky's notions that radically changing climatic conditions were responsible for the decadence of a once glorious civilization permitted him to share their feelings of disgust for the contemporary inhabitants of the Andean high plateau, or *altiplano*:

> the Andean Altiplano was not always, as it is today, a desolate, arid and cold region. It was not always extremely poor in vegetation and inhabited in part by groups of apparently inferior races, possessing scant civilization, like those who today speak Aymara, Quechua, Puquina, Uru, etc. These groups are completely deviod of culture at the present time; they scarcely know how to scratch the soil to provide themselves with their miserable daily bread. They weave coarse cloth to protect their bodies against the inclemency of the weather and they lead a wretched existence in clay huts which seem, rather than human dwellings, the caves of troglodytes. (Posnansky 1945:33)

Posnansky created a new myth for Tiwanaku, one that placed it at the center of ancient intellectual ferment and achievement in the Americas. Essentially he styled the civilization of Tiwanaku as a golden age of innovation and transformation, similar in social impact, if not in cultural content, to that which occurred in the Old World in sixth century B.C. Attica.

As one might imagine, Posnansky's myth was well received among the social elites of mid-twentieth century Bolivia, and Latin America in general. It simultaneously fashioned a seemingly substantial scientific rationale for considering Tiwanaku one of the great civilizations of the ancient world, thereby promoting the ruins as a national and regional symbol, and, at the same time, shored up the intellectual underpinnings supporting the repressive system of patron-client relationships and economic domination that characterized the social relationships between European and Indian. Reading Posnansky's weighty volumes permitted the Europeanized upper and middle classes to feel a romantic sense of national pride in the heroism, nobility, and splendor of the ancients without the messy inconvenience of attributing those past glories to the direct ancestors of the Indians whose repression was an essential cog in the economic engine of modern Bolivian society. After all, the contemporary Indian was merely a debased and pale reflection of the past – according to Posnansky, a retrogression in the scale of human evolution – worthy, perhaps, of pathos, but most certainly not of a true measure of dignity and participation in modern society.

If Posnansky's manipulation of mythic Tiwanaku was distinct from that of Castelnau, Nadaillac, and Chalon, his fundamental message was the same: the contemporary Indian could not possibly have been the creator of Tiwanaku civilization. For that we must look to an exotic, entirely distinct, and certainly more accomplished source culture. Even today, Posnansky's myth retains a certain resonance in Bolivian society where positive change in class and racial attitudes creeps along at glacial pace. Despite the research of modern archaeology that has thoroughly debunked Posnansky's climatic, cultural, and hyper-diffusionist interpretations, an astonishing number of his acolytes in Latin America still keep the flame burning, recapitulating his exegesis of Tiwanaku history and culture, clinging to a vision they see as accurate, fitting, even noble.

But, of course, Posnansky and the nineteenth-century adventurers with whom he shared a common intellectual and social formation, do not have a monopoly on mythologizing and flights of speculative fancy. More recently, one can find any number of fanciful decipherments of the meanings encoded in Tiwanaku stone sculptures. One sculpture alone, the famous Gateway of the Sun, a stunning ceremonial portal carved from a single gray andesite block, has inspired a host of ingenious, if preposterous interpretations (Figure 1.4). Common to these reconstructions of the Gateway's symbolic content is the belief that the monument records events from a profoundly distant past. One such interpretation makes the astonishing claim that the Gateway of the Sun is an astronomical document in stone that records the eclipses, equinoxes, solstices, and peculiar cosmic geometry of a "pre-lunar" world of unfathomable antiquity, perhaps hundreds of thousands of years old:

> the great gateway is indeed a calendar – a calendar, moreover, that has not its like in the world. It will be shown that this Calendar is also the oldest in the world – nay, that it has actually come down to us from "another" world ... our Moon was not yet the companion of our

Figure 1.4   The "Gateway of the Sun" at Tiwanaku. (Photograph by H. Boero Rojo).

Earth at the time when the Calendar of Tiahuanaco was devised. (Bellamy and Allan 1948:18)

Another not only ascribes to Tiwanaku and the Gateway a similarly fantastic geological date, but also attributes the city's immense cut-stone architecture and sculpture to creative, laser-wielding extra-terrestrials (Von Däniken 1969).

Again, in these more recent myths of Tiwanaku, the common tie that binds them all is the serene conviction that the ancestors of the native inhabitants could not have created the remarkably beautiful, monumental assemblage of buildings and sculptures that constituted the ceremonial core of old Tiwanaku. The stubborn persistence of these latter-day myths is truly breathtaking. In 1988, while conducting excavations in the ceremonial precinct of Tiwanaku, my staff and I were stunned by the sight of a small group of self-proclaimed "Druids" who suddenly disrobed before the Gateway of the Sun and proceeded to dance stiffly around the great icon. One can only imagine the fevered, convoluted beliefs concerning Tiwanaku and its greatest sculptural image that these modern Druids hold.

This disparate catalog of fantasia regarding the ancient people of Tiwanaku is by no means complete. The city and its monuments have exercised an extraordinary hold over the imagination of those who have journeyed to the high plateaus of Bolivia to view, and to reflect upon these ruins at the top of the Andean world. Perhaps the legends and fantasies that have encrusted Tiwanaku through the centuries may be attributed, in part, to the exceptional aura cast by the city's dramatic physical setting. Situated in an overpowering landscape of high steppe and rugged, snow-shrouded mountains, at 3,850 meters, Tiwanaku maintains the distinction of being the highest urban settlement of the ancient world. The panoramic, windswept vistas opening out from the site toward the surrounding, silvered ramparts of glaciated mountain peaks and the intense cobalt-blue waters of Lake Titicaca impart an undeniable air of mystery and of melancholia. The sight of gigantic stone sculptures and architectural blocks shattered into utter chaos and ruin evokes a palpable, almost visceral sense of profound antiquity and the passage of great events, now unremembered and lost to us.

The modern mythographers have interjected their own peculiar gloss on this forgotten history of the people of Tiwanaku. But their slovenly, illogical myths about Tiwanaku are little more than arcane mystifications which offer nothing of substance to the serious student of this ancient civilization. If not for the grotesque, insidious subtext of racism that undergirds virtually all of these latter-day myths, they could be dismissed as mildly amusing footnotes in the annals of Andean archaeology.

Myth, History, and the People of Tiwanaku

The indigenous myths concerning Tiwanaku, on the other hand, permit an authentic entrée into the meaning of Tiwanaku in the ancient Andean world. These products of the native mind, even though transformed through the filter of the alien culture of the Spanish chroniclers, inform this inquiry into the nature and significance of ancient Tiwanaku. But much of the basic material for this reconstructed history of the people of Tiwanaku must come through the efforts of archaeology and its allied disciplines. The text of this history will emerge from the creative interplay between the fragments of myth and ethnohistoric documents available to us, and from the substantive discoveries of archaeology.

Much of the archaeology of Tiwanaku remains to be done. The past several years have witnessed, however, a renaissance of scholarly work on the complex phenomenon of Tiwanaku. This book draws heavily upon my own ongoing systematic research in the city of Tiwanaku and in its near hinterland: the high plateau heartland of the Tiwanaku state. The results of other recent field projects in areas outside of the core *altiplano* zone in southern Peru, northern Chile, and north-western Argentina promise to dramatically alter current perceptions regarding Tiwanaku's role in the geopolitics of the ancient Andean world. Fresh, compelling interpretations of the social characteristics, political economy, and cultural history of Tiwanaku are forthcoming. This book represents an initial foray into the dense, pluriethnic thicket of that ancient world in an attempt to make sense of its structure, historical evolution, and ultimate denouement. The trajectory of Tiwanaku's history offers us insight into the particular social and cultural elements that constituted an ancient Andean society, but it also informs us about more general processes of social change. As we shall see, there may even be a contemporary application of what was once the principal technology of agricultural production in the Tiwanaku state: a rare and special case in which direct knowledge of the past has an immediate, tangible impact on the present.

Reconstructing the story of ancient Tiwanaku requires a multi-dimensional approach, a creative, but judicious integration of anthro-pological, historical, and ecological research. In what follows, I will synthesize evidence from ethnohistory, native mythology, linguistics, conventional and experimental archaeology, and the ecological sciences to draw as convincing a portrait of the people of Tiwanaku as is currently possible. The following chapter offers a brief précis of the fundamental sources available to us in shaping this historical reconstruction.

Contemporary ethnography, too, has a significant role to play in the array of information and methods that will give substance to this portrait, for, in a real sense, the people of Tiwanaku never vanished completely. Their cultural and biological descendants remain on the ancient lands of the Tiwanaku realm, tilling the soil of the high plateau and fishing the great lake of Titicaca. Llama caravans bearing aromatic and hard woods, resinous shrubs, and blocks of pure salt still come down to the shores of the lake as they have for at least 100 generations, although today they are much attenuated, slowly dis-appearing before the onslaught of motorized traffic along primitive roads that are penetrating even the most desolate stretches of the high plateau. Complex rituals of agricultural and livestock fertility continue to be performed by the *yatiri*, spiritual leaders of the rural Aymara, whose performances, prayers, and sacrifices at planting and harvest ceremonies, and at a myriad of other moments of life crisis, ensure the health, productivity, and survival of their communities. The present shares with the past virtually identical physical landscapes and many of the same natural resources. We can still witness technologies of rural production that have persisted almost without change for centuries and a human population dispersed across the high plateau in small villages and hamlets in a pattern of settlement that would not have been alien to the Tiwanaku eye. Many essential truths about Tiwanaku still remain embedded in the indigenous communities of the *altiplano*.

Nevertheless, despite the tenacity of this simulacrum of the past, the immensely strong forces of acculturation will irrevocably erode the social landscape of the high plateau. Young families from indigenous villages are pouring into the increasingly chaotic cities of Bolivia and Peru attempting to escape the bitter realities of rural poverty, and in the process they are changing their lives and the special identity of their cultural heritage forever. Our living mirror of the past diminishes and grows more opaque each year. But this image and linkage to a rich past still exists, and we can learn much about pre–Colonial Andean reality by acutely observing and participating in the new social worlds being created daily in mountain valleys and high plateaus.

2

The Sources

and this people's lack of writing is the reason there is no knowledge
of who the people that built these great foundations and strongholds
were, or how much time has gone by since then. (Pedro de Cieza de
León [1553] 1959:283)

Cieza de León's despair that the native Andeans had left no written
record of their history, so that he could give no certain account of
when Tiwanaku had been built and by what manner of people, was
mitigated by his inquisitive nature, and by his perceptive observations of the tangible vestiges that remained to him. When presented
with oral traditions, myths, and legends preserved only in the minds
of the living inhabitants of Tiwanaku, and with the physical remains
of a ruined city, Cieza became an ethnographer and an archaeologist.
Much like a contemporary scholar of prehistory confronted with a
nonliterate society, he turned to the living informants to probe their
memories, and to record their own interpretations of the ruined,
ancient city in which they lived. He walked among the ruins and
carefully noted patterns of preservation, drawing remarkably pres-
cient inferences from them. He was right to judge Tiwanaku as a ruin
more ancient than those of the recently destroyed Inca empire. His
methods and his observations anticipate those of the modern archaeologist grappling with the seemingly intractable cypher of the distant
past.

How can we gain access to societies lost to us in a past without
written record? What methods and sources yield plausible, if not
certain, insights into the workings of now extinct societies? The an-
swers to these questions are not simple, and they shift with changing
cultural and temporal contexts.

The Ethnohistoric Evidence

In the Andean world, and particularly in the old highland core of the Inca empire, we are fortunate to have available abundant ethnohistorical documentation concerning indigenous populations. These documents, commissioned or produced from the earliest stages of European conquest and domination in the Andes, represent a rich and virtually inexhaustible panorama of information on indigenous myths, marriage patterns, religious ideologies, and the myriad forms of political, economic, and social structures evolved by the distinct ethnic groups native to the ancient Andean world.

The thematic range, information content, and purpose of these documents are incredibly diverse: personalized chronicles of conquest and life among the newly vanquished natives written by the early European conquistadors; vast, and nearly overwhelming quantities of administrative records generated by the Spanish colonial bureaucracy including tribute and taxation lists, land titles, population censuses, and *encomienda* grants; litigation records from disputes over land, labor, and taxes brought before the courts of the colonial government by both European and Indian; and, of course, ecclesiastical records of baptisms, marriages, and deaths among native converts to Christianity. The darker side of Christian proselytization also yields rich information. Accounts of native religious "superstitions" uprooted by brutal and justly infamous campaigns of inquisition and torture, recounted in graphic detail in texts like Polo de Ondegardo's *Informaciones acerca de la religión y gobierno de los Incas* ([1571] 1916) and Arriaga's *Extirpación de la idolotría del Peru* ([1621] 1968), offer deep insights into native Andean spirituality. Contemporary historical scholarship in the Andes has only skirted over the surface of this daunting corpus of materials. Extracting the jewels of new information on the native reality embedded in the obscure, repetitive, and frequently misleading dross of bureaucratic language that characterizes this documentary mass requires the patient, dedicated ministrations of the professional ethnohistorian. Only in the past two decades have we truly begun to reap the benefits of this most patient and specialized art.

Throughout the course of this book, I will incorporate important insights drawn from recent ethnohistorical investigations into both Inca and non–Inca societies in the Andes. Of particular relevance to the story of the people of Tiwanaku is extensive material on the fifteenth and sixteenth century Aymara kingdoms around Lake Titicaca published in an invaluable document entitled *Visita hecha a la provincia de Chucuito* by Garci Diez de San Miguel ([1567] 1964).

Since its modern publication in an accesible form, this document has been assiduously mined by ethnohistorians and archaeologists for insights into the prehispanic organization of native societies under Inca rule. The Spanish *visitas*, or inspections, were a combination of population censuses and interviews with local political leaders "who described many of the details of their religious structure, political organization and tribute payments under Inca rule" (Morris and Thompson 1985:29). Careful analysis of such *visitas*, when combined with intensive archaeological research, permits reasonable inferences concerning the political, economic, and religious constitution of the pre–Inca social landscape as well. They are irreplaceable touchstones for an historical reconstruction of ancient Tiwanaku.

Perhaps the most important general conclusion that may be extracted from the Garci Diez *Visita* is that the Aymara kingdoms, or *señorios* of the fifteenth and sixteenth centuries were characterized by a form of political and social organization referred to as dual organization, or the moiety system, in which a society is segmented minimally into two bounded, complementary units with distinct political leaders. Although this organizational system results in a bipartition of society, the two halves of the total social unit created by this segmentation were not precisely equal in ritual, political, or economic status. That is, this form of dual organization does not form a society with two corporate groups that are mirror images of each other. Rather there persist elements of asymmetry that generate grounds for ranking, resulting in a system of social statuses arrayed in a hierarchy. John Murra's (1968:117) analysis of one of the most powerful of these *señorios*, the Lupaqa, makes this point quite explicitly: "Like most other people of the Andes, including the Inca, the Lupaqa had two lords at every level of authority. The power, prestige and income of the two moiety leaders were equivalent but not identical."

As Murra noted, this system of asymmetric dual organization was not a feature exclusive to the Aymara polities of the late prehispanic period. Many indigenous Andean societies were organized in this fashion, with an explicit and thoroughgoing division of social space, ideological structures, ritual behavior, and economic activities into complementary, but hierarchically ranked segments. Such a system of dual corporate organization has been documented for the north coast of Peru for the period immediately preceding the Spanish conquest (Netherly 1984), and many ethnographers describe homologous systems that persist (although reduced in scale of regional action in comparison to some of their prehispanic counterparts) among contemporary Andean communities (Albó et al. 1972; Duviols 1973; Isbell 1978; Platt 1986 among others).

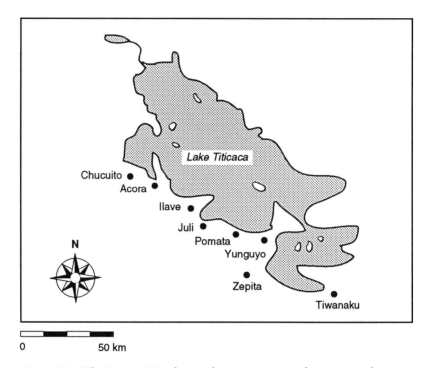

Figure 2.1   The Lupaqa Kingdom and its seven principal towns, or cabeceras, *located along the western shore of Lake Titicaca. (Based on Stanish 1992: Figure 6).*

For the case of the Lupaqa, the kingdom's geopolitical landscape was organized hierarchically beginning with two lords, called *mallku* [glossed as lord, or lordly in Aymara]: Qari and Qusi. These two *mallku* politically controlled, or at least extracted tribute from, seven *cabeceras*, or capitals of territorial provinces identified with seven large archaeological settlements along the western shores of Lake Titicaca (Figure 2.1). These seven provinces, as well as the kingdom as a whole, were segmented into upper and lower moieties, referred to in Aymara as Arasaya and Masaya. Two officials subordinate to Qari and Qusi ruled at each of these levels. In theory in this system the two highest lords retained certain rights to human and natural resources in all seven of the provinces. The two subordinate lords at each of the seven *cabeceras*, in turn, claimed rights of access to resources within the boundaries of their individual territories. The dualistic structure of the socio-political and economic organization of the Lupaqa *señorío* is illustrated graphically in Figure 2.2.

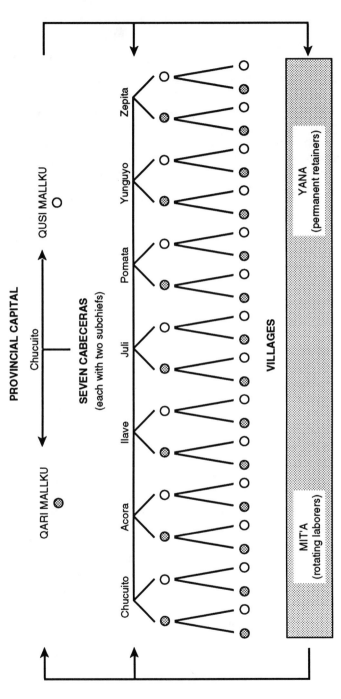

Figure 2.2 *Dual political organization of the Lupaqa Kingdom. Note in particular the cycle of reciprocity between elites and commoners.*

One of the essential resources claimed by these political leaders was human labor: for construction and maintenance of agricultural terraces and canals, for planting and harvesting crops, for production of textiles, pottery, and metals, and for military service, among other public tasks. There were two principal forms of labor service that were mobilized by the various political leaders of the Lupaqa: the *yanapaqhuna* or *yana* and the *mit'anni* or *mit'a*. The *yana* were the class, or perhaps more accurately, status relationship of permanent retainers to the nobility. This status relationship was well established in the Inca state in which *yana* were much like vassals in a feudal state. They were attached to the households of individual Inca lords and owed personal fealty to them. In return for personal service to their liege lords, the *yana* were generally exempted from tribute obligations assessed against the ordinary citizens of the realm. A similar relationship between personal retainers and nobles seems to have obtained for the Lupaqa.

The second form of labor obligation, called the *mit'a*, was highly variable in kind and length of service. This was a system of labor taxation that was assessed against heads of households, that is, against the bulk of commoners under the authority of the moiety leaders. The *mit'a* system, which was also a fundamental institution of the Inca and other pre–Inca Andean states, was administered principally through local officials of the various ethnic groups subject to the Lupaqa. These local officials would select from among the pool of eligible taxpayers (married heads of households) in their community on a rotational basis to supply the designated quota. In this way, the labor obligation was distributed equitably both among the different local ethnic groups in the province, and within the groups themselves. No individual taxpayer was forced to serve the *mit'a* more frequently than another, and, apart from some special exemptions such as the *yana*, all communities and ethnic groups participated in the system, contributing labor service according to the size of their population.

Local autonomy in implementing the *mit'a* labor tax was one of the special characteristics of the system that enhanced its efficiency and flexibility. But there was another principle in this system of taxation that reveals its character as a quintessential native Andean institution. To the indigenous peoples of the Andes, the *mit'a* was not perceived as a simple, one-sided tax debt assessed by their political superiors. Rather they viewed the *mit'a* as a complex skein of reciprocal obligations. If the government compelled them to contribute labor in public projects, or in the private estates of the ruling elite, then the state had the obligation during the period of labor service to provide the taxpayer with food, drink, clothing, tools, and housing if the project was distant from the home community.

To the commoners, the *mit'a* was a variant of an ancient pattern of reciprocity among family, kinsmen, and neighbors referred to as *minka* that, even today, remains a vital principle of social relations in rural Andean communities. In this system, for instance, a newly married couple, with the aid of local officials, may call on their relatives and friends to help them build their first home. In return for this donated labor, the couple, and perhaps their immediate family, provide food, drink, and hospitality while the job is completed. They also incur a future obligation to contribute some equivalent service to those who participated in the house-raising. This mix of mutual labor service and hospitality permits individuals to mobilize labor beyond that available in their households and contributes to community solidarity.

The Garci Diez *Visita* also furnishes us with rich details on a particular economic strategy of the Lupaqa kingdom (again built upon pre-existing patterns of economic behavior grounded in simpler village-based life) that entailed establishing colonies in lands distant from the regional and provincial capitals around Lake Titicaca. These colonies were founded in order to directly exploit distinct production zones in a variety of ecological settings with natural resource endowments different from those of the cold, high plateau of the Lupaqa homeland. Colonies were established in the lush, semi-tropical valleys east of the great Andean mountain chain, as well as on the arid western slopes of the Andes and Pacific coasts of Peru and Chile. A principal motive force for establishing these colonies was to gain direct access to arable land in temperate climatic zones that were capable of supporting production of maize, chile peppers, coca, and other warm lands crops that could not be grown at extreme altitude. This special relationship of environmental stratification and political economy that has deep temporal roots in the south-central Andes will be treated in greater detail in the following chapter. Here I wish only to underscore by these examples relating to the Lupaqa kingdom that the ethnohistorical documents available to the modern scholar are indispensable for interpreting the archaeological evidence which remains the core source of our information on the ancient people of Tiwanaku.

The Archaeological Evidence

In many respects, despite international recognition of its importance as one of the key archaeological sites in the ancient Americas, the archaeology of Tiwanaku remains in an incipient state of development. The first formal plans of the site, actually little more than sketch maps, were drawn by the nineteenth-century explorer Ephraim Squier (Figure 2.3). Squier's (1877:300) brief sojourn in the ruins of Tiwanaku led him to conclude that:

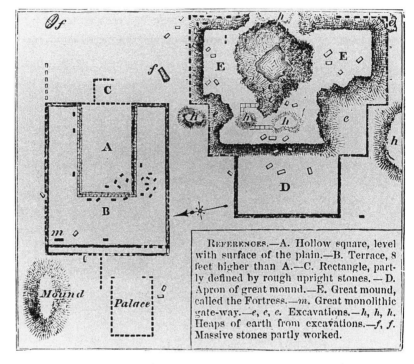

REFERENCES.—A. Hollow square, level with surface of the plain.—B. Terrace, 8 feet higher than A.—C. Rectangle, partly defined by rough upright stones.— D. Apron of great mound.—E. Great mound, called the Fortress.—*m.* Great monolithic gate-way.—*e, e, e.* Excavations.—*h, h, h.* Heaps of earth from excavations.—*f, f.* Massive stones partly worked.

Figure 2.3   Late nineteenth-century map of Tiwanaku's ruins by Ephraim Squier (1877).

we find nowhere in the vicinity [of Tiwanaku] any decided traces of ancient habitations, such as abound elsewhere in Peru, in connection with most public edifices. . . . This is not, prima facie, a region for nuturing or sustaining a large population and certainly not one wherein we should expect to find a capital. Tiahuanaco may have been a sacred spot or a shrine, the position of which was determined by accident, an augury, or a dream, but I can hardly believe that it was a seat of dominion.

Squier's comments are fascinating in that they represent one of the first expressions of the notion that Tiwanaku was not a true city, but rather a sparsely populated ceremonial center: a focus of religious pilgrimage, but not of dense resident population. Furthermore, Squier attributed the implicit marginality of Tiwanaku as a population center to its location in the rigorous environment of the high plateau. This attitude that Tiwanaku's environmental setting was inherently unproductive and inhospitable, and that therefore the site itself never attained true urban proportions, or importance as "a seat of dominion" remains a strong theme in the interpretations of some contemporary archaeologists and historians (Schaedel 1988:772–3). Squier's interpretations of Tiwanaku as essentially a vacant ceremonial center echo similar conceptions proposed for many Mayan settlements in the tropical rainforest of the Peten in Guatemala. As in the case of Tiwanaku, the conclusion that Mayan society was essentially non-urban was generated by the underlying notion that this society had evolved in a difficult and agriculturally unproductive environment (here, the humid tropics characterized by thin, acidic soils and a choking vegetation cover). In the case of both the Mayan and Tiwanaku civilizations, these subjective judgments with respect to the relative productivity of the natural setting were reinforced by a paradoxical concern for mapping and exploring only the major, public architecture of their principal settlements. It is not terribly surprising, then, that the archaeologists and explorers who worked under difficult environmental conditions in the bitterly cold, windswept Andean high plateau or in the suffocating heat of the Mayan tropical jungles and who concentrated their energies on the magnificent temple mounds and palaces developed a similar image of these civilizations as theocracies organized as loose congeries of sparsely populated ceremonial centers.

The theme of Tiwanaku as a ceremonial center lacking large resident populations was reiterated in the subsequent archaeological research of Wendell Bennett during the 1930s. Bennett (1934) conducted the first systematic excavations within the monumental precincts of Tiwanaku, and developed a cultural chronology based on changes in ceramic styles over time. Bennett's achievement in establishing the first stratigraphically based ceramic chronology for Tiwanaku cannot be overestimated. His quadripartite stylistic sequence of ceramic phases (Primitive Tiahuanaco, Classic Tiahuanaco, Decadent Tiahuanaco, and Post Tiahuanaco/Inca) formed the basis for contemporary formulations of Tiwanaku cultural chronology. Nevertheless, Bennett's excavations, which were restricted by the Bolivian government to ten test pits each of which was to be no larger than ten square meters, were placed exclusively within the area of monumental architecture at the site. On the basis of this work and his discovery of an enormous, intricately carved stone stela in the center of a structure referred to today as the Semi-subterranean Temple, Bennett (1934:480) concluded that Tiwanaku was "distinctly a ceremonial site, composed of an aggregation of temples" that were built sequentially over long periods of time. Bennett came to understand the expansion of Tiwanaku cultural influence into Peru, Chile, and Bolivia as essentially religious in character, a cult of high prestige directed by "priest leaders" whose principal temple and oracle center was the site of Tiwanaku itself. Like Squier, he did not believe that Tiwanaku ever achieved urban proportions.

Apart from the pioneering studies of Bennett in the early 1930s, serious archaeological research on a substantive scale at Tiwanaku and its proximal affiliated sites began only within the past three decades. This work, organized and executed during the 1960s and 1970s primarily by Bolivian nationals under the aegis of the *Instituto Nacional de Arqueologia de Bolivia* (INAR), again focussed primarily on the highly visible architectural ensembles of Tiwanaku. However, this period of large-scale excavations generated substantive new information on the morphology, function, and chronological context of the city's cultural evolution (Ponce 1972). Based on the results of this research, the Bolivian archaeologist Carlos Ponce Sangines was able to establish, for the first time, empirically based warrants for considering Tiwanaku a true urban settlement. Ponce calculated that Tiwanaku was, in fact, a city of substantial size, approaching nearly 4.5 square kilometers. Completing deep stratigraphic excavations in the great temple of Kalasasaya enabled Ponce to refine the ceramic chronology sketched out by Bennett. Ponce's formulation of five phases of ceramic development now forms the foundation for the Tiwanaku cultural sequence (Figure 2.4).

My own involvement with Tiwanaku archaeology began in 1978. That year I was fortunate to begin a pilot project sponsored by the Bolivian National Institute of Archaeology that was intended to explore the archaeological sites and features in Tiwanaku's immediate rural hinterland. One explicit goal of this project was to investigate the technology and organization of agricultural production worked out by the people of Tiwanaku over the course of a millennium. This project gradually expanded to incorporate large-scale multidisciplinary investigations at four major settlements of Tiwanaku civilization within a 30 kilometer (km) radius of the Tiwanaku Valley (Tiwanaku itself, Lukurmata, Pajchiri, and Khonko Wankané), excavations in smaller villages and hamlets within the Tiwanaku sustaining area, systematic mapping and exploration of major agricultural features such as preserved field systems, aqueducts, canals, and dikes, and even experimental rehabilitation of Tiwanaku field systems by contemporary Aymara Indians (Kolata 1986; Kolata 1991; Kolata and Ortloff 1989; Ortloff and Kolata 1989).

Many of the results of this research on Tiwanaku's remarkably sophisticated system of intensive agricultural production are described in Chapter 6. Other insights into the nature of Tiwanaku vernacular and elite architecture; the economic and political relationships between

PERIODS	TIME SCALE	NORTHERN TITICACA BASIN	SOUTHERN TITICACA BASIN
Late Horizon	1500	Inca	Inca
Late Intermediate	1000	Colla, Lupaqa, Collagua Tiwanaku V	Pacajes Mollo Tiwanaku V
Middle Horizon	500	Tiwanaku IV	Tiwanaku IV
Early Intermediate	AD / BC	Pukara	Tiwanaku III Tiwanaku II Tiwanaku I
Early Horizon	500	Yaya-Mama Religious Tradition Late Qaluyu	Yaya-Mama Religious Tradition Late Chiripa Middle Chiripa
Initial Period	1000 / 1500	Early Qaluyu	Early Chiripa

Figure 2.4   Chronological chart for the south-central Andes, from the Initial Period to the Late Horizon [Inca conquest]. (Based on Browman 1978; Kolata 1983; Mohr-Chavez 1988; and Ponce 1972).

city and countryside; the diet of Tiwanaku urban and rural populations; the kinds of occupational specialties practiced within hamlets, villages, towns and cities; the degree of stratification of Tiwanaku society into distinct social classes; and many similar questions concerning the daily lives of the people of Tiwanaku are incorporated throughout this book. All of these insights are based on concrete kinds of archaeological evidence and analytical techniques: detailed compilation and interpretation of maps and plans of human settlements; intensive excavation of dwellings, temples, and cemeteries; careful technical analysis of artifacts derived from excavations such as ceramic vessels, stone, bone and wood implements, metal jewelry, and the like.

The increased tempo of archaeological investigations during the 1980s, both in the Bolivian high plateau core area and in more distant regions that were heavily influenced by the ebb and flow of Tiwanaku culture, has made this first synthetic rendering of Tiwanaku civilization feasible. Despite this attempt to merge diverse bundles of evidence derived from multiple lines of investigation into a coherent historical account, in many respects Tiwanaku's nature and cultural significance in the ancient Andean world remains an enigma. But this is the excitement and the challenge of archaeological and historical research: the subject matter constantly changes as new data are produced and incorporated into the interpretive enterprise. We are forced by the nature of the inquiry to continually respond to fresh information, and to constantly reformulate our analytical perspectives. The archaeologist cannot afford the luxury of dogma. The field investigations are ongoing, and many new discoveries to be made over the course of the next few years will surely alter my portrait of the people of Tiwanaku. This is not to say that all our current interpretations are merely casual, mutable speculations. Rather they are like a partially completed building with some essential structural elements laid down, but with much more finish work to be done. We have the basic blueprint and, although unforeseen changes and modifications will undoubtedly affect the plan, we can nevertheless envision the principal contours of the final structure.

The Linguistic and Ethnographic Evidence

The reconstruction of the history, character, and meaning of Tiwanaku turns principally on archaeological and ethnohistoric evidence. Nevertheless we do have access to other critical sources of information that bear directly on the question of Tiwanaku and its historical trajectory. If, as I suggested earlier, the imprint of the people of Tiwanaku is still to be traced no matter how ephemerally in the lifeways of contemporary populations on the high plateau, then the study of living communities and of indigenous languages will offer essential insights in our efforts to reconstruct ancient Tiwanaku. But in using the data of contemporary ethnography and of historical linguistics to draw inferences concerning a now distant past, we must also remain keenly aware of the profound social traumas and cultural transformations that have affected the Andean peoples over the course of the past five centuries. We cannot uncritically assume a kind of unmediated cultural isomorphism between the rural villages of today and the settlements of similar scale that constituted the fundamental webwork of Tiwanaku social life 1,000 years ago. Equally, though, we cannot fail to be struck by the extent to which life in the isolated high plateau hamlets of contemporary Bolivia and Peru evokes an intense, autochthonous image of what was local reality in a time now long past.

The methodological dilemma of how and to what degree to regard living peoples and languages as a looking glass into the past is not simple. We must treat the data of ethnography and of historical linguistics critically and with due caution, conscious of their limitations for historical reconstruction, and aware of the assumptions which underlie their application. For instance, with respect to the use of language distributions to interpret Andean cultural history, Isbell (1983–4:242) perceptively notes that application of historical linguistic data hinges on two critical assumptions that require close scrutiny and testing: First, the archaeologist "can somehow recognize the prehistoric material cultural remains produced by the ancestors of modern language speakers," and second, linguistic variation corresponds with "variation in material culture, and . . . the degree of difference in material culture is a suitable predictor of the degree of difference between the languages of human groups." Clearly these are rigorous assumptions, fraught with many potential exceptions because of essentially random historical occurrences not directly perceivable in the archaeological record.

For instance, language replacement that was not accompanied by changes in basic technologies, or other manifestations of material culture, has occurred in many regions of the world with relative frequency. Replacement may be the result of absorption, or assimilation into a dominant ethnic group, or of the gradual adoption of a lingua franca among different ethnic groups to facilitate commerce. Cases of language replacement are well documented in the Andean world. Historically, the Macha of northern Potosí in the Bolivian *altiplano* have adopted Quechua in place of Aymara without radically changing their domestic economy, or patterns of settlement. In the pre-hispanic context, there are several instances of the imposition of Quechua by the Inca state on local communities, which subsequently abandoned their native tongues for the imperial language. Similarly, discriminating the tangible material objects produced and used by prehistoric groups and then associating these objects with the ancestors of a particular modern language group is an extremely difficult proposition. We cannot blithely ignore the problems of using linguistic data for reconstructing prehispanic culture history, but, at the same time, we should not dismiss these data as entirely intractable. The occurrence of a particular Aymara or Quechua toponym (place names), for example, provides essential clues to the prehispanic distribution of that language. Mapping multiple examples of such toponyms might then provide us with a bounded distribution that can be correlated with independent material data, such as ceramic styles, or particular technologies characteristic of a given archaeological culture (see, for example, Bird et al. 1983–4).

Given our lack of written evidence, we cannot be certain what language the people of Tiwanaku spoke. In the late prehispanic period we do know that at least four principal languages were spoken in Collasuyu, the southern quarter of the Inca realm whose core was the great high plateau and its adjoining valleys. Uru-Chipaya was spoken around the shores of Lake Titicaca and Lake Poopó and along the banks of the Desaguadero River connecting these two bodies of water: the region that Nathan Wachtel (1986) refers to as the "aquatic axis" of the south-central Andes. Pockets of Uru-Chipaya speakers were also located on the Pacific coast of southern Peru and northern Chile. Only a handful of people still speak the ancient Uru-Chipaya language. Puquina was spoken in the arid Peruvian coastal valleys south of Arequipa, across the mountainous highlands of southern Peru and northwestern Bolivia and into the humid, sub-tropical eastern slopes of the Andes. Puquina is now an extinct language. Aymara, one of three languages in a group referred to as Jaqi, is today the dominant indigenous tongue of highland southern Peru and Bolivia with over 3 million native speakers. In the past, Aymara, or more generally Jaqi, may have been spoken as far north as the mountainous regions east of modern Lima (Hardman 1979, 1981). Quechua, today spoken by over 20 million native Andeans, was the language of the late Inca empire. Quechua dialects are spoken from northwestern Argentina to Ecuador with a continuous highland distribution from the region south of Cuzco into northern Peru. The origins and history of the various Quechua dialects are the subject of heated scholarly debate (see, for instance, Torero 1970; Stark 1976, 1979; Bird et al. 1983–4; Isbell 1983–4 among others), but it seems clear that the Quechua spoken in enclaves throughout southern Bolivia and northwestern Argentina was the result of expansion by the Inca empire into those regions (Figure 2.5).

It is likely that at least three of these languages were spoken by the various ethnic groups that were incorporated in the Tiwanaku state: Uru-Chipaya, Puquina and proto–Aymara. The question of which of these was the dominant language remains unresolved. Arguments based on the distribution of toponyms and other lexical markers have been formulated to demonstrate that Puquina was the original language of the Tiwanaku people (Torero 1974; Hardman 1979, 1981). However, a reasonable case on similar distributional grounds can also be made for proto-Aymara (Bird et al. 1983–4). Both of these arguments attempting to link a language with the people of Tiwanaku share the core assumption that the spatial distribution of the distinctive Tiwanaku art style, represented in sculptures, painted pottery, metals, wooden objects, and textiles, reflects the aggressive expansion of a single ethnic group that imposed linguistic uniformity in its direct sphere of influence. Most scholars do agree that Uru-Chipaya was

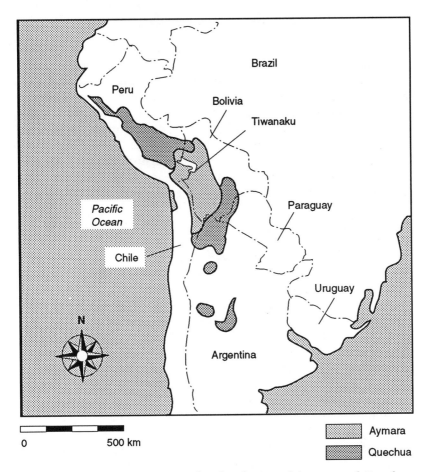

Figure 2.5 Approximate geographic distribution of Aymara and Quechua languages in the south-central Andes (ca. 1532). (Based on Bird et al. 1988: Figure 1).

more specialized and restricted in its distribution than either Puquina or proto-Aymara, and therefore less likely to represent the mother tongue of Tiwanaku.

Although the linguistic data are still ambiguous, and not easily shaped into certain conclusions, they do provide another glimpse and a possible entrée into life in the Tiwanaku realm. Accordingly, I will use the data and controversies of historical linguistic reconstructions and of contemporary ethnography in this book to help illuminate, in so far as possible, the origins and character of the pluriethnic world of ancient Tiwanaku.

The Paleoecological Evidence

Human populations have dramatic, transforming effects on their environment. To realize how profound and interrelated these transformations are, we need only look to our own industrial activities that have generated a chain reaction leading from atmospheric ozone depletion to possible global warming trends to negative impacts on critical staple crops and human health levels. Large-scale human impact on environments are not a peculiar product of the industrial world. The advent of intensive agriculture and city life throughout the pre-industrial world produced the technological and demographic conditions that induced long-term, transformative changes in local physical environments. For instance, irrigated agriculture, even when managed well, frequently resulted in hypersalinization of soils that caused serious problems for archaic states which relied on dependable agricultural production for their economic well-being. The civilizations of southern Mesopotamia and the Indus Valley are trenchant examples of societies that generated some of the conditions of their own decline through intensification of irrigation systems to the point at which soil salinization became irreversible, permanently damaging the arable land that was the fundamental source of their food supply. The pre-industrial Mayan civilization of Central America radically altered their rainforest environment through construction of massive agricultural systems and intense episodes of city building and urban renewal. The famous collapse of Mayan civilization around A.D. 900 may be attributed, at least in part, to humanly induced alteration of a fragile tropical forest environment (Rice and Rice 1984).

Careful, interdisciplinary analysis of the paleoecological record can provide us with a measure of the physical impact of human populations on their environment. For instance, there are fine-grained analytical techniques that furnish indices of deforestation, or the contribution of populations to local and regional soil erosion and sedimentation of lakes, rivers, and estuaries. These indices and rates of environmental transformation calculated from the paleoecological record can, in turn, generate provocative questions and hypotheses regarding the effects of culturally induced environmental changes on the constitution of human societies. In general, culturally induced environmental changes, whether deliberate alterations of physical landscapes or unintended by-products of large-scale human activities, cause substantial stress in human societies. Often such changes negatively affect the capacity of societies to sustain economic production and growth. Societies experiencing such stresses may respond in a number of ways. They may develop technological innovations that reduce or overcome the stress.

They may fission into smaller population units, or reorganize their political institutions thereby reducing stress by structural transformation. Or, like the Maya, they may simply collapse.

In short, a rich body of data invaluable for reconstructing the history and structural transformations of archaic civilizations remains encapsulated within the paleoecological record. All too frequently for lack of interdisciplinary collaboration these data lie dormant and underexploited. In the case of the Tiwanaku heartland, we are now in a position to incorporate the results of recent, systematic paleoecological research conducted in conjunction with my own multi-disciplinary project at Tiwanaku and in its immediate hinterland. At various points throughout this book, I will introduce insights into the changing man–land relationships gained from this multi-disciplinary research that characterized the emergence and development of Tiwanaku civilization. I will pay particular attention to the far-reaching and subtle effects of the massive, artificial agricultural landscapes created by Tiwanaku to sustain its urban populations and to generate economic surplus on the historical trajectory of Tiwanaku civilization. The history of agricultural reclamation and collapse played out against a background of both gradual and radical environmental changes is intimately associated with the story of the people of Tiwanaku. Given the multiple, interpenetrating relationships of environment and human society, I will first bring into sharp relief some of the connections between the natural and social worlds that helped to shape the special character of the ancient Andean world.

3

The Natural and Social Setting

At some point in the relentless drive to industrialization, the Western mind severed the connection between the rhythms of nature and the daily patterns of social life. Nature and environment for the hyper-urbanized populations of the modern world have been transformed into abstracted, increasingly romanticized ideals: one political cause among many, but no longer an experienced daily reality. The dwellers in megalopolis have lost immediacy and involvement with the chain of events that links them to their food supply. In the industrial world, food is transformed from its raw state into convenient commodity packets, unseen by its consumers, and purchased without consciousness of the processes of production.

This sense of alienation from nature, except as a kind of nostalgic, recreational icon, inhibits us from grasping the profound sense of connectivity to the agricultural cycle of the seasons that was the most distinguishing characteristic of civilizations in the pre-industrial world. In that world, now all but lost to us, philosophical and religious conceptions were born of and firmly rooted in a rich agrarian heritage. Social relationships, patterns of work, ideologies, systems of artistic expression were all products of an ancient cultural landscape of which the technology, sociology, and ritual of farming was the pivot. We can spontaneously appreciate the products of these pre-industrial civilizations, but in order to truly understand their nature and meaning, we must learn to perceive them on their own terms. We must attempt an imaginative reconstruction of the conditions of ancient life.

In the first instance, such a reconstruction demands the capacity to revivify in the mind a sense of what it means to live in a society directly and inextricably bound to the imperatives of agriculture. To achieve this, we must conceptually strip away the seemingly endless layers of food industry intermediaries and governmental agencies that today insulate us from the primary acts of tilling, planting, weeding, and harvesting a field. We must imagine a world in which virtually the entire population resides, generation after generation, in small villages and hamlets scattered across the countryside. A society in which perhaps 90 percent of the population earn their living from farming, petty craft production, and local barter, and live under constant threat of agricultural catastrophe and famine. The primitive splendor and cosmopolitan character of the great cities of antiquity disguise the realization that the foundations of archaic states rested upon the nitty-gritty pediment of rural agriculture.

Recreating the conditions of ancient life begins with a detailed understanding of the physical setting, the juxtaposition of landscapes and natural resources, in which the drama of the rise and decline of civilizations played itself out. This does not entail simply cataloging the resource endowments of environmental zones inhabited by ancient populations. Rather, we seek a more complex understanding of the relationship between preindustrial humans and their environment.

To what extent did the unequal distribution of natural resources affect patterns of human settlement and production, and the structure of social institutions, such as trade and marketing? What kinds of environments and resources were valued by the indigenous culture? Which of these were harnessed for economically productive purposes? Do we find relationships between ethnicity and the exploitation of specific ecological niches? What was the role of technological innovation in transforming perceived boundaries between productive versus marginal or wastelands? How did long-term environmental change affect the course of civilization, and can we define the impact and discover the resulting social responses?

These are some of the fundamental questions that I will address throughout this exploration of the remarkable civilization created by the people of Tiwanaku. The essential point of departure for understanding the dynamic relationship between landscape and human society in this Andean civilization is appreciating the breathtaking diversity and peculiar structure of the natural environment in which it evolved. To a significant degree, the spatial organization and political economy of Tiwanaku society was rooted in a dramatic, highly differentiated landscape that can best be portrayed as a true ecological mosaic. This metaphor of a mosaic, which emphasizes the diversity of ecological niches exploited by Tiwanaku, however, should not obscure the underlying general organization of biotic, climatic, and natural resources zones that characterizes the Andean natural environment. In what follows, I will begin with a consideration of this environment from a macroregional perspective (essentially the entire

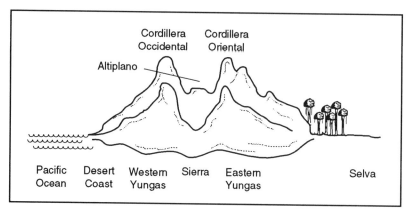

Figure 3.1   Cross-section illustrating the five principal physiographic divisions of the Andean world: desert coast, sierra, altiplano, yungas, and selva (or tropical forest). Note that the yungas, divided into east and west segments, refer to warm lands on the eastern slopes of the Cordillera Oriental and the western slopes of the Cordillera Occidental, respectively.

central and southern Andes), and then gradually narrow the focus to generate a finer grained portrait of the specific environmental life zones and resources routinely used by the people of Tiwanaku. Tiwanaku was a predatory, expansive state society, one of the first empires in the Andes. Its resulting sphere of geopolitical action was extensive, overlapping the boundaries of its core region in the Andean high plateau. For this reason, an appreciation of the entire range of ecological settings in the Andean macroregion is essential to fully understand the underpinnings of Tiwanaku's state and local economies.

Structurally, the Andean natural environment can be divided into five principal physiographic regions: the desert plains of the Pacific coast; the mountainous highlands, or *sierra* basins; the high plateau, or *altiplano* of southern Peru and Bolivia; the humid, eastern slopes of the Andes, or *montaña*; and the true tropical rainforests of the Amazon basin (Figure 3.1). Proceeding east to west from the Amazon basin across the mountainous highlands down to the Pacific coast, climate, precipitation, and vegetation patterns change dramatically, with a general trend toward increasing aridity until one reaches the strip of coastal desert that forms the western edge of the continent from northern Peru to central Chile. The Pacific coastal deserts of Peru and Chile are among the most forbidding tracts of land on earth. The only relief from the monotonous gray-brown desert landscape is offered by a series of coastal rivers cascading down the western slopes of the

Andes. These rivers, naturally enough, have become oases for coastal peoples over the millennia, yielding a series of fertile bands in an otherwise sterile and hostile environment.

The perpetual aridity of the Peruvian and north Chilean coast is brought about by the interaction of rain-laden southeast trade winds, cold ocean currents, and the coastal landscape (Figure 3.2). As the southeast trades blow along the coast, the cold waters of near-shore currents keep the ocean air cool and hold evaporation to a minimum. However, as this mass of air reaches the littoral, pushing up against the ramparts of the Andean massif which towers within sight of shore, it is warmed by the higher temperatures of the land, increasing its capacity to retain moisture. Consequently, little rain falls on the narrow coastal strip. Flowing over the westernmost chain of mountains, the wind is forced upward, through atmospheric levels of diminishing pressure. As the pressure is reduced, the air expands and cools. Decreasing temperature lowers the capacity of the air to retain water, and at altitudes around 2,000 meters the saturation point is reached. Regular annual rainfall occurs above this altitude in the highlands (Robinson 1964:240). Some of this water eventually returns to the coast in the form of runoff in mountain streams and rivers. The levees and natural flood plains of these rivers originating in the highland collection basins are the fragile life lines of the coast, permitting year-round cultivation of food and tree crops. With the advent of widespread artificial irrigation in the Andes at some point in the second millennium B.C., these naturally watered floodplains were extended laterally to incorporate entire valleys and, eventually, multiple valley networks into large-scale agricultural production systems.

The deep, cold waters of the Pacific Ocean play a different, but equally critical role in the economic environment of the coast. The interplay of several coastal currents results in an upwelling of waters bearing a tremendous load of chemical nutrients from the ocean depths that sustains a variety of marine plants. The plants, in turn, provide forage for millions of other organisms, and eventually, this great food chain terminates in a bountiful harvest of marine produce. Exploitation of these vast, renewable marine resources is, without a doubt, an ancient Andean pattern (Moseley 1975), one that continues to this day (Idyll 1973).

The characteristic horizontal banding of the Andean landscape along the desert coast is replicated along the vertical axis, eastward from the coast into the mountainous highlands. These vertical bands of life-zones, unlike the radical alternation of sterile desert and fertile river valley along the coast, are the product of altitude, and therefore the variation in micro-environments assumes more subtle forms,

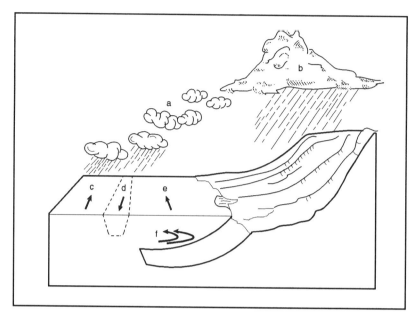

Figure 3.2   A schematic cross-section of the Pacific coast's physiography and ocean current system. Moisture-carrying clouds moving off the Pacific Ocean are warmed by the land mass, and a temperature inversion inhibits further precipitation (a), leaving the coast dry but cool. Upon reaching the higher, cooler elevations of the Andes, the clouds yield rain above 2,500 meters (b). The coastal waters off Peru are swept northward by the oceanic current (c) and the narrow coastal current (e), while the normally small counter current (d) pushes in the opposite direction. Upwelling waters (f) from the ocean depths carry rich nutrients that support abundant marine life. (Based on Moseley 1975: Figure 21).

grading one into the other. This climatic stratification is the result of altitudinal change correlated with variation in temperature, precipitation and topographic relief. Microclimatic variation in the Andes can almost invariably be linked with changes in altitude.

Immediately east of the arid coastal strip, the zone from the western foothills of the Andean chain up to the sierra basins is a highly dissected, desolate terrain dotted with stunted shrubs and an assortment of magnificent, bizarrely shaped cacti. Very few vestiges of past agricultural activity can be found in this bioclimatic tier, and it is likely that human exploitation was restricted to hunting small mammals and perhaps collecting a few plants, some of which, like the mescaline bearing columnar cactus, were used for medicinal and ritual purposes. Above this zone lies a rolling, transitional landscape of steppe covered with grasses and groves of trees, such as the native pine. In the central Andes, this more heavily watered transitional steppe gives way to multiple intermontane basins hemmed in by the two great mountain chains that form the Andes: the Cordillera Occidental (western) and the Cordillera Oriental (eastern) (Figure 3.1). These high mountain valleys were heavily populated in the prehispanic past and became the core territory for the Inca empire. The indigenous populations of the intermontane basins farmed the rich alluvial soils of the valley floors and extended the spatial reach of food cultivation by constructing contour terraces, frequently connected with irrigation canals which drew water from mountain springs at higher elevations.

Immediately south of Cuzco, the two imposing mountain chains diverge significantly. Interposed between them is an anciently uplifted high plateau, the great Andean *altiplano,* which lies between 3,000 and 4,000 masl. The *altiplano* proper, defined by the relatively flat depression between the two towering *cordilleras,* runs for over 800 kilometers from north to south, from southernmost Peru to northwestern Argentina, and ranges between 120 and 160 kilometers from west to east. This enormous plateau, incorporating thousands of square kilometers, comprises the largest area of interior drainage in highland South America. The geologic processes of tectonic uplifting and orogenesis that created this vast, enclosed drainage basin also generated extensive fresh water lakes. The *altiplano* and the lakes were formed in the Miocene with the rise of the Andes (James 1971), and attained present form in the Pleistocene (Lavenu 1981). Since formation, the lakes of the *altiplano* have been disappearing through evaporative loss. Today only Lake Titicaca on the northern end of the high plateau and Lake Poopó to the southeast remain significant bodies of water (Figure 3.3).

Over the past 100,000 years, Lake Titicaca has been as much as 100 meters above its current level (Servant and Fontes 1978). Some sedimentological studies suggest lake-level fluctuations of 50 meters during the past 12,000 years (Wirrmann and Oliveira Almeida 1987). In historical times, the lake level has fluctuated as much as 5 meters within a two-year period. The last major fluctuation, generated by torrential rainfall, occurred between September 1985 and April 1986 when the level of the lake rose nearly three meters, inundating many square kilometers of the littoral zone in Peru and Bolivia and destroying at least 11,000 hectares of agricultural fields. In contrast, Lake Poopó is currently suffering the ineluctable evolutionary fate of the once imposing paleolakes that covered virtually the entire *altiplano*

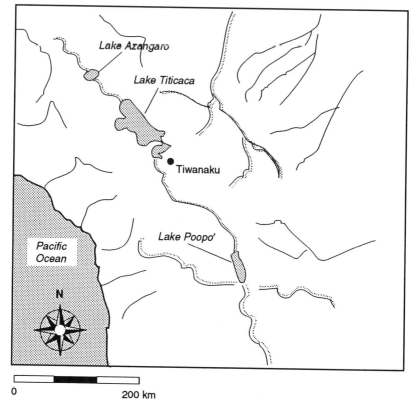

0   200 km

*Figure 3.3   The Bolivian altiplano, from Lake Titicaca to Lake Poopó.
(Based on Wachtel 1986: Figure 15.2).*

during the Miocene: it is becoming increasingly shallow and saline each century. In a relatively short geologic time, Lake Poopó will be rechristened the Salar Poopó, or the salt pan of Poopó, like its counterparts to the southwest, the *salares* of Coipasa and Uyuni, remnants of once gigantic fresh water lakes now converted to deposits of solid mineral salts.

Precipitation on the *altiplano* decreases from north to south. The region around Lake Titicaca, although subject to periodic, potentially catastrophic downpours, receives an annual average rainfall of around 700 millimeters which falls principally in a wet season between December and March. Farther south, precipitation drops off dramatically, and the region of the Salar de Uyuni experiences consecutive years when no measurable rain ever falls. Like precipitation, the terrestrial vegetation of the *altiplano* is sparse and decreases in a marked cline from north to south. The principal natural vegetational associations of the *altiplano* consist of tough alpine bunch grasses which provide forage for the llama herds of the local Aymara populations as well as construction materials for houses and sheds, and hardy evergreen shrubs like the *tola*, a resinous plant that burns to an incredibly hot fire and has been used as a source of fuel by *altiplano* inhabitants for millennia. Interspersed among the grasses and shrubs one can find the occasional cactus, and a wide range of delicate herbs, mosses, and lichens, frequently growing in mutualistic relationships with the alpine grasses.

Within the greater *altiplano* region, the Lake Titicaca basin was the most productive environment for human populations. The immense water surface of the lake (8,600 square kilometers) and its great depth (greater than 200 meters at points) create a moderating influence on local temperatures. Milder temperatures in the near-shore environment, along with predictable and more abundant rainfall, converted the Lake Titicaca basin into an enormous engine of agricultural production. Not surprisingly, the lake district has sustained high population densities since the emergence of sedentary populations over 3,000 years ago.

The Lake Titicaca basin was a pivotal hearth for the domestication of important, high-altitude adapted food crops. Most indigenous crops of the *altiplano* are derived from the same families as the natural vegetation. Apart from multiple varieties of potato, many of these native food crops are unfamiliar to the Westerner: tubers like *oca*, *ulluco* and *mashwa*, grains like *quinoa*, and *cañiwa*, and legumes like *tarwi* and *jiquima*. Over the course of the millennia, the prehispanic populations of the lake district developed a variety of sophisticated technologies for intensifying agricultural production. These included artificial canalization of rivers and *quebradas* to regulate groundwater, erection of check dams, aqueducts, and dikes to divert or impound water on agricultural fields, excavation of massive raised agricultural fields in the perennially inundated landscapes along the rim of Lake Titicaca, and construction of contour terraces on steep hills that conserved precious soils and ground moisture and significantly reduced erosion. These indigenous technologies of intensification are a fascinating topic in themselves and their history and function are the subject of Chapter 6.

Juxtaposed with this terrestrial landscape of intensive agricultural production was the rich aquatic resource of the lake itself. The near-shore waters of the lake harbored vast numbers of migratory waterfowl including ducks and flamingo that were taken with snares or darts. These shallow waters were also the niche for many aquatic plants such as *totora*, a tuberous, edible reed that was also employed as an industrial crop to thatch houses, weave shirts, and build small watercraft. Other aquatic plants like water milfoil, widgeon grass, and water weed were dredged as forage for domesticated animals, a practice that continues today in rural communities along the lake edge. Deeper, colder waters farther offshore offered the promise of abundant harvests of fish. Along with exotic species introduced during the twentieth century such as rainbow trout, these native fish are still avidly sought today and sold fresh from the boats in local markets.

Beyond the moderating influence of Lake Titicaca, intensive forms of agricultural production are rare as the landscape gradually becomes more arid and desolate toward the southerly reaches of the Bolivian high plateau. Here enormous barchan sand dunes loom across the horizon, driven forward inexorably by the ferocious windstorms of the *altiplano*. Saltating sand which can rapidly choke rudimentary canals and increasingly saline soil conditions place nearly intolerable burdens on the farmer. Agriculture in the southern *altiplano* is a desultory affair. The isolated, chronically poor villages of the region plant little more than *quinoa*, an astonishing, crimson-colored grain that is saline tolerant, and highly resistant to the brutal, ultraviolet solar radiation characteristic of the high plateau. In certain locales, native inhabitants developed artificial techniques for manipulating river water to enhance agricultural production. In the region of the Chipaya ethnic group west of Lake Poopó, for instance, villagers construct small diversion structures and dikes of sod blocks to impound the icy waters of the Lauca River which tumble down from quiescent, snow-capped volcanoes along the nearby Chilean border. This simple form of irrigation may permit the Chipaya to harvest a single crop of *quinoa*. At other times, the vagaries of precipitation reduce the depth of the mountain snow pack, the river level falls, and the *quinoa* withers.

Given these debilitating, risky environmental conditions, the core of the southern *altiplano* economy was not intensive agriculture as it was farther to the north. Here economic livelihood, social and ritual life, and even philosophical conceptions of the indigenous inhabitants revolved around pastoralism. The vast, gently undulating plains of the region were the natural habitat of the Andean camelids: llama, alpaca, guanaco, and vicuña. The earliest Paleoindians hunted these animals for their meat, fat, and wool since their entry into the South American continent some 14,000 years ago. Llama and alpaca were domesticated in this region perhaps as early as 7,000 years ago (Fernández 1974). These two domesticated animals rapidly became the cornerstone of the *altiplano* economy, particularly in the south.

Even in the agriculturally productive northern *altiplano*, sixteenth-century documents reveal that the Aymara kingdoms controlled immense herds of llama and alpaca. These animals were bred carefully, primarily for their wool, which was woven into a variety of textile products: tunics, bags, hats, slings, and the like. The textiles in turn were used as clothing, exchanged for food and other products, or used to discharge social obligations. These Andean herd animals were also a readily available source of food and industrial products. They grazed on the ubiquitous, tough grasses of the high plateau, transforming otherwise economically unpromising plants into a rich source of consumable animal fats and meat.

Virtually all parts and by-products of these animals were exploited for some purpose. Whole llamas were sacrificed in religious ceremonies and auguries were taken from the quantity and disposition of body fat. Llama fat itself was a critical source of food energy and an essential symbolic element in rituals. Llama bones were transformed into utilitarian tools: hide scrapers were shaped from mandibles hafted on wooden shafts, while knives, needles, and awls were produced from long bones. Llama dung, or *taquia*, became an important source of fuel in this treeless, desert environment. Finally, the llama became the *altiplano* dwellers' essential means of transporting bulk commodities long distances over daunting, perilous terrain. It was, in fact, the only efficient pack animal in the ancient Americas. By the end of the prehispanic era, llama caravans made up of as many as 2,000 animals were ranging widely over Collasuyu, transporting textiles, pottery, metals, and salt. Understanding the people of Tiwanaku requires grasping the fundamental economic, social, political, ideological, and even emotional role of llama and alpaca pastoralism in their lives.

Immediately to the east of the Andean *altiplano*, crossing the great eastern mountain range, which in Bolivia carries the name Cordillera Real, we move quickly into a world entirely different from the bleak, forbidding plateaus of tenuous subsistence agriculture and llama herding. Wild rivers originating in the ancient glaciers of the *cordillera* cut and gouge the hard rock of the mountains in spectacular displays of headward erosion. Waterfalls cascade violently for hundreds of meters down the vertiginous eastern slopes of the Andes which become increasingly humid and forested as one descends through roiling banks of damp fog from the high mountain passes. Gnarled, evergreen shrubs, dripping with parasitic wild orchids, cling tenaciously to the fractured black shale and basalt-clad mountainsides. Enclaves of nearly flat land with deep, rich soils are encrusted in the tortuous, almost chaotic jumble of rock formations that form the eastern edge of the Andean chain. These are the opulent hot lands of the *montaña*, or *yungas* as the Aymara call them.

The upper margins of the *yungas* abut the treeless, windswept steppe referred to by the Indians as the *puna*, a high, cold land over 4,000 masl that was used anciently for pasturage. The lower margins merge gradually with the true tropical rainforest of the Amazon basin. The *yungas* are a zone of radical landscape transition, of movement from the dry, frozen edge of glaciated tundra where biological activity seems virtually paralyzed, dispersed, and energy conserving, to the suffocating humid heat of the tropical forest swarming with insects and redolent with the organic smells of decaying plant and animal tissue. Nowhere in the world is this transition between radically divergent biozones completed so abruptly and so dramatically as in the *yungas*.

The natural vegetation of the *yungas* is an exuberant mix of trees, shrubs, vines, wild fruits: a classic subtropical montane forest. The wide variety of hard and soft wood trees of the *yungas* such as walnut, mahogany, cedar, and ironwood palm, have been extracted for timber for countless generations. Other aromatic woods and shrubs like sasparilla, saffron, and cinchona (the tree that produces the anti-malarial compound quinine) were exploited for their medicinal and ritual properties. Today huge quantities of native and exotic tropical fruits are taken from the *yungas* to supply the highland cities of Bolivia and Peru: avocados, bananas, pineapples, mangoes, guavas, melons of all kinds, papayas, and the less familiar chirimoya and tumbo among many others. Strawberries, oranges, lemons, and coffee grow cheek by jowl with maize, hot peppers, manioc, and potato. Virtually the entire roster of wild and cultivated plants flourish in the rich soils and mild climate of the *yungas*.

The constraints to agriculture in the *yungas* are not set by climate or soil, but rather by topography. Arable land in the *yungas* is at a premium: the broken, tectonically folded landscape concedes little in the way of flat land to the hopeful farmer. Here labor intensive terracing is a way of life, and it significantly expands the amount of land that can be reclaimed for agricultural production. Even in the Andes, however, the most resourceful and energetic farmer cannot carve terraces out of sheer mountain cliffs. When the crops are brought in, they must still be hauled out of the *yungas* over the terrifying, snakelike gravel roads that wind upward over the high mountain passes to the urban markets. Today enormous ten-ton diesel trucks laden with people and produce grind their way ponderously in low gear up the grade, churning dense clouds of dust and gravel. On the return trip, they hurtle back down the narrow, switchbacked mountain road with wheels grazing the edge.

Until the advent of motorized traffic, the products of the *yungas* were brought out by a more tranquil and less perilous mode of transport: on the backs of people and llamas. Before the Spanish conquest, the lords of the *altiplano* commissioned native caravan drivers to move the highly prized products of the warm lands to the cities on the shores of Lake Titicaca. From the upper reaches of the *yungas* came potatoes and *quinoa*. The middle elevations produced huge harvests of maize, beans, squash, peanuts, chili peppers, and cotton. The hot valley floors and tropical forests brought fine hardwoods, resins, honey, medicinal and hallucinogenic plants, the pelts of wild animals and brilliantly colored tropical bird feathers to be sewn into the costumes of the native elite.

Arguably the most precious commodity of the *yungas*, sought out with fervor by the lords of the lake, was a plant indispensable to the daily life of their people, one associated with spirituality and the supernatural: coca. Coca was, and still is, avidly traded and consumed by the natives of the high plateau. Mixed with lime made from the ashes of carbonized plants, shells, or minerals, coca is chewed slowly throughout the day, releasing small quantities of the alkaloid compounds that can relieve fatigue brought on by long hours of manual labor at high altitude. But coca is more than an analgesic. It serves a central role in the ritual and social life of the Aymara communities. Offerings of dry coca leaf, cigarettes, crystal rock candy, ground minerals, herbs, and llama fetuses are carefully arranged on *mesas*, symbolic tables of textiles stretched on the ground. Later these offerings are burned by the *yatiris*, the ritual representatives of the community, to supplicate the mountain deities for rainfall and fertile fields. Coca leaf is also used in divination rituals to predict the future, and to assess whether communal decisions are auspicious: their color, shape, and the way they fall on the ground after being tossed in the air are all important attributes for interpreting the response of the coca augury. Coca leaf is placed in the mouth of the dead during mourning ceremonies. For the living, coca represents the *sine qua non* of social reciprocity. If a young man solicits help from family and community members to till a field, or roof a house, proper etiquette demands that he have an ample supply of coca to offer through the day.

Given its centrality in the social and spiritual life of the natives, it is not surprising that the ancient polities of the *altiplano* like the state of Tiwanaku strove mightily to control prime coca producing lands in the *yungas*. The Tiwanaku elite established extensive coca plantations both in the *yungas* region and in the subtropical valleys farther to the southeast such as Cochabamba. In fact, the desire to control huge supplies of coca may have been a key motive in the predatory expansion of the state. This possibility, of course, contains a certain irony for contemporary Bolivians. By 1990, the *yungas* and the Chaparé region of Cochabamba were under seige by narcotics enforcement agents battling drug lords for control of the coca production. Clandestine trafficking in coca and coca paste, the essential ingredients of rock cocaine, has overwhelmed the legitimate agrarian economy of these areas. Attempts to destroy coca fields have failed, and production continues to rise in the absence of economically viable alternative crops. While the drug war rages over a modern narcotic derivative, the divine coca of the native Andean continues to play an integral role in agricultural rituals, in community events, and in the daily life of the individual.

Beyond the *yungas*, at the easternmost fringe of the Andean world, the ancient tropical forests of the Amazon basin begin. This environment of immense, high canopy forests and sluggish, sediment laden rivers replete with exotic animals was alien to the native Andean. The Inca empire's attempts to politically incorporate and extract tribute from tropical forest groups were utter disasters. Inca armies became hopelessly bogged down in the trackless interior expanses of the forests. Without familiar open horizons to guide them, they thrashed about in disarray attempting to engage the locals in pitched battles that would lead to capitulation, or at least in the diplomacy of intimidation that the Inca had used so effectively in their highland homelands (Hemming 1970). The ferocity, cunning, and strategic sophistication of the Amazonian groups, insulated in their immense, densely covered world of forests and rivers, frustated the much vaunted imperial war machine.

The Inca withdrew. Saving face, they defined the eastern border of their empire, and therefore symbolically the known world, as the montane forests of the *yungas*. Beyond that mountainous edge was beyond the pale of civilization – a barbaric, inchoate world of true savages. Despite this paroxysm of self-deluding ethnic pride, the pragmatic engines of commerce ground on. Although beyond the pale of civilization, the Amazonian groups were not outside the profitable circuits of trade that linked the tropical forest lowlands with the Andean highlands. As they had for centuries, enormous quantities of tropical forest products flowed upstream into the urbanized world of the Andes. The coveted blue, yellow, and crimson colored feathers of parrots, kingfishers and macaws, jaguar pelts, monkeys, placermined gold, hallucinogenic plants, resinous woods, and foodstuffs were all moved to higher elevations into the stream of Andean commerce. The relationship between the Andean and Amazonian worlds was essentially one of down-the-line exchange, of intense intercourse at the frontiers, of the movement of commodities and information on the margins. But no colony of Andean civilization was established in the tropical forest; no outpost of Andean ideology was exported to or embraced by the Amazonian peoples. They inhabited separate, but tangentially connected realities. In that respect, the tropical forest was never physically exploited by native Andeans directly. Rather it played a more passive role from the perspective of the Andes, a wild, intractable, but seductive source of precious raw materials.

Ecology and Economy

To this point I have canvassed the broad contours of the ecological mosaic that was the natural arena of adaptation for the people of Tiwanaku. Each of the five principal physiographic zones of the south-central Andes from the Pacific coast to the tropical lowlands incorporated within its boundaries myriad microclimatic zones and subtle variations in precipitation, hydrology, topography, soil quality, animals and plants. The classificatory knife can mince finely indeed. Botanists and geographers have systematized the Andean natural environment in multiple ways, from Pulgar Vidal's (1946) "eight natural regions of Peru" and Troll's (1968) 10 "geo-ecological" tiers, through Tosi's (1960) 34 life zones, to Weberbauer's (1945) 15 regional and 150 local ecological zones. However the individual pieces of the ecological mosaic are sliced, the key point is to grasp how these pieces are distributed and structured, and the manner in which local configurations of the ecological mosaic affected the technology and organization of production in the ancient Andean world. For throughout this debate there is consensus on one thing: in that world environment and economy were inextricably linked.

The most influential general formulation of the relationship between ecology and political economy in the south-central Andes was formalized by the anthropologist John Murra. Murra (1972) suggested that many different ethnic groups in the Andes, particularly those in the south, maintained a cultural ideal of economic self-sufficiency through control of a maximum number of altitudinally stratified ecological tiers. An underlying asssumption in this model is that the different resource endowments of highlands versus lowlands generated a kind of selective pressure for direct colonization of multiple, distinct production zones. The inhabitants of highland basins over 3,000 meters in elevation were severely constrained by the kinds of food crops they could cultivate at altitude. Agriculture at high altitude in the Andes

Table 3.1   Temperature, precipitation and altitude ranges for the principal native Andean crops

	Annual Mean Temperature °C	Annual Rainfall (dm)	Altitude (m)
Aracacia xanthorrhiza (arracacha)	15–23	7–15	850–956
Arachis hypogaea (peanut)	11–27	3–40	46–1000
Capsicum annuum (chili pepper)	9–27	3–40	2–1000
Capsicum frutescens (chili pepper)	8–27	30–40	385–1000
Chenopodium quinoa (quinoa)	5–27	6–26	28–3878
Cucurbita ficifolia (squash)	11–23	3–17	850–956
Cucurbita maxima (squash)	7–27	3–27	385–1000
Cucurbita moschata (squash)	7–27	3–28	28–1000
Erythroxylon coca (coca)	17–27	7–40	450–1200
Gossypium barbadense (cotton)	9–26	5–40	320–1006
Ipomoea batatas (sweet potato)	9–27	3–42	28–1000
Lagenaria siceraria (gourd)	15–27	7–28	850–956
Manihot esculenta (manioc)	15–29	5–40	46–1006
Nicotiana tabacum (tobacco)	7–27	3–40	57–1000
Oxalis tuberosa (oca)	12–25	5–25	850–1700
Persea americana (avocado)	13–27	3–40	320–1750
Phaseolus lunatus (lima bean)	9–27	3–42	28–1000
Phaseolus vulgaris (common bean)	5–27	3–42	2–3700
Psidium guajava (guava)	15–29	2–42	28–1000
Solanum tuberosum (potato)	4–27	3–26	2–3830
Tropaelum tuberosum (mashwa)	8–25	7–14	850–3700
Ullucus tuberosus (olluco)	11–12	14	3700–3830
Zea mays (maize)	5–29	3–40	2–3350

(From Moseley 1992: 30, Figure 12).

is inherently risky, prone to debilitating frosts, hail, wind, droughts, and floods. Only the hardy, high-altitude adapted tubers and grains grow readily in this dour environment. In starkest numerical terms, approximately 95 percent of the principal Andean food crops can be cultivated below 1,000 meters, but only 20 percent reproduce readily over 3,000 meters (Table 3.1).

The implication of this differential resource distribution is clear: in order to enhance the variety and quantity of their foodstuffs, and thereby reduce the risk of subsistence agriculture, people living at high altitude sought access to the products of lower, warmer climatic zones. The most highly prized of these temperate land crops were maize and coca. Maize was significant as both a bulk food product, and as the principal ingredient of *chicha*, or maize beer, an essential component of ceremonial feasts hosted by political leaders throughout the ancient Andean world. Coca, of course, was the pre-eminent ritual plant of the Andes, indispensible for the entire panoply of formal, communal ceremonies related to agricultural and animal fertility, to transitions in the human life cycle, and for a multiplicity of informal rituals performed by individuals and households.

In most of the pre-industrial world, the problem of differential resource distribution is resolved by long-distance trade organized through a complex of merchants and markets. These mechanisms typically result in a flow of desired commodities through relatively long, indirect chains of barter over which the end consumer exercises little control. Although highland Andean peoples participated in such merchant-mediated networks, they relied more heavily on direct appropriation of desired resources through a strategy of maintaining autonomous production forces in as many ecological zones as possible. The distinct commodities produced in these ecological zones were extracted, processed, and transported entirely by members of a single group. This economic strategy enhanced community self-sufficiency by directly ensuring the diversification of production, and by eliminating the uncertainty engendered by potentially fragile trading relationships and by the manipulations of merchant brokers.

Given that the principal axis of environmental and natural resource variation in the Andes derives from altitudinal change, this economic strategy of direct access to a maximum number of ecological zones by a single group has been called "verticality," or the vertical economy. Even today one can see rural communities, particularly along the eastern slopes of the great Andean *cordillera*, maintaining use rights simultaneously to pasture lands for llama and alpaca in the high, cold meadows of the mountains above 4,000 meters; to potato, *oca* and *quinoa* fields in the mountainous basins over 3,000 meters; and to plots of maize, coca, and other warm lands crops in regions well below 2,000 meters.

The exploitation of altitudinally stratified resources in the Andes takes many specialized forms, but we can identify two principal variations on the theme that capture the essence of this remarkable economic strategy. The first of these is what we may refer to as compressed verticality (Brush 1977). In this form of the verticality strategy, a single village or ethnic group resides in a physical setting that permits easy access to contiguous, close-packed ecological zones. Different crop zones, pasture lands, or other localized resources such as sources of salt, honey, or fruit trees are within one or two days walk of the parent community. Generally, this parent community is situated above 2,000 meters in an agriculturally productive mountain basin. Individual members of the community, or, at times, the entire village, may reside temporarily in one of the lower ecological zones to manage the extraction of products unavailable in the high-altitude homeland.

The village maintains temporary dwellings on a number of ecological tiers and rotates residence among them in accordance with the agricultural and pastoral cycle of the seasons. The efficiency of this system relies heavily on group solidarity and the sharing of reciprocal obligations. Communities engaged in this form of verticality are characterized by strong bonds of kinship and by an ethic of self-help.

The second principal form of the verticality strategem resembles compressed verticality in that a single group maintains residences in multiple, altitudinally stratified environmental zones. However, in this variation on the theme, which has been aptly termed the "vertical archipelago," the ethnic group or village exploits resources in zones that are non-contiguous and widely dispersed, forming a series of independent "islands" of production (Murra 1972). In some contemporary villages engaged in this strategy, community members must trek up to 10 to 14 days from their home base in the mountains to reach distant fields in the tropical lowlands.

Although contemporary expressions of the vertical archipelago economy still exist, this form of verticality was most highly elaborated in the precolumbian world in the context of complex social formations, such as the indigenous Aymara kingdoms of the Lake Titicaca basin. In these kingdoms, the vertical archipelago was transformed into a formal, specialized system of production in which satellite communities from the home territory were sent to reside permanently as colonists in distant eastern *yungas* and Pacific coastal settings. There these colonists grew crops and extracted products for their own consumption, and for transshipment back to their high-altitude compatriots. By establishing this policy of permanent colonization, these polities enhanced the efficiency of their economic system by producing crops and other goods simultaneously in multiple ecological niches. In this system, food crops, raw products, and other commodities, rather than people, circulated through the archipelago.

The colonists from the highlands frequently shared the resources of the foreign territories in which they were resettled with the indigenous inhabitants, at times adopting the dress and customs of the locals (Salomon 1986). These colonists however, maintained basic rights to marriage, residence, familial lands and property in their communities of origin in the distant highlands. The number and kind of colonists maintained by the *altiplano* kingdoms in the various islands of production was highly variable, but could range from single, extended families of a few people to entire village communities.

Over the past decade, concepts of compressed, extended, and microverticality, multiethnic exploitation of economic islands arrayed in vertical archipelagos and even horizontal archipelagos have gained currency in the explanatory frameworks that seek to link economy and ecology in the Andes. Such concepts are valuable for understanding the economic and social worlds of the people of Tiwanaku, even if they are not the entire story. At the least, judicious application of these concepts focuses our attention on the variety of strategies that the Tiwanaku state employed to reduce risk and to achieve stability in economic production, and the manner in which this Andean ideal served to structure the people of Tiwanaku's perception of their own social and natural landscape.

The complexity and variability of the ecological setting inhabited by the people of Tiwanaku was more than matched by diversity in the ethnic, occupational, and cultural affiliations of the populations who shared their environment. Understanding the people of Tiwanaku entails appreciating, for instance, the profound cultural impact generated by the potentially uneasy and conflictive relationships between farmers and herders, or by the wealth differentials, status distinctions, and social hierarchies that emerged historically among ethnic groups competing over basic natural resources. The linkage between human society and environment in the Andes was never simple or mechanical, and it is the exploration of the rich textures and the dynamics of diversity in the social and natural worlds of the people of Tiwanaku that shapes this book.

4

Tiwanaku Emergence

About 14,000 years ago, the first humans laid eyes on the vast, high plateau around Lake Titicaca. These Andean pioneers were descendants of the earliest migrants to the New World who had passed over the Bering Straits from northeast Asia many generations before. As best we can reconstruct from the fragmentary evidence available to us, these early native Americans were organized in small, highly mobile bands that ranged widely over the landscape, hunting game animals and foraging to earn their livelihood. Only a few archaeological sites in the high plateau preserve remnants of their ancient actions: a small campsite here, a station for butchering game there, perhaps the remains of a quarry, or tool manufacturing site.

The historical connection between the people of Tiwanaku and their distant hunting and gathering ancestors was extremely remote. But these first inhabitants of the high plateau developed essential strategies and techniques for making a living at the top of the Andean world that remained virtually unchanged for millennia and would not have seemed alien in the rural reaches of the Tiwanaku state. One economic strategy worked out by the first Andeans was a pattern of transhumance, or seasonal nomadism between highland and lowland ecological zones. Over the past decade, Chilean archaeologists in particular have developed a general theory that explains early cultural evolution in the southern Andes in terms of an ancient, pervasive economic system that selected for continuous interregional exchange of people and basic resources (animals, plants, and mineral products) (Núñez 1962, 1965, 1971). Given the highly compressed elevational extremes of northern Chile, it is not surprising that this theory is, in many respects, a generalized extension of Murra's verticality concept.

Specifically, these archaeologists believe that, from about 8000 B.C. on, the Pacific coastal populations of northern Chile, who had by then established a stable maritime adaptation, were actively involved in an economic interaction with contemporaneous populations living at high altitudes in the inter-Andean basins and Bolivian *altiplano* to the east. At first, and for several millennia, this highland-coastal interaction took the form of seasonal nomadism. That is, at regular intervals during the year, populations that lived seasonally on the coast exploiting the rich biomass of the near-shore environment would journey into the inter-Andean basins and puna grasslands to hunt for vicuña and guanaco.

At some point before the fourth millennium B.C., the form of vertical economic integration changed as agriculture and fully domesticated llamas and alpacas were added to the economic repertoire, apparently first in the highlands and somewhat later on the coast. With agriculture, both highland and coastal communities established permanent sedentary settlements, the former based on a developing agro-pastoral economy, the latter on a productive agro-maritime adaptation. According to this scenario, however, vertical social interaction between highland and coast did not cease with the development of these more stable, diversified subsistence bases. On the contrary, the ancient highland-coast connections were intensified and expanded through the vehicle of organized llama caravans. After 1000 B.C., large pack trains of llamas traveling along these vertical axes between the established villages and towns of the highlands and coasts were a common scene throughout the southern Andes (Núñez and Dillehay 1978).

Over time and space, these llama caravans were organized in different ways. Most often, the Andean caravans were operated by politically independent pastoral societies. These pastoral nomads followed well-established trade routes, visiting predetermined, sedentary communities on the coast and in the high, Andean basins in a fixed seasonal round. The social relationships that bound the nomadic pastoralists with their sedentary trading partners was most likely some form of kinship or fictive kin arrangement, rather than an impersonal market linked to the value of commodities alone. Stable, reciprocal kinship bonds were essential to a system that entailed high risk ventures over the trackless, desertic wastes of the southern Andean *altiplano*: *caravaneros* would not hazard a perilous journey without the assurance of a guaranteed consumer for their products and, just as importantly, family-style hospitality at the end of the trail. During times of political expansionism, however, such as with the Tiwanaku state, many of the traditional trade routes came under the jurisdiction of centralized authorities. Although some independent pastoralists may have continued to operate their caravans autonomously at these times, the most lucrative trade routes surely became state monopolies.

Extensive Tiwanaku economic colonies in regions with abundant arable land point directly to such a conclusion (see Chapter 7). The caravans that linked the state-implanted colonies with the capital could only have been operated directly by the state itself, or in intimate collaboration with agents of the state. The great south Andean caravans brought about an extensive interregional exchange of people, products, and political and religious ideologies. In archaeological terms, the caravans were mechanisms of long-distance diffusion that was reflected materially in art styles shared over widely separated geographical regions, in highland colonies on the coast, and in a diverse array of trade items distributed throughout the southern Andes.

The earliest inhabitants of the high plateau pioneered a strategy and established a pattern that preadapted subsequent *altiplano* populations to extensive social and economic interactions with their lowland dwelling contemporaries. Naturally, the form and intensity of these vertical interactions changed within the context of local historical events and processes, but highland-lowland relationships always formed a salient feature of the social landscape in the southern Andes. In a real sense, then, these first Andeans laid the necessary foundations for the efficient systems of economic production and distribution that came to characterize the mature Tiwanaku state. But when do we first begin to glimpse specifically Tiwanaku, or Tiwanaku-like social and ideological patterns in the core territory of the Lake Titicaca basin? When and in what social context does the emergence of Tiwanaku as an identifiable cultural phenomenon take shape?

In the past decade, archaeological research on the *altiplano* of Bolivia and southern Peru has demonstrated the existence of several early, yet remarkably sophisticated regional cultures that flourished in the first and second millennia B.C. These regional cultures shared some basic organizational features: an economy based on a mixed pastoral-agricultural regime, with secondary reliance on hunting and on exploitation of the rich resources of Lake Titicaca, and a village-based settlement pattern. During this period, as well, we see the first material evidence for the emergence of regional ideologies. Shared ideological concepts, and perhaps even a common religious system in the Lake Titicaca basin, can be inferred from a basin-wide tradition of monumental stone sculptures, the elaboration of public architecture in the form of standardized temple complexes, and the diffusion of a religious iconography that apparently relates to the personification and worship of natural forces. Unfortunately, the transformative social processes that preceded this first and second millennia B.C. explosion of cultural complexity and sophistication in the Lake Titicaca basin remain virtually unknown.

Painfully little field research in the area has been directed toward the basic problems of plant and animal domestication, and with certainty we can now state hardly more than that these processes occurred. A clear understanding of the causative agents behind this second millennium "break through" in the Titicaca basin, reflected in the achievement by native populations of a demographic and cultural critical mass, remains elusive. But the picture begins to clarify after about 300 B.C. We know that around this time the centers of two of these early cultures, Pukara and Tiwanaku begin to coalesce into settlements that reach truly urban proportions, far outstripping other societies in terms of ideological prestige, economic power, and political influence. These two growing urban centers eventually eclipsed the other regional cultures of the Titicaca basin whose origin they had once shared.

Tiwanaku Precursors

One of the earliest and most recently described archeological complexes of this critical second millennium B.C. period is that of Wankarani (Ponce 1970, 1980). The Wankarani complex consists of a series of villages centered in the high plateaus north and northeast of Lake Poopó (Figure 4.1). The economy of Wankarani villages was typical of the *altiplano*, a combination of subsistence agriculture (primarily of potato and *quinoa*) and camelid pastoralism, similar, in many ways, to that of the Chipaya Indians who inhabit this region today. I have seen the Chipaya coax, with great skill and ingenuity, a single crop of potatoes and *quinoa* from their salt-encrusted fields. Despite chronically low yields, in these environmental conditions the Chipaya surely rank among the best farmers of the traditional world. Given the hostility of their environment for agricultural production, it is not surprising that llamas and alpacas play a pivotal role in Chipaya life, and one can imagine that the care and breeding of enormous camelid herds was likewise a cornerstone of Wankarani economy.

Ponce (1980) notes that some Wankarani villages have been found at lower altitudes near the valley of Cochabamba. He concludes that these villages were established to exploit resources such as wood and rich farmlands suitable for temperate land crops like maize that were not readily available on the high plateau. The geographical distribution of Wankarani settlements expresses a simple variation on the Andean theme of vertical control over distinct, altitudinally stratified resource zones. The material culture found associated with Wankarani villages – monochrome ceramics, basalt stone tools (particularly agricultural

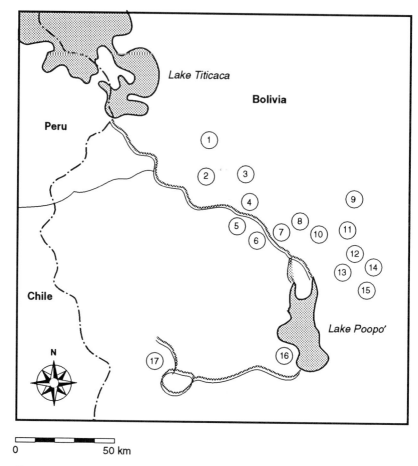

Key:
(1) Wankarani, (2) Sicasica, (3) Kellakellani, (4) Kelkana, (5) La Joya, (6) Kella Kollu,
(7) Pukara (de Beden), (8) Toluma, (9) Upsa-Upsa, (10) Upsa-Lullo, (11) Spulturas,
(12) Jikilla, (13) Machacamarca, (14) Sokotina, (15) Wilake, (16) Takawa, (17) Pakasa.

*Figure 4.1   The distribution of Wankarani sites north and northeast of Lake
Poopó. (Based on Gisbert 1988:5).*

hoes), and distinctive stone effigies in the form of llama heads (Figure
4.2) – appears standardized across these ecological zones, implying
some kind of ethnic, or cultural unity cross-cutting environmental
boundaries.

Wankarani villages themselves consisted of a cluster of circular
adobe houses with thatched roofs. House clusters were often encircled

Figure 4.2 An example of a Wankarani stone effigy llama head. (Museo National de Arqueología, La Paz, Bolivia. Photograph by Alan Kolata).

by an adobe wall to form the quintessential Andean *cancha*, or farm-house enclosure (Figure 4.3). We can infer from this configuration that houses were occupied by nuclear or extended families, while the larger clusters as a whole reflect a minimal *ayllu* or lineage grouping. The scale of Wankarani settlements was highly variable. The number of houses in Wankarani sites that have been investigated to date range from 15 to 780, leading Ponce (1980:14) to calculate population sizes between 75 and 3,900 persons. If confirmed by future work, these demographic projections indicate that at least some Wankarani settlements grew to such substantial size that they might be referred to as true towns. One precocious feature of Wankarani society, fully consonant with this respectable level of nucleation, was metallurgy. Copper-smelting slags were discovered in the earliest strata at the site of Wankarani itself, and these have been dated between 1200 and 800 B.C. This is the earliest *prima facie* evidence for the smelting of copper ores in the Andes, which in itself may reflect the

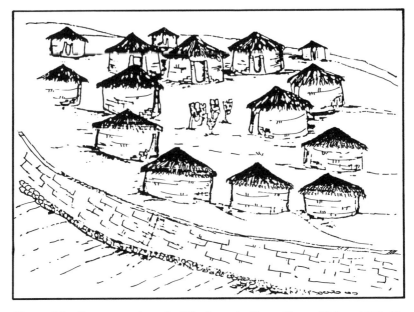

Figure 4.3   Reconstruction of a Wankarani village. (From Gisbert 1988: 7).

emergence of another form of social complexity: the division of labor by occupation.

The order-of-magnitude variability in the scale of these settlements raises the possibility of political hierarchies within Wankarani society. Were the larger, town-size settlements regional capitals controlled by particularly powerful lineages? Was Wankarani a hierarchical, chiefly society dominated by a few charismatic *kurakas*, analogous to Melanesian "big men"? Regrettably, the present state of our information does not permit any definitive conclusions on this point. But the lack of identified architecture in the form of disproportionately large or sumptuous elite residences, elaborate temples, or cult centers in Wankarani sites militates against the notion of strong political and religious hierarchies. Religious activities in Wankarani society seem to have revolved around interior household shrines and were not played out in obvious public forums. Numerous stone anthropomorphic and llama head effigies have been found within ordinary Wankarani houses, and these were apparently the focus of personal worship by families and *ayllus*. Although thematically similar in subject matter, each effigy has an idiosyncratic style of representation. That is, Wankarani never promulgated an elite, or corporate art style that can be associated with class divisions, or with formal, politically inspired cults. Perhaps these icons can best be interpreted as *ayllu* tutelary deities focused on the fertility and health of llama herds.

The distribution of settlements with a uniform material culture also implies that Wankarani society was not the product of rudimentary, closed corporate communities. Wankarani peoples ranged far and wide across the Bolivian *altiplano* and adjacent Andean valleys, forming what may very well have been a regional confederation, or at least an ethnically defined network of *ayllus* that maintained close communication and interaction. The intimate association of Wankarani with camelid pastoralism suggests that the principal vehicle of that regional communication was organized llama caravans. Caravans streamed out across the *altiplano* into the adjacent temperate valleys (and even as far as the Pacific coasts of northern Chile), moving slowly from village node to node exchanging desired raw materials and finished products. The result of this regional communication was more than the redistribution of commodities. It also entailed the exchange of information, ideologies, and most likely marriage partners. Reciprocal kinship ties, commercial relations, and shared cults bound the network of *ayllus* even more tightly together as an interdependent social and economic collectivity.

Farther to the north, a cultural complex similar in some ways to Wankarani was evolving around the southern shores of Lake Titicaca. This complex was first defined by one of the pioneers of Andean archaeology, Wendell Bennett (1936), who excavated at the type site of Chiripa. Bennett's excavations revealed that the site was an artificial mound faced by stone retaining walls on at least three sides. Arranged around the sides of the mound were a series of subterranean houses that faced a centrally located open courtyard (Figures 4.4a, 4.4b, and 4.5). Bennett recovered a variety of ceramic wares from the mound, which he referred to as a temple, and from its encircling houses. These ceramic types included Inca and Tiwanaku, as well as a new, stratigraphically earlier style that he called Chiripa. The Chiripa style was characterized by abundant utilitarian vessels, such as plain cooking pots, and a vibrant, polychrome ware, frequently embellished with fine-line incisions and modeled representations of human or feline faces and other animals (Figure 4.6). These elaborately decorated ceramics also appeared in exotic forms, such as trumpets, whistles, and incense burners, that were related to ritual or ceremonial activities.

More recent work on the Chiripa complex extends its known range of occurrence around the southern and eastern shores of Lake Titicaca, including a heavy occupation of the Copacabana peninsula (O. Rivera 1978). A Chiripa occupation that may be larger than the type site

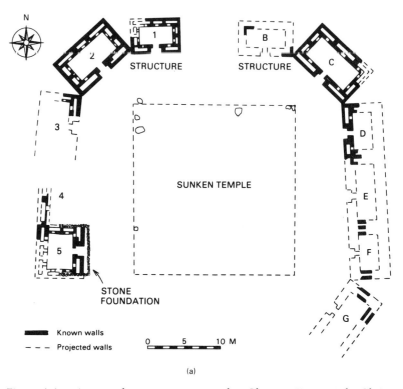

Figure 4.4a   A map of structures excavated at Chiripa. (From Mohr-Chávez 1988: Figure 3).

itself underlies the later Tiwanaku period architecture at Lukurmata (Kolata 1989). Recent excavations at Chirpa established a three-phase chronological sequence (Figure 2.4) for the site (Browman 1978; Mohr-Chavez 1988). The earliest occupation of the Chiripa mound carries radiocarbon dates around 1300–1200 B.C. The pottery of this Early Chiripa period exhibits a distinct similarity to that of Wankarani, where plain and polished utilitarian wares were common. Later occupations, between 900 and 100 B.C., enlarged and refurbished the mound: during this period, the stone retaining walls and subterranean houses were constructed. This later period is associated with exotic polychrome and modeled pottery. At some time between 500 and 100 B.C., a rectangular sunken court (measuring about 23 meters on a side and 1.5 meters deep) was constructed on the summit of the mound. Colored floors of red and yellow clay were laid down continuously from the house structures to the interior of the sunken court. Carved stone plaques were set into the walls of this semisubterranean

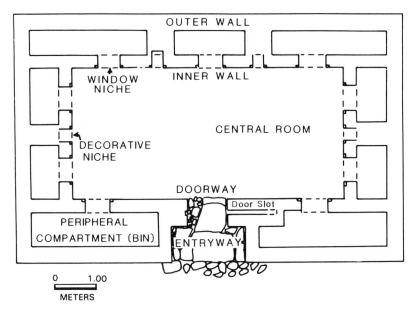

Figure 4.4b   Plan of House 2 at Chiripa. (From Mohr-Chávez 1988: Figure 2 and Bennett 1936: Figure 22).

court, and sandstone stelae with serpent, animal, and human motifs were erected in its interior (Figures 4.7a and 4.7b).

These architectural reconstructions were substantial undertakings that required the organization of a corporate labor pool and, quite likely, the participation of specialists in stone cutting and carving. More importantly, for the first time in the Lake Titicaca basin, we have in these Middle and Late Chiripa constructions our first tangible evidence for the monumental, public expression of ideological and religious concepts. Unlike the Wankarani stone llama effigies which were used in family or *ayllu* rituals within private homes, the large Chiripa plaques and stelae were clearly intended for public viewing. They were set in unroofed, open-air courtyards within structures that were designed explictly for the display of these religious icons. Furthermore, the Chiripa stelae and carved stone plaques are stylistically similar to numerous other sculptures distributed around the Titicaca basin, suggesting a particularly intense level of regional communication around the lake during the first millennium B.C. This communication took the form of shared religious beliefs, and, most likely, political and economic interdependence.

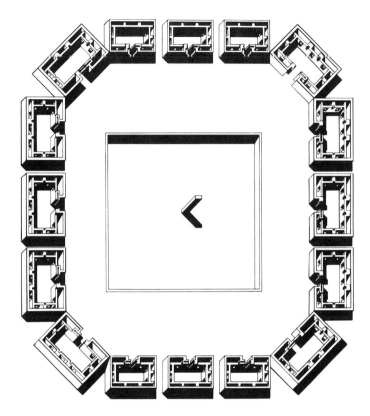

*Figure 4.5   An idealized reconstruction of the Chiripa Mound. (From Conklin
1991: Figure 9).*

Why did the people of Chiripa emphasize public rituals within the
context of impressive temple complexes while the Wankarani peoples'
religious expression apparently remained focused inward on household
shrines? These are the kinds of provocative, but essentially unanswer-
able questions that historians, particularly of non-literate societies,
frequently confront. It is possible that there were considerable differences in the scale and complexity of social organization between
Chiripa and Wankarani that generated this distinction between public
and private religious traditions. Chiripa may have been a society with
a greater degree of social integration and an emerging sense of a
great tradition focused on a shared ideology that demanded religious
proselytism.

The distinction between public and private religious traditions may
also have stemmed from long-standing ethnic differences. Despite a

Figure 4.6   Representative pottery of Chiripa. (Redrawn from Bennett 1936: Figure 28).

generalized similarity in material culture, the ceramic traditions of these two societies are radically different, hinting at significant variations in language, social outlook, and cultural and artistic conceptions. Based on the distribution of native languages in the *altiplano* during the sixteenth century, we might speculate that Chiripa was ancestral to the Pukina, or Uru-Chipaya speaking groups documented ethnohistorically for the lake district, while Wankarani reflects a Jaqi,

Figure 4.7a-b Two examples of Chiripa stone sculpture executed in the Yaya-Mama style. (Fig. 4.7a is from the Museum für Völkerkunde, Berlin, cat. number V A 60591. Fig. 4.7b is from Mohr-Chávez 1988: Figure 4a).

or proto-Aymara language group. Of course, we are on rather shaky grounds making these kinds of correlations between archeological cultures and historic populations, and in this we can make no definitive claims. Yet, the distinct ecological, geographic, and economic orientations of the Chiripa and Wankarani peoples intensifies the striking feeling of ethnic difference that one perceives when confronting the divergent cultural remains they left behind.

Like Wankarani, Chiripa subsistence entailed a dynamic interplay between camelid pastoralism and the *altiplano* agricultural complex focused on the cultivation of high-altitude adapted tubers and grains. However, the Chiripa subsistence base was graced by a third, hugely productive resource: Lake Titicaca. Vast quantities of the remains of fish, waterfowl, and aquatic plants are found in Chiripa middens of all phases. The distinctive ecological distribution of Chiripa sites – directly on lake beaches or only short distances inland – testifies eloquently to the importance of these lacustrine products in the Chiripa economy.

The rich resources of Lake Titicaca did not by themselves underwrite the development of large sedentary populations, differentiated social organization, monumental architecture, and corporate art styles in the highlands of the southern Andes. But the lake did act as a catalyst for the interpenetrating set of economic, political, and social interactions that resulted in the evolution of complex society in the region. Chiripa represents the first direct evidence for an organized, corporate authority capable of planning and constructing monumental stone architecture. In the southern Andean highlands, all subsequent developments of truly monumental architecture, together with its cultural correlates (a stable, surplus-generating economy, large populations, and corporate authority), occur only in and around the Lake Titicaca region. Apparently, the Inca origin myth of emergence from Lake Titicaca reflects more than simple poetry.

It may be that the special natural resource endowment of Lake Titicaca conferred a competitive advantage on formative period societies like Chiripa, propelling them into more complex social formations by providing a readily extractable source of surplus products. The fixed resources of the lake district readily permitted *in situ* development of sedentary villages specialized economically in reclaiming wetlands for agriculture and in extracting the wild resources of Lake Titicaca itself. Farther to the south in the more arid high plateau of the old Wankarani homeland, on the other hand, the need to exploit discrete, dispersed ecological niches selected for a more mobile, pastoral lifestyle. It is not surprising that Wankarani settlement patterns and material culture reflect an obsession with domestic herd animals, such as the llama and alpaca. Chiripa and Wankarani, then, may very well represent two divergent ethnic groups that spoke mutually unintelligible languages (Pukina versus Aymara) and specialized economically in exploiting distinct ecological zones (agro-lacustrine versus agro-pastoral).

On the opposite, northern shores of Lake Titicaca, a second lake-oriented culture developed during the first millennium B.C. This culture is defined by the archeological complex of Qaluyu, a low habitation mound that extends over several hectares and is associated with another distinctive ceramic style. The distribution of this early style, which dates to about 1000 B.C., extends as far north as the site of Marcavalle, near Cuzco (Rowe 1963). The Qaluyu ceramic style has some generalized affinities with that of Chiripa, emphasizing incised geometric designs and polychrome painting. Although it has not been fully explored, the early Qaluyu habitation mound's relatively large size implies occupation by a substantial population. Like Wankarani and Chiripa, Qaluyu represents an early agro-pastoral society of the *altiplano* capable of supporting sedentary populations and of organizing political and economic relationships with distant, often environmentally different regions. At some point around 200 B.C. a second occupation of the mound at Qaluyu is associated with a distinctive, polychrome ceramic style called Pukara. At this time, the mound appears to have been deliberately rebuilt in the form of a catfish, an undertaking that implies an increased labor investment in architecture, as well as a reorganization of cultural concepts regarding the meaning of that architecture. The scale of this increased interest in labor-intensive architectural projects designed according to a master plan is fully apparent at the neighboring site of Pukara itself, which, in many respects, reflects a quantum leap in the nature of corporate undertakings in the Titicaca basin.

The site of Pukara lies some 75 kilometers northwest of Lake Titicaca's northern shore. In the period between 200 B.C. and A.D. 200, Pukara grew to truly urban proportions (Mujica 1978) and took on a distinctly cosmopolitan character, with elegant public buildings and finely constructed private houses. The main architectural complex, which was erected on artificial terrace, consists of several large ceremonial structures (Figure 4.8). These structures, built with dressed stone block foundations and adobe superstructures, were a well-balanced set of spacious inner courts flanked by smaller, regular rooms. The central structure of this complex was a temple composed of a rectangular sunken court enclosed on three sides by a series of smaller rooms. An extensive residential zone sprawled out on the plain below this elevated civic center, which was presumably the

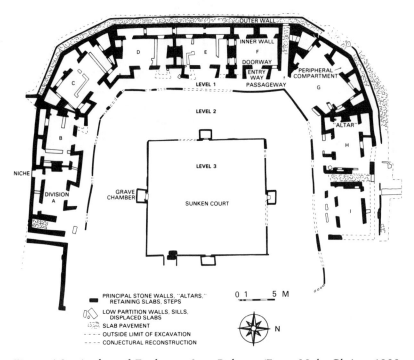

Figure 4.8   A plan of Enclosure 2 at Pukara. (From Mohr-Chávez 1988: Figure 9).

administrative and religious center of power for the Pukara polity. The residential zone is packed with stone foundations of houses and covered with fragments of Pukara-style ceramics covering an urban-scale area of approximately four square kilometers. There is little doubt that Pukara was, at one time, one of the most important cities of the southern Andes – a major religious and secular power. Although Pukara as a planned city emerged by about 200 B.C., it continued to flourish into the fourth century A.D. In its heyday from 200 B.C. to A.D. 200, Pukara dominated a large rural hinterland that was inhabited by farmers, herders, and specialized fishing communities living in smaller towns, villages, and hamlets.

The cultural and technological sophistication of Pukara was expressed most clearly through its impressive architectural achievements and through its remarkable stone-carving tradition that far surpasses that of Chiripa in terms of technical skill and sophistication in design. Pukara stone carvers created both full round and flat relief sculptures (Figures 4.9 and 4.10). The carvers used champlevé and incision

Figure 4.9   Front and back views of a fragment of a Pukara-style stela from
Wiraqocha Orqo. (From Chávez 1988: Figures 6a-b).

Figure 4.10   Three faces of the upper portion of a Pukara-style stela, from
Wiraqocha Orqo. (From Chávez 1988: Figures 6a-c).

0   5
                                                          cm

Figure 4.11 A fragment from a Pukara incised ceramic bowl. (From Chávez 1988: Figure 3; Photograph by Alan Sawyer).

techniques to fashion the relief carvings on rectangular stone slabs, or stelae. The flat relief sculptures tend to portray a variety of animals, such as fish, felines, lizards, and serpents, with incised surface detail representing cosmological or mythical symbols. One stela with a notched upper end portrays a magnificent human head wearing an elaborate crown with feather and feline appendages (Valcarcel 1935: Figure 9). The sculptures carved in full round are relatively realistic portraits of humans, most often depicted holding or wearing trophy heads.

The motifs of the Pukara stone-carving tradition, as well as the manner of executing these motifs with an incision technique, are closely matched in the Pukara ceramic tradition, particularly in elaborately modeled and polychromed types (Figures 4.11, 4.12, and 4.13). The Pukara ceramic style, like its sculptural counterpart, is complex, technically sophisticated, and bold. Provocatively enough, it incorporates

Figure 4.12   Two polychrome incised ceramic trumpets from Pukara. (From Chávez 1988: Figure 11; Museo Nacional de Antropología y Arqueología, Lima, cat. numbers P/8425 (58), left, and Pu/234765, right).

Figure 4.13 Fragments from three Pukara ceramic vessels. (From Kolata 1983: Figure 6.4).

many of the themes and motifs that have been considered emblematic of the art style of Tiwanaku. The predominant Pukara vessel forms are similar to those from Tiwanaku: flat-bottomed, open bowls, globular jars, *keros* (ritual drinking cups) with raised center bands, elongated trumpets, and fully modeled human heads. Feline and human faces with incised and painted designs were often modeled in relief on Pukara vessels in a manner evoking that which was to become a hallmark of Tiwanaku.

There is a fairly tight geographical association that links the stone sculptures to their ceramic counterparts: both are found primarily in the Peruvian department of Puno. However, examples of stone sculpture carved in the pure Pukara style have been discovered as far north as Chumbivilcas in the department of Cuzco, some 150 kilometers from Puno. Monumental sculpture in a Pukara-like style also occurs to the south around Tiwanaku's heartland on the southern shores of the lake.

Even farther afield, in the north coastal valleys of Chile, tapestries woven in a Pukara style with motifs such as trophy heads, frogs, rayed feline heads, and complex, stepped-pyramid forms have been recovered from burial mounds (Figure 4.14). These burial mounds pertain to a cultural phase referred to locally as Alto Ramirez which was fully contemporaneous with Pukara (M. Rivera 1977). The precise nature of the relationship between the Chilean Alto Ramirez populations and the evolving urban centers of the Lake Titicaca region is unclear. At that time, the growth of large cities in the *altiplano* may have stimulated brisk trading between coast and highlands. The highland centers would undoubtedly have cast an avaricious eye on the abundant natural resources of what is now Chile, particularly on its rich mineral deposits and the products of its temperate agricultural lands. Because of the striking stylistic resemblances between the textiles of Alto Ramirez and the corpus of Pukara art, it is possible to suggest that the city of Pukara maintained satellite economic colonies on the north Chilean coast. This notion of *altiplano* colonization of the north Chilean coast is certainly consonant with the later appearance of Classic Tiwanaku (c. A.D. 400–600) materials in the same valleys, a development that was clearly the result of highland colonization schemes. Alternatively, given that the Pukara-style materials in northern Chile derive almost exclusively from rich burial mounds, we may be witnessing here a pattern of patron-client relationships between *altiplano* and coastal *kurakas*, a kind of emerging culture of the elite that shared an ideology and exchanged symbols of that ideology in the form of textiles, clothing, and other emblems of their special status. Rather than establishing permanent Pukara colonies on the Chilean coast, Pukara and Alto Ramirez *kurakas* and their retainers sojourned between coast and *altiplano* on occasional trading expeditions, exchanging valued commodities, and, just as importantly, marriage partners that built kinship networks. In this latter scenario, the presence of Pukara on the Chilean coast (and elsewhere outside its *altiplano*

Figure 4.14   Pukara-style textile with frog iconography from the site of Alto Ramirez in the Azapa Valley, Chile. (Museo San Miguel, Azapa, Chile).

heartland) was less the result of an imposed social and political order and more the product of a mutual, opportunistic exchange of goods, services, ideas, and kin. However we interpret the nature of Pukara influence outside of its *altiplano* core territory, it is evident that this dynamic *altiplano* city was the most powerful and well-integrated political force of its time in the southern Andes. For the first time, with Pukara we see evidence of a corporate art style in the service of elites that had extensive impact throughout the Titicaca basin and the adjoining coastal regions of southern Peru and northern Chile: a pattern that was to be repeated in an even more intensified fashion by the people of Tiwanaku.

Since Julio Tello (1942) first brought attention to the specific similarities that link the corporate art styles of Pukara and Tiwanaku, the exact nature of the relationship between these two vigorous societies has been sharply debated. Recent work by Bolivian archaeologists exploring the precursors of Classic Tiwanaku civilization at Tiwanaku itself has greatly clarified the problem. Previously, the design similarities between the Pukara and Tiwanaku styles, such as running profile figures carrying staffs, modeled feline heads on ceramic bowls, and emphasis on trophy head representations, were thought to be associated at Tiwanaku strictly with the Tiwanaku III (c. A.D. 100–400) and Tiwanaku IV (c. A.D. 400–800) phases of the site's cultural chronology. Given the accepted dates for the floresence of Pukara, this interpretation suggested that the Pukara corporate art style coalesced entirely independent of and prior to Tiwanaku. Excavations by the Bolivians in the Kalasasaya, one of the monumental temples in Tiwanaku's ceremonial precinct, however, revealed the existence of ceramic assemblages that predate the Tiwanaku III period and show specific resemblances to Pukara pottery: decoration in black, yellow, and red paint, design units demarcated by incision, motifs such as a feline depicted with its face in front view and its body in profile. These new assemblages carry radiocarbon dates that range between 400 B.C. and A.D. 100, placing them contemporaneous with the earlier manifestations of Pukara in the northern Titicaca basin. In this scheme, Pukara and Tiwanaku corporate art styles were evolving at essentially the same time, perhaps deriving their impetus and inspiration from a third style ancestral to both.

One possible candidate for this hypothesized ancestral style that was the root of both Pukara and Tiwanaku art was an ancient stone-carving tradition that appears to be indigenous to the entire circum-Titicaca basin. This tradition, characterized by a sculptural style christened the "Yaya-Mama" group by Karen and Sergio Chavez (1975), finds its most intense expression in the southern, Bolivian side of Lake Titicaca, in the vicinity of Tiwanaku and the Copacabana peninsula. The inference may be drawn that the old Tiwanaku heartland was an ancient, persevering, and influential focus of stone-carving. The carved monuments of this Yaya-Mama group relate to a pan-Titicaca basin ideology that codified the beliefs of an animistic religious tradition, one that clearly intended to express and celebrate the intimate connections between humans and their life-giving environment. The iconography of these sculptures is complicated and exuberant, combining densely packed images of stylized humans and animals, particularly serpents, lizards, and toads, with abstract geometric figures. The stela illustrated in Figure 4.15 perfectly captures the essence of the Yaya-Mama style. The two principal faces of this sculpture represent, on one side, a female with breasts clearly depicted, and on the other, a male. Other Yaya-Mama stelae present similar images of a male-female pair. Flanking these human figures on the lateral sides of the stela are two pairs of undulating, double-headed serpents. Each pair of serpents is arrayed in such a way that one serpent is above the waistband of the human and the other below. The human figures appear to be standing upon gnarled, plant, or tree-like representations. Although symmetrical in the overall design field, the details of the images expressed on the principal faces of the sculpture vary noticeably: the two humans, for instance, wear different neck and head ornaments, and they seem to stand on different kinds of plants.

The extreme remoteness in time and cultural tradition of these sculptures makes it difficult to interpret the full meanings of these images. In truth, we can only offer reasonable conjectures based on what we know of more recent Andean religious traditions and social organization, and, of course, it is perilous, something akin to standing on intellectual quicksand, to project meaning so distantly backward in time. Nevertheless, we have few alternatives if we wish to understand the cultural and historical substratum that underlies the emergence of Tiwanaku.

The most salient visual feature of the Yaya-Mama sculptures is their expression of the social and biological principles of duality and the complementarity of the sexes. Duality is clearly portrayed in a number of ways on these sculptures. In the case of the stela illustrated in Figure 4.15, we can see the principle of duality expressed multiply in the symmetrical representation of the two stylized humans, one side male, the other female, in the two pairs of serpents, in each serpent itself possessing two heads, in the spatial distribution of the serpent-pairs, with one serpent placed above the horizontal waistband and the other below, and in the pair of plant representations at the feet of the humans. There is, in short, an almost obsessive concern for displaying dual, opposed figures, plants, animals, and humans, in this sculpture. Both the sexual dichotomy and complementarity of the human male-female pair are effectively conveyed through the convention of carving the images on opposed faces of the sculpture. The images look out in different directions, but they are carved of the same block and the carved waistband encircles the entire sculpture, relating one human to the other. The male-female pair are simultaneously opposed, but conjoined by form and by design. There is both tension and repose here. Duality and complementarity extend to the

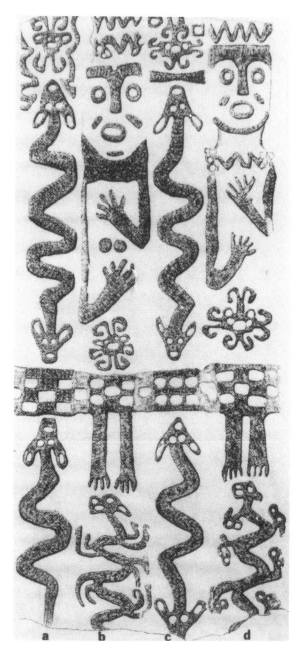

Figure 4.15 Rollout drawing of the Yaya-Mama stela from Taraco, Peru. (From Mohr-Chávez 1988: Figure 5).

plants and animals depicted on the stelae, hinting that, to the pre–
Tiwanaku peoples who created these images, the principles of organization of the social world of humans extends to the natural world of
plants and animals. If nature and society were organized fundamentally
in the same way, to understand nature one had only to look to society,
and to understand human society, one needed to observe nature. So,
in a real sense, an encompassing vision of a basic duality and complementarity between nature and society was encoded in the images on
this stelae.

There are most likely other, more specific meanings embedded in
these images. One could speculate that the obsessive representation
on the Yaya-Mama sculptures of serpents and toads, almost to the ex-
clusion of any other animals, reflects a concern for water, since these
creatures are conceptually linked to the *altiplano* rainy season (they
emerge most noticeably after a heavy afternoon downpour) and to
sources of fresh water, such as springs, subterranean pools, and rivers.
The vibrant, undulating serpents on the stela we have been considering
certainly convey the sense of a flowing, swirling river, and the fertiliz-
ing power of water. Perhaps this stela was meant to capture for its
human creators the concentrated essence of fertility: an icon worshiped
for the purpose of increasing human and natural abundance. However we interpret the specific meanings of these images, it is clear that
the same fundamental theme expressing the interdependence of the
human and natural worlds reoccurs in the religious architecture and
art created by the people of Tiwanaku. The roots of Tiwanaku religious ideology clearly reach back to an ancient concept of spirituality that was keenly sensitive to the rhythms and nuances of the
natural world, a concept densely conveyed in the sculptures of the
Yaya-Mama religious tradition.

Tiwanaku Emergence

Despite the fragmentary state of the archeological record, we have
managed to reconstruct some of the essential, precursor elements to
Tiwanaku's emergence as the pre-eminent city and state of the Andean
high plateau. One of these critical elements was the development of
broad, regional communication and exchange of ideas as well as commodities. In many respects, pan-Titicaca basin participation in a shared
religious tradition was one of the central struts of the deep, cultural
structure upon which Tiwanaku drew for its subsequent expansion.
The precedence of the Yaya-Mama religious tradition must have been
a powerful force for legitimizing the aggressive religious, cultural,

and economic proselytism that came to characterize Tiwanaku's expansion. Contrary to the unreconstructed imperialist's point of view, it is the shared beliefs and practices of a coherent ideology, and not a preponderance of naked force, that bind pluralistic societies into durable political and economic formations.

Another of the precursor elements to the emergence of Tiwanaku was the development after 1000 B.C. of an interacting network of villages around Lake Titicaca graced with vital, expanding economies. The natural resource endowments of the lake district powered these village economies, permitting a stable, abundant food supply. Each of these villages had access to a rich suite of natural resources that enabled them to diversify production and reduce their risk of exposure to the catastrophic famines that are common to small-scale, isolated societies in marginal environments. The cornerstone of these villages' economy was the effective merging of three distinct kinds of subsistence occupations: farming, fishing, and herding. None of these villages was tied to a stagnant, monolithic economy of farming, or fishing, or herding alone. The primary production of this tripartite economy generated sufficient surplus to stimulate a whole range of secondary, wealth-producing occupations: the manufacture of utilitarian craft goods and tools, local and long-distance trading, the production of public sculptures or luxury items for conspicuous consumption, and many others besides. These village economies were generating their own wealth by adding new work to old, by layering new divisions of labor onto old ones.

The Lake Titicaca villages in the time just prior to the emergence of Tiwanaku were behaving like proto-cities, generating food surpluses and transforming these surpluses into new products and services. It is key to note here that the cornerstone activities of fishing, herding, and farming themselves took place in distinct ecological zones, required different technologies of production, and demanded different seasonal schedules, occupational skills, and forms of labor organization. Work in the agricultural fields entailed an intensive, but uneven investment of labor through the year. It was heavily seasonal and required considerable village cooperation and coordination of labor. Most work took place in two intensive bursts of activities: field preparation and planting (August–November) and harvest (April–May). Early agriculture in the Lake Titicaca basin was focused on the wetlands and marshes on the shores of the lake, and along the better watered courses of rivers. Both land and labor resources were concentrated, one spatially and the other temporally. In contrast, fishing and herding were occupations pursued in a more diffuse manner. Unlike agriculture, the exploited natural resources were not concentrated, but rather distributed widely and relatively evenly over the environment. Locating good pasturage in the high *puna* for llama and alpaca herds, for instance, required movement across a fairly extensive area, and the work of herding, unlike farming, was never geographically fixed. Similarly, the work of managing herds was not as concentrated and collaborative as that of agriculture. The herds required constant attention, but this work could be delegated to a relatively few specialists who could live among and move with the herds. Fishing was similarly diffuse in terms of the environment it exploited and in the kind of labor organization that was required: the work was mobile (although less so than herding), constant, and not subjected to marked seasonal variation. Like herding, fishing was an occupation that was delegated to specialists.

By organizing and implementing these three distinct kinds of basic occupations, the pre-Tiwanaku villages and towns around Lake Titicaca created an inherent form of social complexity that conferred on them competitive and adaptive advantages. They were able to diversify their subsistence portfolio and reduce the risk of catastrophic food crisis. Diversification and stabilization of the village economy stimulated more and different kinds of work and new divisions of labor. In this reciprocal process, accelerating, new divisions of labor further intensified village social complexity, creating new occupations, new structures of work, and substantial new wealth. New wealth and differential access to that wealth gradually moved the original village economies outside of their closed, corporate communities into the broader world. The previously autonomous, self-sufficient villages became profoundly dependent on other communities to sustain their new found sources of wealth, and with that interdependence came inevitable culture change, in economies, in aspirations, in power relations. The villages around Lake Titicaca between about 1000 and 200 B.C. were reaching a "critical mass" of accelerating social complexity. This social complexity, marked by diversified economic activities, multiple divisions of labor and broad regional exchange of goods, services, and ideas, lay at the root of the emergence of true urban life in the early state of Tiwanaku.

But how did one proto-city of this period come to assert its dominance over others in the Titicaca region? What spurred Tiwanaku on to pre-eminence and not, say, Chiripa or one of any number of similar villages strung out along the lake edge? In truth, this question is not readily answerable. From the archaeological record, we can piece together the necessary preconditions for the emergence of a pre-eminent settlement, but we cannot easily specify why a particular settlement assumed that role. There are many instances of great cities and capitals emerging through a complex chain of historical contingencies, chance, and the charisma of individual leaders. The precise geographical and topographical location of an important city may result from widely shared beliefs regarding the meaning and cultural role of cities, rather than from fortuitous pragmatic factors, such as location along a navigable stream or astride a lucrative trading route. For instance, René Berthelot argued that the predominant factor in the location and nature of the Chinese city was a complex of shared ideas and cosmological conceptions which he referred to as "astrobiological principles" (Wheatley 1971). These "astrobiological principles" treat human reality (and the built-city environment) as a function and replication of a celestial archetype. The necessary parallelism between the humanly constructed, animate environment and the physical universe necessitates performance of cyclical rituals in specific, propitious locations to maintain harmony between nature and human society. These principles reached their most formal expression in the geomantic tradition known as *feng-shui*, a distinctive Chinese system of ideas in which certain configurations of the landscape were believed to retain and conserve the life-essence. A passage in the *Chou-li*, a text dating most likely to Han period China, succinctly captures the essence and implications of shared cosmological concepts on the form and location of cities: "Here where Heaven and Earth are in perfect accord, where the four seasons come together, where the winds and rain gather, where the forces of *yin* and *yang* are harmonized, one builds a royal capital" (Wright 1977:47).

There are numerous such instances of cultural concepts dominating the conscious or unconscious location and configuration of important cities. Given this, it is impossible to determine with any degree of confidence why the proto-city of Tiwanaku, and not other similar settlements went on to achieve pre-eminence. We can, of course, eliminate certain of the more specific economic explanations for Tiwanaku's emergence as a capital. Tiwanaku's location conferred no particular resource advantage on the city. In fact, one could argue on economic grounds alone that a lake-side settlement such as Chiripa should have held competitive advantage over Tiwanaku given the former's direct access to the considerable natural resources of Lake Titicaca. Tiwanaku was not located near the site of concentrated natural resources, such as a particularly rich obsidian resource, that might have generated extraordinary wealth. Monopolized control and distribution of a precious commodity is one clear path to rapid economic growth that was exploited by many cities throughout the pre-industrial world. This does not seem, however, the route that Tiwanaku took toward pre-eminence. The basic natural resources on which a society might build wealth along the southern rim of Lake Titicaca are fairly uniform. There was, in other words, no unique economic advantage to the location of the proto-city of Tiwanaku.

To be perfectly frank, we are left mostly with conjecture to explain the specific rise to pre-eminence by Tiwanaku. We do know that the social environment of the southern Titicaca basin was one of distinct competition among groups of villages and towns. There is considerable stylistic variation in the ceramics being produced and consumed by these villages, and these styles seem to have fairly restricted geographic distributions. For instance, the Chiripa style is found almost exclusively along the southern shores of Lake Titicaca and rarely in interior sites. A second formative period ceramic style contemporaneous with Chiripa in the Tiwanaku Valley is restricted to inland sites on or near the alluvial plain of the Tiwanaku River, and is never found in the lake-edge environment of Chiripa (Albarracín-Jordan and Mathews 1990). This mutually exclusive distribution of distinct ceramic styles suggests the presence of two social groups, perhaps differentiated by subtle ethnic differences, who had colonized and specialized in the exploitation of distinct ecological zones. We have discovered several distinct, geographically restricted formative period ceramics in the Tiwanaku hinterland, implying that there may have been a number of such competing groups. This social environment of diverse villages and small, proto-cities striving for broader access to natural resources outside the specific ecological zones that they had originally colonized selected for substantial conflict and inter-village rivalry.

Originally, Tiwanaku's pre-eminence may have been the product of aggressive raiding in the territories of other villages and towns and the eventual incorporation of these territories into Tiwanaku's local domain. However, Tiwanaku's growing power and prestige was most likely not maintained by virtue of aggression alone, but by conversion of the emergent capital into a shared center of moral and cosmological authority, a place of pilgrimage and wonder. The transformation of the formative period village of Tiwanaku into a ritual center of the first order occurred at some point between A.D. 100 and 300 with construction of the first truly monumental structures in the Lake Titicaca basin. Given that the formative period settlements of the region shared broadly similar cosmological and religious beliefs, exemplified by the Yaya-Mama religious tradition, once Tiwanaku had started aggressively on its path to power, there was probably little local resistance to its emergence as the pre-eminent center of Titicaca basin civilization. However we explain the origins and dynamic of Tiwanaku's emergence, it is abundantly clear that by A.D. 300 the city was functioning as the principal political and ritual center of the Lake Titicaca basin. By about A.D. 500, Tiwanaku was the nexus of an intensely interacting network of cities, and the capital of an expanding empire that maintained its economic and political power for some 500 years before finally disintegrating around A.D. 1000.

5

Taypikala: The City at the Center

Cities are inherently unstable and evanescent. What may begin as an ad hoc frontier garrison of an empire transforms itself into an administrative center of great regional significance, perhaps coming to rival the capital itself in terms of the essential elements of urban success: economic and demographic growth, political power, and social prestige. Cities grow at a sometimes cancerous clip, and just as readily they decay, dominated by economic and political forces of regional and national proportion. The residents of the urban landscape are rarely masters of their own fate. They are bound inevitably to broader social networks that determine their success or failure as participants in this most complex kind of human community. The city is a dynamic congeries of political, economic, and social institutions that is shaped and reshaped by historical circumstance.

Social and political forces related to the emergence of specific forms of command hierarchies, to competition among elite interest groups, to the tension between rural and cosmopolitan realities, played important roles in shaping the form and internal organization of Tiwanaku. Tiwanaku, its secondary cities, and their surrounding rural sustaining areas were bound together in symbolic landscapes, in a geography of the sacred that structurally recapitulated basic social formations and generated a perduring sense of participation among urban and rural populations. This is not to suggest that there were no serious tensions, cross-purposes, or contradictions among distinct social classes in these cities or between city dwellers and their country kin. Conflict and coalition building among distinct interest groups within these cities was surely an important force that brought form to both the social and physical environments of the urban landscape.

Tiwanaku at its apogee was not simply an *altiplano* village writ large. The city's conceptual and social roots resided in the fundamental organizational forms of *ayllu* and moiety relationships that undergirded native Andean civilization. But as it gained religious prestige as the paradigmatic ceremonial center of the high plateau, Tiwanaku was transformed qualitatively: it became, in Mumford's (1961:36) words, "a new symbolic world, representing not only a people, but a whole cosmos and its gods." The structuring of the city by principles embedded in a perceived cosmovision extended to its physical, built form, but, more importantly, to the actors who created that form as well. The concept of cosmological order pervaded the social and political organization of Tiwanaku society.

The mystique of Tiwanaku in late prehispanic Andean society was intimately associated with its role as a place of origin in cosmogonic myths. It was in Tiwanaku that the creator god Viracocha ordained a new social order, and it was from Tiwanaku that the primeval couple were sent out along symmetrically opposed migratory paths to call forth the nations of the Andean world from the *huacas* of springs and rivers, rocks and trees. In these myths of creation and radiation, Tiwanaku was simultaneously origin point and *taypi*, the place of emergence and of necessary conjunction.

The archaic city was organized as a self-reflexive representation of universal order: the perceived order of the cosmos was mapped into the ideal order of society, and from this ideal flowed moral authority and social stability (Wheatley 1971). The city, then, was not merely an astonishingly rich economic engine of production, a generator of new goods and services. It was also a visual and conceptual tool of socialization, a generator and arbiter of new ideas, norms, and ideologies. The location and built form of Tiwanaku directly reflects these latter elements of urban meaning.

The city was founded near the southern shores of the great lake of Titicaca, the enormous inland sea ringed by glaciated mountain peaks that was the sacred locus for many indigenous myths of creation. As we have seen, in the sixteenth century the Aymara considered the fertile axis formed by the lake as the *taypi*, the essential conceptual and physical zone of convergence between the principles of *urco* (symbolically associated with the qualities of west, high, dry, pastoralism, celestial, male) and *uma* (symbolically associated with the qualities of east, low, wet, agriculture, underworld, female). Importantly, these essential qualities or principles of reality were tangible and observable features of the physical landscape. This was no vaguely ambiguous concept. Rather it was a lived and constantly re-experienced reality embedded in the most concrete and salient characteristics of landscape and the evocative symbolic associations inhering in that landscape.

The *altiplano* dweller can gaze westward from atop the Chila mountain range in the valley of Tiwanaku toward the immense, high, arid plains of the *Urcosuyu* countryside. Crossing the lake from Tiwanaku toward the east, one can climb the side of Mount Illampu and look down from a high mountain pass toward the *yungas*, the humid, cloud shrouded valleys that cling to the eastern slopes of the Andean chain: the lands of the *Umasuyu*. From either mountain vantage point, the glistening, cobalt-blue surface of the lake marks the axis of ecological transition from one zone to another. The continuity and orderliness of the cosmos demanded that these complementary, opposing principles of *uma* and *urco*, which were themselves an interpenetrating skein of natural and cultural qualities, be brought into creative conjunction: that the structural faultline between them be seamed in some fashion. This was the conceptual and symbolic role of *taypi*, and Tiwanaku was the central representation of the *taypi*; the principal icon emblematic of the physical zone of necessary convergence. Tiwanaku was the *taypikala*, the stone in the center.

In many ways, the urban nature of Tiwanaku remains an enigma. A city of such huge spatial reach and protracted temporal occupation is seldom explored in depth, simply because the logistics of large-scale archaeological investigation are so daunting. Space and time conspire to keep the face of urban Tiwanaku veiled and unobserved. Only in the past two decades have archaeologists begun to systematically explore the internal character and structure of the city. Even then the focus of research was fixed squarely on the principal monumental architectural complexes that characterize the urban core. The zone of domestic residences ringing this core area remained virtually uninvestigated. Only in the past few years have we come to understand something of the character and function of ordinary dwellings in the city and in its urban satellites. Household archaeology in Tiwanaku remains in a nascent stage.

Beyond the inference that they existed, we know virtually nothing about the processes and networks of craft production and artisan workshops that supplied Tiwanaku with its elite mortuary ceramics, stone sculpture, lapidary work, and precious objects of metal. No urban storehouses have been definitively identified, although some elaborate circular structures with double-paved floors in the northern extremity of the city may represent just such a warehousing facility. Nor do we have unambiguous evidence of architecture housing administrative activities. Despite these constraints to full understanding of how the city looked and worked, sufficient new evidence has been generated in the past few years to give us substantive insights into the urban concept of Tiwanaku. By counterposing empirical data with what one might call informed conjecture, this chapter will sketch the broad contours of that concept. Here I will describe the architectonic arrangements that define the monumental core of the city and suggest something of their meaning for the people of Tiwanaku. If not quite a complete and richly detailed day in the life of urban Tiwanaku, this chapter will offer a few, sharp vignettes, sufficient to convey a tangible sense of the place.

Sacred Geography and Urban Design

Tiwanaku, most especially its civic-ceremonial core, was a regal city, redolent with the symbolism of power, both sacred and secular. The city was the principal seat of Tiwanaku's ruling lineages, the locus of the royal court, and the holiest shrine of the imperial religion. The city itself was simultaneously an icon of Tiwanaku rule and a cosmogram that displayed symbolically in the spatial arrangement of its public architecture and sculpture the structure that framed the natural and social orders. It was conceived as the *axis mundi*, the city at the center that bound together the complementary universe of the sacred and the secular. It was, for the people of Tiwanaku, the ultimate nexus of wealth and power, social identity and prestige, cult and command.

The architectural form of Tiwanaku, together with its public en-semble of monumental stone sculptures, intensified the mythic aura of the city, embuing it with a quality of the supernatural: a sacred space beyond the strictures of the profane world in which it was embedded. The ceremonial core of Tiwanaku was surrounded by an immense artificial moat that restricted easy access to its centrally located public buildings (Figure 5.1). The intent behind this reshap-ing of the high status urban landscape through construction of a physical barrier of water was not to provide the Tiwanaku elite with a defensive structure against marauding barbarians or the potentially hostile lower classes of the city as Posnansky (1945:120–1) believed. Rather, the concept was precisely to evoke the image of the city core as an island. But not just a common, generic island. The notion was to create, at the cost of a huge investment in human labor, an image of the sacred islands of Lake Titicaca which were the *situs* of cos-mogonic myth: the points of world creation and human emergence. The moat generated a dramatic visual cue that emphasized the ritually charged nature of social actions that were played out in the center. Essentially, in moving from the landlocked outer ring of Tiwanaku's vernacular architecture across the moat into its interior island circle of temples and elite residences, the visitor to the city moved from the

Figure 5.1 Oblique, low altitude aerial photograph of the central civic-ceremonial precinct at Tiwanaku, looking east. The Akapana pyramid is the large mound on the right side of the photograph, with the Kalasasaya and the Semi-subterranean Temple immediately to the left.

space and time of ordinary life to the space and time of the sacred. The interior sacred core was symbolically a human re-creation, or perhaps more aptly, re-representation of the place and time of human origins.

In the Andean world, as in many other indigenous cosmologies, the time of origins was not a vague, temporally distant historical event to be remembered and commemorated in yearly ceremony. Rather, cosmological time was cyclical, regenerative, and re-created by human agency. Humans existed in the sacred time of cosmology, as well as in the profane time of daily life. The ceremonial inner core of Tiwanaku was constructed as the theatrical backdrop for the recurrent social construction of cosmological order. And, of course, the parallel message embedded in this architectonic text was the appropriation of the sacred by a subconstituency of society: the Tiwanaku elite.

Within the ceremonial core of Tiwanaku were constructed not only the principal temples of the city, but also the palatial residences of the ruling class. By living within this sacred inner precinct of the city, this elite was claiming for itself the right, and assuming the obligation to intercede on behalf of society with the divine, with the supernatural, to maintain harmony in the natural and social orders. The lineages of the elite conjoined historical time (the linear experience of time lived here and now) with cosmogonic time (the cyclical, regenerative time of myth). As Robert Ellwood (1973:3) suggests, the figure of the king, and the symbolic process of kingly accession played the pivotal role in merging the powers of myth and history on behalf of society in the archaic world:

> [kingly accession] brought the cyclical eternal-return time of nature and its seasons together with time as history, the time of society which could only approximate repeating itself in the line of kings. Fundamentally, then, the rite of accession is an act of civilization. However primitive the society, it catches up the temporal paradox which underwrites civilization. The rites seek to impose upon human society a continuity with nature.

Although we are lacking primary, native texts and thus no access to the names of Tiwanaku's kings, their lineages, or their individual deeds, the peculiar architectural and sculptural arrangements within the inner regal core of their capital city permits us to reconstruct a plausible theory of meaning regarding the built environment of which they were the principal authors and patrons. This interpretation of urban design and meaning, in turn, gives us insight into the nature of rulership in Tiwanaku society.

To the tourist, Tiwanaku appears as a city without an obvious internal plan. A few monumental structures built of stone loom isolated above the surface, dramatic landmarks in an otherwise seemingly featureless plain shrouded in the tough bunch grass of the high plateau. The eye is drawn to these salient monuments, and the tourist's invariant paths toward them cut across and ignore the ancient logic of circulation now interred beneath the surface. Yet walking from one structure to another, the more observant visitor realizes that the ground undulates underfoot, dropping from time to time into large hollows, or suddenly stepping up onto low platforms. Ancient public plazas and private courtyards persist in vague tracery, deteriorating, but still detectable. Weathered stone pillars project from the earth marking the corners of ruined buildings now deeply buried under fine-grained sediment. The sedimentary products of erosion from ancient adobe structures and from the surrounding mountainous landscape deposited over the centuries obscures much of what was once the internal urban order of Tiwanaku. But there still remain lines of sight along walls and between structures perceivable to the eye accustomed to look for such alignments. Enormous segments of polished sandstone, granite and andesite drains, sophisticated technological artifacts from Tiwanaku's system of fresh water supply, lie scattered about with no immediately understandable relationship to each other. Ironically, only the intact, deeply buried network of subterranean sewer lines offers clues to the original plan of the city's hydraulic infrastructure.

Despite these physical impediments to deciphering the shape of the ancient city, the underlying concepts of social order that brought form to Tiwanaku are gradually emerging from the evidence of new research. We can now extract some of the general organizing principles that structured the capital, and trace those which carried over to the internal design of Tiwanaku's satellite cities. Such a comparison generates insights into the construction of political, economic, and social hierarchies, and provides an entrée into the meaning of symbolic representation expressed through the medium of architectural display on an urban scale in Tiwanaku society.

The Concentric Cline of the Sacred

Earlier, I alluded to the key element of one such organizing principle embedded in and shaping Tiwanaku's urban order: the civic-ceremonial core of the city evoked the image of a sacred island, the island of universal origins and human emergence. Tiwanaku's moat served to physically demarcate the concentrated, sacred essence of the city. The moat acted as a psychological and physical barrier, setting up by its very shape, dimensions, and symbolic representation, a concentric hierarchy of space and time. Passage across the moat represented a change of both spatial and temporal frames of reference, a movement into the place and time of ethnic origins.

The contradiction inherent in its meaning to the people of Tiwanaku must have been clear to them: the central island of cosmogonic myth was believed to be the point of origins for all humans, but at Tiwanaku, only *some* humans, the elite of Tiwanaku society, appropriated the special right of residence in this sacred core. The barrier of water, then, also marked a point of transition that distinguished the residences of elites from those of commoners: social inequality and hierarchy were encoded in Tiwanaku's urban form.

There was, in other words, a principle of urban order at Tiwanaku that we might describe as a concentric cline of the sacred that diminished in intensity from the city core to its far peripheries. Within this

Figure 5.2   High altitude aerial photograph of Tiwanaku. Note the series of moats surrounding the civic-ceremonial core of the city, particularly in the eastern sector.

framework of urban order keyed to conceptions of the sacred, the inhabitants of Tiwanaku occupied physical space in accordance with their relative social and ritual status. At the highest level, ritual status was identified and partially merged with political authority. The upper echelons of the Tiwanaku elite monopolized for their residences the innermost, and most sacred, core of their artificial island. The notion that there was some image of concentricity in the mind of the people of Tiwanaku which shaped conceptions of proper order within their capital is reinforced by the presence of two additional, although partial moats situated farther to the east of the primary moat completely encircling Tiwanaku's monumental architecture (Figure 5.2). The precise meaning of these moats is not clear. They do not have obvious technological functions, although it is possible that they served to drain excess groundwater and seasonal rainfall away from inhabited portions of the urban landscape. But, given the correctness of my interpretation of the meaning of Tiwanaku's principal moat, I would suggest that the essential purpose of the moats toward the city periphery was to symbolically mark social boundaries, to further differentiate the ritual status of the urban residents by their relative positions along what I have referred to as the concentric cline of the sacred. Movement from the east of Tiwanaku toward the civic-ceremonical core of the city entailed passage across a nested, hierarchical series of socially and ritually distinguished spaces.

In extracting this sort of symbolic text from architectural space, we perhaps run the risk of forcing the interpretive enterprise beyond the limits of credulity. But the problem of believability here turns on the fact that we are unaccustomed to perceive our own Western urban environments as embued with this kind of symbolic coherence. Our image of the city is one of almost chaotic fragmentation, many disparate parts that make, at best, a mechanical, ill-fitting whole. Movement through the Western city from periphery to core does not offer the same sense of the inexorability of revealed truth that was frequently designed into the archaic city. The social elite of London and New York never validated their status by emulating and symbolically appropriating the cyclical, reproductive powers of nature. There is an almost insuperable cognitive gap between the archaic, agrarian mind and the mind of the industrial world: they inhabit and are engaged by separate realities.

Then too we must recall that cities and urban design played a distinct role in the agrarian world of archaic states. These were fundamentally non-urban, or even anti-urban societies. The bulk of the population in archaic states resided in the countryside, dispersed in small villages and hamlets. The dominant social reality of these archaic states was one which turned on the cyclical, seasonal rhythms of rural life, radically removed from the cosmopolitan world of the elite. The cities that did exist in these societies were few, and consequently exceptionally special. Most were important centers of pilgrimage for the inhabitants of the countryside: a necessary nexus of religious tourism and venal commercialism. At the same time they were the distilled essence of elite belief, the focal points of publically expressed concepts of universal order. To exert any moral authority over the rural hinterlands, they needed a coherent, immediately understandable design that directly, perhaps even with exaggerated, chiaroscurolike effect, expressed a sense of man's, and still more specifically, one's own ethnic group's place in the world. Ironically this sense of place, expressed with monumentality in the architecture of the cities, explicitly evoked a rural sensibility. The life of farms and fields in the countryside provided the model for the essential relationship between humankind and nature that profoundly influenced the internal design and social order of the city. The symbolic text written into the design of these cities was one which attempted to identify, or to harmonize the productive, yet potentially destructive, forces of nature with the culturally created order of human society. The rural hinterlands of cities in the archaic world tangibly produced both food and symbolic meaning for urban populations. Such intense symbolic and historical relationships between urban and rural realities seem alien or quaint

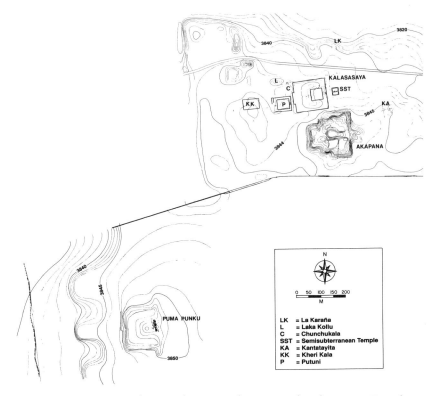

Figure 5.3   A map of Tiwanaku's central ceremonial architecture. (Based on Posnansky 1945, vol. I: Plates I and VI).

to us now, disintegrated under the heavy burden of industrialization and the globalization of economies. But we must vividly re-create in the mind these relationships if we are to grasp the social principles that brought form and meaning to cities such as Tiwanaku.

The Solar Path: From Mountains to the Lake

A second principle of urban organization at Tiwanaku crosscuts what I have termed the concentric cline of the sacred. This is a principle of organization that derives from cardinality, and more fundamentally from the perceived path of the sun across the urban landscape. The major structures within the civic-ceremonial core of Tiwanaku are aligned generally to the cardinal directions, as a whole 4.5 degrees west of true north (Figure 5.3).

The perceived solar path establishes an east-west axis that bisects the city, and furnishes the principal avenue of circulation. This solar path emerges from and dissolves back into two salient geographic features to which indigenous peoples in the Valley of Tiwanaku still orient themselves: the glacier shrouded peaks of the Cordillera Real, particularly the three peaks of Mount Illimani, to the east (the emerging sun) and Lake Titicaca to the west (the waning, setting sun). The great snow-capped peaks and the lake are readily visible from the flanks of the mountains that enclose the valley, but both can be glimpsed simultaneously from the city of Tiwanaku on the valley floor *only* from the summit of the Akapana, Tiwanaku's tallest terraced platform mound. The summit structures of the Akapana (and the elite who resided there) must have been embued with considerable symbolic power derived, in part, from this unique visual frame of reference. From this summit alone could one track the entire celestial path of the sun from its twin anchors in the mountains and the lake.

That the elite of Tiwanaku were conscious of, and purposely manipulated this solar element of sacred geography to invest their capital with social and spatio-temporal symbolic meaning seems certain from key aspects of the architectural design of the Akapana, and its companion terraced mound to the southwest, the Puma Punku. As Cieza de León recounted in clear reference to the Akapana and Puma Punku, these two "sepulchral towers of the native lords of Tiwanaku" have their "doorways [facing] the rising sun" (Cieza de León [1553] 1959:284). Although not mentioned by Cieza, each of these structures possessed a second staircase, directly opposite those referred to in his account. That is, as we now know from recent excavations at these two structures, both Akapana and the Puma Punku possess axial, twin staircases constructed centrally into their east and west facades. The concept of east-west axial entry ways were also design features of the Kalasasaya, Chunchukala, and Putuni complexes in Tiwanaku's civic ceremonial core. What is interesting about these sets of axial staircases, apart from their simple presence and location, is that they differ dramatically in terms of architectural elaboration. In these structures, both sets of western staircases are significantly smaller in scale than their eastern counterparts. Furthermore, in the case of the Pumapunku, Chunchukala, and Putuni complexes, the western staircases lack the elaborate, monumental carved stone jambs and lintels that grace the eastern entries. It is likely, although not yet demonstrated archaeologically, that this architectural pattern applies to the Akapana as well. This differential architectural treatment, which signified substantially different investments of labor and capital, implies that these buildings, and more specifically their points of entry and egress, architectually encode a culturally significant symbolic, or status hierarchy. That is, I suggest that in Tiwanaku's system of sacred geography reflected in principles of urban design, east was symbolically of higher status then west, and that this symbolic hierarchy derives, ultimately, from the symbolism of the solar path: the ascending sun of the east is energetically more powerful than the waning sun of the west. As we shall see, this axial symbolism intersects with the sculptural program within Tiwanaku's civic-ceremonial core, which, in turn, relates to the institution of kingship in Tiwanaku society.

As with the concentric principle of urban organization, the principle of axiality generated by the solar path differentiated social space in Tiwanaku. In effect, the solar path conceptually divided the city into two hierarchically ranked segments with distinct symbolic associations: the east conceptually linked to the celestial realm, the rising sun and high prestige, and the west evoking images of the chthonic realm, the setting sun and lesser prestige. Curiously, the prestige hierarchy of directionality that I infer for Tiwanaku on architectural grounds is the inverse of the sixteenth-century Aymara sacred geographical divisions of the Lake Titicaca basin into *urco* and *uma*. Recall that *urco* was associated with the west and the celestial sphere and evoked principles of strength, superiority, maleness, aggression, mobility, and the pastoral lifestyle. *Uma*, on the other hand, was linked with the east and a sedentary, agricultural life-style, and conveyed to the Aymara notions of fertility, passivity, and the female principle. Although rather speculative, this inversion suggests an intriguing possibility: the ethnic identity and court language of Tiwanaku elite may have been Pukina, rather than Aymara. The former, identified in ethnohistoric documents with the east and with agricultural reclamation of the wet lands of Lake Titicaca, would likely have symbolically encoded space in a manner quite distinct from the Aymara, and perhaps invested the east with greater symbolic prestige.

The Twin Ceremonial Centers

Cross-cutting the east-west axis generated by the solar path, there was a further bipartition of social and symbolic space at Tiwanaku into northern and southern segments, to form, with the solar axial partition, a division of Tiwanaku into four quadrants. At the most general level, we can assume that these quadrants replicated symbolically the four quarters of the known Tiwanaku world. Such a symbolic division is common to archaic cities, particularly archaic cities of empire throughout the world (see, for instance, Wheatley 1971). We know that the Inca capital of Cuzco was organized symbolically in just such a fashion (Hyslop 1990; Zuidema 1990) having been partitioned into two hierarchically ranked sectors, *hanan* Cuzco and *hurin* Cuzco, and further subdivided into quadrants defined by the four principal roads leading out to the provinces. The Cuzco quadripartition rendered the capital an audacious microcosm of the empire, as well as an architectural metaphor for, or perhaps more concisely stated, a cosmogram of the Inca universe (Zuidema 1990).

Tiwanaku's north-south division may be inferred from the distribution of its two principal terrace-mounds: Akapana to the north and Puma Punku to the south. These two temple-mounds constitute the most visually salient features of Tiwanaku's urban design. But, they do not stand isolated as individual monuments. Rather, each terraced mound forms the central piece of an orchestrated tableau of sacred architecture and monumental sculpture. The complex flanking the northeast side of the Akapana is the clearest and most complete example of this concentration of ceremonial architecture. The individual elements of this architectural tableau (Kantatayita, Semi-subterranean Temple, Kalasasaya, Chunchukala, and Laka Kollu) were, most likely, constructed at different times, but they were always oriented to, or composed around, the imposing physical presence of the Akapana platform. These flanking structures, along with the Akapana itself, were the dramatic theatrical backdrops, or staging areas for some of Tiwanaku's most iconographically rich and visually arresting sculptures.

Similarly, although less massive than the Akapana complex, the Puma Punku platform was the visual, and, one can infer, symbolic lynchpin of a second, southern ceremonial complex within the city of Tiwanaku. The Puma Punku, although utterly shattered and in virtually complete ruination, is one of the most beautiful and architecturally complex structures ever created in the ancient Andean world. Its principal, eastern entry court was graced by massive, but delicately carved door jambs and lintels, and by a series of monumental figural sculptures. In fact, this court was probably the original location of the justifiably famous monolithic sculpture referred to as the Gateway of the Sun.

If we accept that Tiwanaku was spatially and symbolically partitioned into northern and southern segments, each with its own core of ceremonial architecture and sacred sculpture, what might this architectonic pattern mean? How was this design linked into broader social and political structures? If we take as a potential model the meaning embedded in the dual division of Cuzco into *hanan* and *hurin* segments, this bipartition reflects basic patterns of social, economic, political, and religious organization. In Cuzco each of these two divisions were associated with specific lineages, or *ayllus*, that were ranked in a hierarchy according to the degree of their kin relationship with the king and his royal lineage. As Zuidema (1990) notes, these *ayllus* possessed territorial rights and access to sources of water within the district of Cuzco and were obligated to perform certain ritual obligations, such as sponsoring the celebration of agricultural rituals, or maintaining a particular shrine according to a complex ceremonial calendar.

John Murra's (1968, 1972) extensive ethnohistorical research established with little ambiguity that a similar principle of dual division of the political landscape operated among the Lupaqa, the Aymara-speaking kingdom of the fifteenth and sixteenth century centered in Tiwanaku's old core territory in the Lake Titicaca basin. We may recall that two principal Aymara lords, Qari and Qusi, were the pre-eminent political leaders of the Lupaqa during the mid-sixteenth century. As might be anticipated under a thoroughgoing system of dual division, Qari and Qusi's domain as a whole, as well as each province, was divided into upper and lower moieties, and two lower ranking lords ruled at each of these territorial levels (see Figure 2.2).

An early Colonial period document from 1547 describes the political situation in the village of Tiwanaku in structural terms similar to that of the contemporary Lupaqa kingdom (Ponce 1971:25). At that time the village and its near hinterland (consisting of the lands of smaller villages and *estancias* or farmsteads that still exist today) were led by a principal lord named Tikuna, assisted by a second *kuraka* named Jichuta, who was of somewhat lower prestige and rank ("la segunda persona"). As Ponce remarks, this is a clear allusion to a moiety system with political and social bipartition. In his dictionary published in 1612 the Italian Jesuit Ludovico Bertonio, who lived in Juli, one of the seven *cabeceras* of the Lupaqa, remarks that the Aymara names of the complementary moieties were "Alasaa" and "Maassa," and that "all of the pueblos [villages] of the *altiplano*" possessed this division. This system of dual division persisted in a remarkably integrated and systematic fashion in the village of Tiwanaku into the nineteenth century as recorded in fascinating detail by Adolph Bandelier (1911:235) who in 1894 questioned the locals regarding their form of political and social organization:

> The reply came that there were only two [divisions], Arasaya and Masaya. These two groups are geographically divided at the village. Masaya occupies the building south, Arasaya those north, of the central square, the dividing line going, ideally, through the center of the plaza from east to west. This geographical division is (at Tiahuanaco) even indicated at church. We saw, when at mass, the principals of the two clusters, each with his staff of office, enter in procession: Masaya walking on the right or south, Arasaya on the left, or north, and take their places in the same order on each side of the altar. After the

ceremony they jointly escorted the priest to his home. But we were told also, that there were other ayllus (and as many as ten) within the parish. This caused me to inquire for the church books . . . and I soon found out what I already had suspected, that the two main clusters just named were not kins or clans, but groups of such, perhaps phratries. This is a very ancient arrangement and existed, among other places, at aboriginal Cuzco, where the river divided the inhabitants into two clusters, Hurin-suyu and Hanan-suyu, whereas there is every probability that the tribe was composed of at least thirteen clans, of ayllus, localized; a certain number of them belonging, through their location, to one and the remainder to the other principal subdivision.

Bandelier goes on to recount that the church records of local marriages in Tiwanaku reaching back to 1694 refer to the same Masaya and Arasaya territorial dichotomy. The importance of the Masaya and Arasaya divisions of the social world to both political authority and ritual activity is underscored in Bandelier's perceptive commentary.

But the question remains: given their remoteness from each other in time, and to a lesser extent, geography, are we on secure ground applying principles and practices of spatial and social partitioning from Cuzco and the early Colonial-period Aymara to Tiwanaku? Are these principles historically contingent, or are they the product of fundamental structures of great antiquity and broad geographical distribution in the Andean region? It would seem that the preponderance of the ethnographic and ethnohistorical evidence confirms the latter proposition, although, as in any circumstance in which we lack primary textual evidence, we can never claim ultimate certainty. But, along with Ponce (1971), I would argue that a Lupaqa-like social, political, and religious structure of dual division did govern Tiwanaku society and resulted in the urban design of twin ceremonial centers that we can perceive in the capital.

An even more provocative question is raised by my conclusion that dual corporate organization structured social, political, economic, and religious life among the people of Tiwanaku. I have already suggested that Tiwanaku was pluri-linguistic and multi-ethnic, with Pukina, Aymara, and Uru groups as the principal players in the creation of Tiwanaku society. How could contrasting and potentially competitive ethnic groups create together a coherent, productive social life?

One possibility is suggested by Duviols's (1973) analysis of the origins of dual division in the Recuay region of the central Andean highlands. Here, according to Duviols, the moiety divisions emerged historically as the result of the expansion of highland, mobile herding groups (the *llacuaz*) into the domain of sedentary agriculturalists (the *huari*). The tensions emerging from this encounter engendered a form of dual division that acknowledged separation between the two groups in terms of economic specialization: the *llacuaz* retained productive control of highland pastures, herds, and crops and engaged in mining and textile production; the *huari*, on the other hand, were responsible for maintaining primary agricultural fields at lower altitude. Although each group controlled unique sets of natural resources, the assured right of access to the complementary goods and services of the other moiety segment was the key to the system. The *huari* and *llacuaz* moiety groups exchanged commodities of economic and ceremonial value and, importantly, established a reciprocal adoption of cult figures, ritual practices, and symbolic frames of reference.

The contradictions inherent in the system are apparent. Each half attempted to maintain its original identity and cultural practices, but, at the same time, it was required by historical or ecological circumstances to effect a conceptual and social merger with the other group. The expansion or dislocation of one group into the domain of the other, or the need to gain access to resources from different environmental zones not under direct community control generated considerable tension and potential for debilitating conflict. The solution was to create a dynamic, although potentially unstable, social organization with community authority invested equally in the two principal moiety leaders.

It is tempting to apply a version of Duviols's analysis to Tiwanaku. Tiwanaku society, and its principle of dual corporate organization, might have been generated by the creative encounter and tension filled interaction between mobile herding groups of proto-Aymara origin with sedentary agricultural groups of Pukina origin, with the latter retaining a measure of higher prestige. In the Tiwanaku situation, the Uru groups as specialized aquatic foragers would have occupied a third, somewhat liminal position of lower prestige beneath that of the more powerful proto-Aymara and Pukina elements, serving potentially as the equivalent of *yanapaqhuna,* or permanent retainers in Tiwanaku's court society. Reciprocal adoption of cults, ritual practices, and symbols systems among Aymara, Pukina, and Uru-Chipaya peoples may have resulted in the vigorous, syncretic art style that we associate with classic Tiwanaku culture.

Concepts of sacred geography and the symbolic integration of natural landscapes were clearly strong forces shaping the urban design of Tiwanaku. In a global sense, we can conceptualize the plan of Tiwanaku as a square (quadripartion) within a circle (the concentric cline of the sacred). The innermost artificial island demarcated by Tiwanaku's principal moat was the heart of elite residence in the city, and the setting for one of the most important shrines: the Akapana. This artificial island represented the concentrated essence of the sacred,

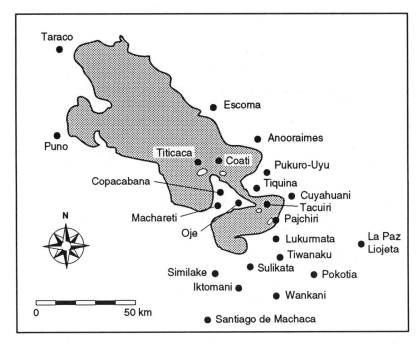

Figure 5.4   The distribution of Tiwanaku regional centers around the southern shore of Lake Titicaca.

and was structured as an orchestrated, architectural allusion to cosmo-gonic myths. At the same time, this sacred core functioned as the cere-monial center for Tiwanaku's northern moiety, linking the concentric principle of design with the principle of dual division and cardinality. Puma Punku to the southwest, then, formed the complementary cere-monial center for the southern moiety. If we have some insight into the overall structure, social partitioning, and symbolic structure of Tiwanaku's urban design, what can we say about the meaning, func-tion, and social characteristics of individual elements in its monu-mental and vernacular architecture?

Tiwanaku's Civic-Ceremonial Core

If there is a single emblem of Tiwanaku elite architectural design, the terraced platform mound constructed around an interior sunken court is its essence. This form dominates the civic-ceremonial core of Tiwanaku and that of its satellite cities such as Lukurmata, Pajchiri, Khonko Wankané, and Oje (Figure 5.4). At Tiwanaku this form finds expression in multiple architectural complexes. The two principal terraced platform mounds at Tiwanaku, Akapana, and Puma Punku, although different in scale and architectural detailing, share this concept, as do, on a less grand scale, the major building complexes of the Kalasasaya, Putuni, Chunchukala, and Kheri Kala. Each of these architectural complexes share, as well, elaborate carved stone monuments, and from excavations undertaken to date, an apparent nonresidential character. That is, for the people of Tiwanaku, the terraced mound with interior sunken court was the standard architectural framework for ceremonial display and public religious expression.

Recent investigations in Tiwanaku's civic-ceremonial core have given us a new and detailed understanding of the physical characteristics and function of its principal architectural complexes. We now know that this core area defined by the great ceremonial moat of Tiwanaku contained not only the largest ceremonial structures, but also elite and royal residences as well. We can capture the essence of the scope and kind of human activities that were carried out in this core area by examining first three principal architectural complexes: Akapana, Puma Punku, and Putuni.

Akapana: The Sacred Mountain

The largest and most imposing single building in Tiwanaku is the Akapana. Perhaps because of its massive and unprecedented scale for the Andean highlands, archaeologists early in this century assumed that the Akapana was a natural hill, a geological feature only superficially modified by the people of Tiwanaku (Bennett 1934; Posnansky 1945). But, as our recent excavations have demonstrated unequivocally, the Spanish chronicler Cieza de León had it right nearly 500 years ago when he described the structure as "a man-made hill, built on stone foundations" (1959:283). The Akapana is, in fact, an entirely artificial construction of transported earth, clay, gravel, and cut stone stepping up in seven, superimposed terraces. The design, techniques, and materials of construction in the Akapana are fascinating in themselves, but even more so for the insight they provide concerning the function and meaning of this impressive structure.

The Akapana conforms to a rather eccentric plan that has been described as one half of an Andean cross (Figures 5.5a and 5.5b). The Andean cross is one of the most ubiquitous, if least understood elements in Tiwanaku iconography, and may be a symbol for the four quarters of the inhabited human world. The structure itself is approximately 200 meters on a side at its maximum extent, and rises to nearly 17 meters in height. The basal terrace is a monumental and

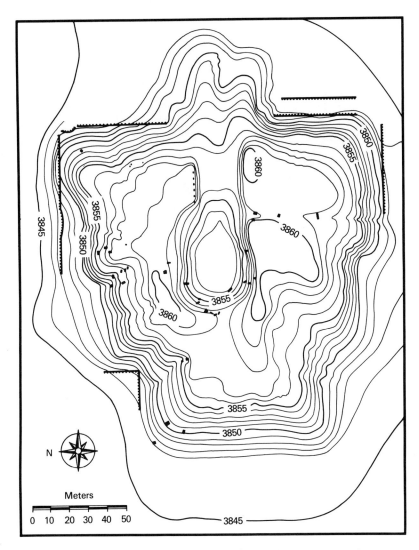

Figure 5.5a   Map of the Akapana pyramid according to Posnansky. (1945, vol. I: Plate VIII).

strikingly beautiful revetment of cut stone with rounded, beveled edges at the joins between blocks. This massive stone foundation replicates (or, more likely, provided the model for) a construction technique employed at the adjacent Kalasasaya complex. In this technique, vertical pillars were erected at the corners of the structure, as

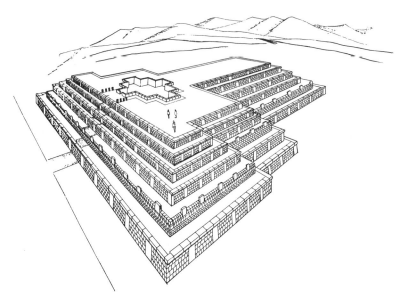

Figure 5.5b   Idealized reconstruction of the Akapana pyramid, as it would have been viewed from the north-east. (Drawing courtesy of Javier Escalante, INAR, La Paz, Bolivia).

well as every few meters along the facade of the terrace. In the case of Akapana, these vertical pillars occur at intervals of approximately three and one half meters. Between the pillars, the architects of Akapana set cut stone blocks in ashlar-like masonry, precision joined without mortar (Figure 5.6). This gigantic revetment wall was then capped with large, rectangular blocks that projected slightly beyond its vertical face, much like modern coping tiles.

The upper six terraces of the Akapana riding on this foundation differ substantially in architectural detail. These upper terraces, for instance, lack the distinctive beveled edges of the stones employed in the basal terrace, and make less frequent use of vertical pillars to mark facade intervals. Instead, these terraces incorporate large, highly visible stone panels into their facades (Figure 5.7). Based on similar architectural elements in the Kheri Kala, Kalasasaya and Kantatayita complexes, we can assume that these panels were covered with iconographically rich metal plaques and textiles, or may themselves have been carved and painted (Figure 5.8). The upper terraces constituted a kind of public, symbolic text, the specific content of which is now irrevocably lost to us. Given the ritual meaning that I ascribe to the Akapana below, the public texts of the upper terrace panels

Figure 5.6   A section of the first terrace on the east side of Akapana, exposed during the 1976 excavations directed by Gregorio Cordero Miranda (INAR). (Photograph by Wolfgang Schüller).

Figure 5.7   Upper terraces on the west side of Akapana.

Figure 5.8   Carved stone panel with a front-faced puma design from Tiwanaku. A similar panel was found by Posnansky (1945: Figure 44) in the Putuni complex. (Miraflores Museum, La Paz, Bolivia; Photograph by Alan Kolata).

most likely made reference to the role of this structure in Tiwanaku's cosmogonic myths. Excavations along these upper terraces also recovered tenon-head sculptures of pumas and humans that were at one time inserted into the facades, punctuating the flat, vertical surfaces of the terrace walls with gargoyle-like projections.

Behind the retaining walls of the seven superimposed terraces, the builders of Akapana laid tons of earth and clay. The outward pressure exerted by this earth fill must have been tremendous, and, in some cases, Akapana's architects devised ingenious caissons of stone to contain the fill. In other interior sections of the upper terraces, we uncovered dome-shaped adobe, tapia, and rammed-earth fill that consolidated some of the materials brought into the construction site. As suggested by Posnansky (1945) decades ago, the bulk of the clay and earth transported to construct the Akapana was excavated from the huge moat surrounding the civic-ceremonial core.

One class of materials used in the construction of the Akapana is unique and provides us with an intriguing, if somewhat speculative, insight into the meaning of this structure for the people of Tiwanaku. Within the construction fill of the upper terraces, interspersed between enormous layers of chunky clay, are thin layers of a bluish-green gravel. These small, water-worn pebbles completely cover the summit of the Akapana. Posnansky (1945:74) attributed this gravel on the summit of Akapana to the detritus left behind by "the great flood which covered Tihuanacu after its destruction." In fact, its presence on the Akapana can only result from human agency. Why would the architects of Akapana go to such great lengths to incorporate this green gravel into the uppermost fill and surface of the structure's summit?

It is apparent that this gravel had no structural role. It constitutes an infinitesimal proportion of the total building's volume and it did not serve as a binding agent for the clay and earth fill. Gravel in this quantity would have been exceedingly tedious to collect and transport to the construction site. The fact that the gravel occurs in distinct layers within the structure and on the summit indicates that it was not simply a by-product, or accidental inclusion in the clayey fill. What, then, is it doing there?, and why would Tiwanaku's architects invest so much labor in purposefully distributing this gravel inside and on top of the Akapana? The answer, I think, stems from the origin and distinctive color of this gravel. This gravel is an erosional product of the Quimsachata and Chila mountain ranges to the south of Tiwanaku, and it occurs naturally in a number of *quebradas* and intermittent streams that flow down from these mountains (Figure 5.9). The source of the gravel is clear to anyone who lives along the base of the Quimsachata range, and its exotic, visually arresting green color immediately attracts even the most casual observer's eye. I believe that the architects of the Akapana selected this gravel for inclusion in the structure precisely because of its potent symbolic associations with the sacred mountains of the Quimsachata range which were important spiritual points of reference, or *huacas*, for the people of Tiwanaku (Reinhard 1987). The gravel was, quite literally, like pieces of the true cross, embued with the spiritual essence of the mountain *huacas*. But, even more, the exotic green color of these stones conveyed an association with the life-giving springs, streams, and subterranean seeps which have their origin in the southern mountain ranges. Not only is the gravel the color of water, it is brought down to the broad plains of the Tiwanaku Valley within these same surface streams and subterranean flows that furnish fresh water to most of the valley. This green gravel condensed in one material the symbolic essence of two Tiwanaku sacred elements: mountains and water.

Such a conclusion, although what I would term informed conjecture, is not without parallel in the ancient Andean world. Haukaypata, one of the two principal plazas in Inca Cuzco, was covered with a layer of sand brought from the Pacific coast nearly 500 kilometers

Figure 5.9   A view of the Quimsachata mountain range, looking southward. The modern town of Tiwanaku, as well as the Akapana and Puma Punku complexes are located in the upper left quadrant of the photograph.

away. The Spanish magistrate Polo de Ondegardo "had the sand removed in 1559 after finding that it was considered sacred by the local residents, who buried gold and silver figurines and vessels in it. Polo also relates that the original earthern surface of the plaza was venerated and carried to other parts of the empire" (Hyslop 1990:37). The sand was apparently sacred because of its association with the waters of the Pacific ocean. One of the places to which the original earth from the Huakaypata plaza may have been carried was the main plaza of the Inca sanctuary on the Island of the Sun in Lake Titicaca. Hyslop (1990:77) notes that "the most detailed historical commentary on the area relates that the plaza [on the Island of the Sun] was called Huakaypata (Aycaypata) and that it was covered with loose dirt, brought in from elsewhere, wherein gold figurines and pottery vessels were buried."

If we accept that the architects of Tiwanaku shared similar concepts regarding the need to sanctify their capital's ceremonial structures through these audacious, labor-intensive schemes of symbolic transference, the question remains, why cover Akapana, and not other structures, with this green gravel? Apart from the obvious, general fact that the Akapana is the most imposing structure at Tiwanaku and the touchstone for the entire northern ceremonial complex, I believe that Akapana was conceived by the people of Tiwanaku specifically as their principal emblem of the sacred mountain. That is, Akapana served as a human-created simulacrum of the highly visible, natural mountain *huacas* in the Quimsachata range.

I infer this symbolic association for several, interrelated reasons. Most simply, the Akapana mimics the form of a mountain, ascending in seven stepped-terraces to visually dominate the urban landscape. Throughout the archaic world, there are countless instances of this kind of symbolic mimesis between pyramidal structures and mountain peaks (Townsend 1979; Wheatley 1971). Then, too, the layers of green gravel physically link Akapana with the Quimsachata range: pieces of the mountains are quite literally built into the structure. But, more subtly, certain structural features of the Akapana intensify the mountain association, and, even more specifically, the link between mountains and sources of water.

Our recent excavations at Akapana revealed an unexpected, sophisticated, and monumental system of interlinked surface and subterranean drains (Figure 5.10). The system begins on the summit with sets of small, subterranean stone-lined channels that originally drained Akapana'a central sunken court. This court is now entirely destroyed by massive seventeenth-century looting operations. The sunken court on Akapana's summit was not roofed, and huge amounts of water collected in the court during the *altiplano*'s furious rainy season between December and March. These stone channels conducted water from the sunken court to a major trunk line that was buried deeper beneath the summit surface. This trunk line probably extended around the four sides of Akapana's summit, but we have direct evidence for it only on the north and west sides. On the west side, we excavated an extensive segment of this subterranean trunk line running in a north-south direction. The drain is rectangular in cross-section, and finely crafted of large (120 by 70 centimeters), precisely fitted sandstone blocks with an interior dimension of 45 centimeters that would have accommodated an enormous flow. The drain as a whole dips northward on a sharp downward slope of 12 degrees. To stabilize the construction on this slope, it is set on a foundation of flagstones, and individual blocks are joined together with copper clamps that were originally poured molten into depressions carved into adjacent stone blocks in the form of a double T (Figure 5.11). This elaborate subterranean trunk line collected water flowing from the channels draining the sunken court on the summit and conducted it inside of the structure to the next lower terrace. Here the water emerges from inside the Akapana onto an exterior stone channel tenoned into the vertical terrace face (Figure 5.12). The water poured over the edge of

Figure 5.10   One of the stone-lined subterranean drains located on the summit of Akapana.

Figure 5.11 In-situ *copper clamp, joining individual stone blocks of Akapana's drainage network.*

Figure 5.12   Exterior stone drain tenoned into the vertical face of an upper terrace at Akapana.

Figure 5.13   A drainage tunnel located in the basal terrace of Akapana.

the tenoned drain onto a stone channel on the terrace, flowed for a few meters on the surface, and then dropped back into the interior of the structure to the next lower terrace through a vertical drain. This process of alternating subterranean and surface flow on the stepped terraces repeated itself until the water finally emerged from the basal terrace of the Akapana through beautifully constructed tunnels (Figure 5.13). Eventually, this water flowing from the Akapana's summit merged into a major subterranean drainage system that was installed three to four meters under the civic-ceremonial core of Tiwanaku. This system itself drains into the Rio Tiwanaku, and, ultimately, Lake Titicaca.

From this spare description alone, it is apparent that the system of draining the Akapana was complex, and, like the case of the green gravel, it was not a structural imperative. A much simpler and smaller set of canals would have accomplished the basic function of draining accumulated rain water from the summit. In fact, the system as installed by the architects of Akapana, although superbly functional, is completely over-engineered, a piece of technical stone-cutting and joinery that can only be called pure virtuosity. There is clearly a dimension to this elaborate drainage network that goes beyond simple utility. A dimension that we can approach by posing a single question: why is the water repeatedly and alternately threaded inside and on the surface of the structure?

The answer to this question lies in considering a more profound mimesis between Akapana and the natural mountains of the Quimsachata range than the general morphological similarity of stepped-terrace mounds and mountain peaks. This deeper symbolic association is grounded in certain natural ecological processes that characterize the Quimsachata range. During the rainy season, almost every day, huge banks of black clouds swollen with rain well up in the deep ravines and inter-montane basins of the Quimsachata range. Sudden, ominous thunderstorms sweep the slopes with torrential rains, driving hail, and violent claps of thunder and lightning. Water rapidly pools in the saddles and peaks along the summit of Quimsachata, and then begins to flow down to the valley floor. But the flow is not direct. Surface water quickly drains into subterranean streams which periodically re-emerge down slope, gushing and pooling in natural terraces, only to tumble again down inside the mountain. The peculiarities of mountain geology and the erosive power of water combine to create this natural alternation between subterranean and surface streams. Runoff from the rains finally emerges from the foot of the mountains in rivers, streams, springs, and spongy, marshy seeps. This fresh water recharges the aquifer of the Tiwanaku Valley and is the source for virtually all of the valley's irrigation and drinking water. In fact, the *altiplano* rainy season is also the principal growing season for major food crops, and the success of agriculture is tied to this critical period of rainfall. Vast tracts of raised agricultural fields developed by the people of Tiwanaku were dependent on this seasonal recharge of surface streams and groundwater (see Chapter 6). At the most primal level, the mountains were sacred because they were the source of water that nourished people and their fields.

Akapana was the sacred mountain of Tiwanaku. It partook of the spiritual essence of the Quimsachata mountain range, the image of which was evoked by Akapana's stepped-terrace shape, by its green gravel mantle, and by its clever, constructed mimicry of the natural circulation of mountain waters in the rainy season. The course of water flow on the Akapana replicated the pattern of nature: pooling, dropping out of sight, gushing onto terraces, emerging at the foot of the mound. In a driving, *altiplano* storm, the large, subterranean drains inside of Akapana may even have generated an acoustic effect, a vibrating roar of rushing interior water that shook the mountain-pyramid, much like the thunderstorms rumbling across the peaks of Quimsachata.

Extending the analogy, Akapana was Tiwanaku's principal earth shrine, an intense icon of fertility and agricultural abundance. Although it may have had a particular association with the mountains of the imposing and immediately visible Quimsachata range, Akapana's location in the civic-ceremonial core of the city suggests yet another kind of symbolic representation. Akapana rests in the center of the island enceinte carved out by Tiwanaku's great, ceremonial moat. Viewed in the larger context of its setting, Akapana becomes the mountain at the center of the island-world, and may even have evoked the specific image of sacred mountains on Lake Titicaca's Island of the Sun. Here another aspect is layered into the meaning of Akapana. In this context, Akapana is the principal *huaca* of cosmogonic myth. It becomes the mountain of human origins and emergence. It takes on specific mytho-historic significance. The Tiwanaku elite who lived within the sacred, moated precinct were appropriating images from the natural order and merging them with their concept of proper social order. They were asserting their intimate affiliation with the life-giving forces of nature through a constructed, mimetic program of architectural and sculptural display.

We know that Akapana served as a key shrine in Tiwanaku religion and elite ideology. But there remain other elements of the structure revealed in recent excavations that add fascinating textures to our understanding of its function and meaning. Although Akapana was a center of cult and ritual behavior, part of its summit was used for living quarters as well. Most of the Akapana summit was taken up by the centrally located sunken court which measured approximately 50 meters on a side. Access to the court was gained by the twin, axial staircases. We can assume that within the sunken court, much like at its counterparts the Semi-subterranean Temple and the Kalasasaya, were placed towering stone sculptures with complex, religiously charged iconography. Flanking the central court, however, at least on the northern side where we completed major excavations, were distinctly secular structures (Figures 5.14a and 5.14b).

Here we uncovered a well-constructed suite of rooms arrayed around a central patio that appear to have served as residences. Although we uncovered no hearths or food preparation areas on the summit, these rooms, as well as the central patio, were filled with large quantities of broken, utilitarian pottery, and botanical remains from the rooms indicate that the inhabitants were eating potato, corn, and possibly more exotic fruits from the subtropical *yungas* zones. Beneath the central patio, a series of burials were uncovered. A file of seated adults, originally wrapped tightly in textile mummy bundles, faced a seated male holding a puma-shaped *incensario*, or incense burner in his hands (Figures 5.15a and 5.15b). Who might the inhabitants of

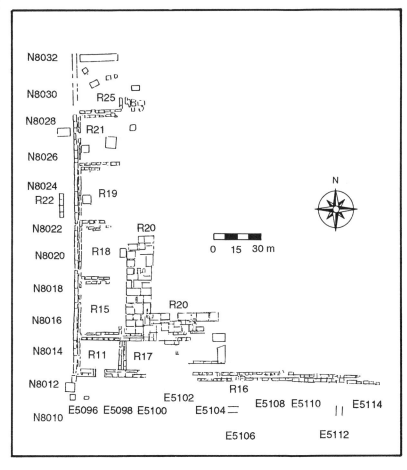

*Figure 5.14a   A plan of the residences located on the summit of Akapana
(north-east sector).*

such a sacred structure have been? The burials under the patio suggest that they were of a relatively elite stratum in Tiwanaku society.
Drawing an analogy from the Inca state, the excavator of this complex
interpreted the rooms as the residences of priests who presumably
served as the principal ritual practitioners for ceremonies that took
place on Akapana's summit (Manzanilla and Woodard 1990). This
seems a plausible conclusion, particularly in light of the manner in
which this residential complex was treated upon abandonment.
    In the southwest corner of the complex, we discovered a major
offering that was associated with the sealing and abandonment of

Figure 5.14b   Six of the Akapana summit structures exposed during 1988 and 1989 excavations. Room 11 is the corner structure in the foreground.

one of the rooms (see Figure 5.14a: Room 11). This offering consisted of fourteen disarticulated llamas, copper pins, plaques, a miniature figurine of a sitting fox (Figure 5.16), hammered silver sheets, a polished bone lip plug, mica, obsidian, quartz, and fragments of complex, polychrome ceramics, including a miniature *kero* or ritual drinking cup, a puma-shaped incense burner, and a vase with an image of a resplendent, crowned figure like that on the Gateway of the Sun. The offering itself was distributed spatially in a mannered, ritualistic fashion: the skulls and upper jaws of the llamas were found in the north and west sides of the room; the lower jaws of these animals were placed in the southeast corner; and the metal objects were concentrated in the northeast portions of the room. The polychrome ceramics, lip plug, mica, and fragments of obsidian and quartz stone tools were found immediately outside the entrance to the room.

The curious, structured distribution of these objects, in many ways analogous to those made today by Aymara *yatiris* when they assemble a melange of dissimilar items on a ritual table of offering, evokes a powerful sense that we have excavated the final remnants of an important ritual. A sample of wood charcoal taken from these materials yielded a radiocarbon date that permits us to fix the date of this

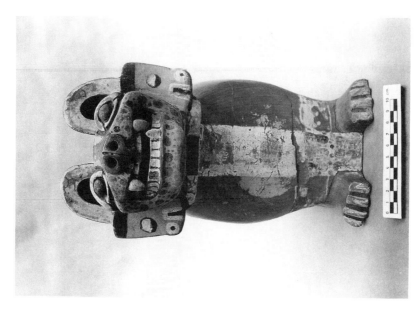

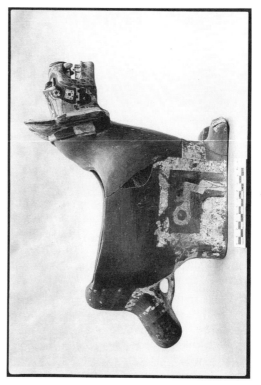

Figure 5.15a and 5.15b   Side and front views of a Tiwanaku incensario, or incense burner, in the form of a puma, recovered during 1987 excavations at Lukurmata. (Photograph by Wolfgang Schüller).

Figure 5.16 Miniature copper fox figurine found in an offering in Room 11, on the summit of Akapana.

ritual event with reasonable confidence between A.D. 1000 and 1300. Given that the offering itself rendered the room inaccessible and that the event occurs at a time of general abandonment in the city, we may be witnessing here a ritual of closure, a ceremony during which the great Akapana earth shrine and the practitioners of its cults were symbolically interred. In any event, the ritualized treatment accorded the sealing off of this room suggests that these habitations on Akapana's summit were not ordinary dwellings.

The summit structures are not the only ones associated with Akapana. Terraces farther down the mound show evidence of surface buildings with foundations of andesite blocks and adobe superstructures. A series of small, but finely wrought buildings were uncovered on the first terrace of the Akapana in excavations by Bolivian archaeologists in the mid-1970s. A number of these appear to be late constructions, perhaps even erected by the Inca after the abandonment of Tiwanaku. The Inca incorporated Tiwanaku as an important shrine in their imperial ideology, and were reputed to have built various structures in the city. But other such terrace structures are clearly associated with the florescence of Tiwanaku.

Excavations on the northwest corner of Akapana revealed a fascinating, and, to date, not entirely understood set of ritual offerings associated with the foundations of the structure and with buildings

Figure 5.17   One of the human dedicatory burials uncovered at the base of Akapana, consisting of two articulated, but incomplete adult males, portions of ceramic vessels, and the partial remains of two llamas.

on the first terrace (Figure 5.17). Here we uncovered a series of twenty-one human burials commingled with llama bones and associated with ceramics that date to the Classic Tiwanaku period. What is curious about the burials is that most are incomplete, but the bones that were present from these skeletons are articulated in correct anatomical position. A good example of this unusual burial practice was an adult male, 21–27 years old, who was found face down parallel to the foundation wall of the Akapana. His spinal column was complete, and his mandible (lower jaw) was in correct anatomical position, but his skull was missing. Another male, 25–30 years old, was discovered laying face down farther along the base of Akapana's foundation wall. Next to him in the same burial was a second young adult male buried face up. Eighteen of these burials lack skulls and several are missing lower limbs, arms, or portions of the spinal column. Among these remarkable burials, only one child was found completely intact and with a fully articulated skeleton (Figure 5.18). But this child, who was approximately two years old upon death, was also discovered laying face down and with legs flexed and crossed. Unlike the other burials of apparently robust, young males, this child suffered from a severe degenerative bone

Figure 5.18 The remains of an infant, approximately two years old, buried face down at the base of Akapana.

disease that left it painfully crippled. This disease was, most likely, the cause of the child's death.

Who were these people, and why were only parts of their bodies buried at the Akapana? At first glance, we assumed that these individuals (many of whom were adult males from 17–39 years old) were dismembered prior to, or shortly after death, conjuring Aztec-style images of sacrifice at the hands of priest-warriors. But the fatal problem with this interpretation quickly emerged on closer examination: none of the bones showed evidence of cut marks, and there is little evidence of intentional physical violence. In lieu of a preternatural capacity to butcher a human body without leaving a mark on adjacent bones, the skulls and other body parts must have been removed *post mortem*, at some time after the corpse and its tough connective tissue had begun to decay. It is possible that these individuals died, or were sacrificed, and their bones were later interred at the Akapana in the form of mummy bundles. Although some body parts, such as the skull and lower limbs, were removed in the process of assembling the mummy bundle, the remaining portions of the skeleton remained articulated in anatomically correct position by the textile wrappings of the bundle.

But why did the people of Tiwanaku remove individual bones, and particularly the skulls from these burials? One clue to this intriguing

Figure 5.19   A small section of the spectacular ceramic offering on a lower terrace of the Akapana.

puzzle comes from a tremendous offering of purposely broken, polychrome ceramics associated with five of these curious partial skeletons. This ceramic cache and its associated burials were uncovered within the destroyed room of a structure on the first terrace of the Akapana. The ceramics are iconographically associated with the Classic Tiwanaku period, and three radiocarbon dates fix the episode between A.D. 530 and 690. These dates, along with the identical burial pattern of partial skeletons, indicate that the offering was contemporaneous with those excavated along the foundation wall of the Akapana, perhaps even forming part of a single, ritual event. The ceramic offering consists of hundreds of fine polychrome vessels fashioned into bowls and *keros* that we found shattered into thousands of fragments (Figures 5.19 and 5.20). The polychrome bowl fragments from this ceramic offering have a consistent, standardized motif: painted bands of stylized human trophy heads (Figure 5.21). The *keros* display painted images of humans elaborately costumed as puma and condor figures. Trophy heads hang from the belts of these figures, or are worked into the elements of masks worn by the dancing celebrants portrayed on the vessels. Not infrequently, human trophy heads appear as the finials of staffs carried by the condor or puma-masked dancers. The trophy heads, although eerily stylized skeletal images, are clearly representations of actual human trophy heads. Cut and polished skulls have

Figure 5.20   An example of an intact kero, one of the vessel forms most
frequently encountered in the Akapana ceramic offering. (Museo Regional de
Tiwanaku. Photograph by Wolfgang Schüller).

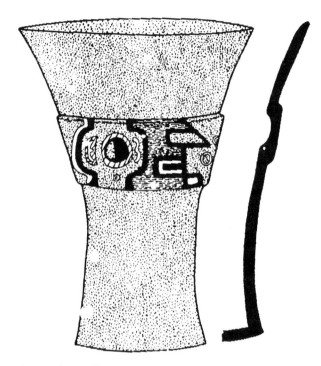

Figure 5.21   A kero *illustrating a stylized human trophy head. (From Sutherland 1991: Figure 8).*

been found in excavations at Tiwanaku, leaving little doubt that the practice of taking heads in battle as trophies was a central symbolic element of Tiwanaku warfare and ritual sacrifice. We know that the Inca took heads in battle and later transformed the skulls of particularly important enemy warriors into macabre drinking cups used to celebrate victory over the vanquished foe (Rowe 1963:279). It is not surprising that the people of Tiwanaku adhered to similar practices.

If we can judge from the testimony of state art, the elites of Tiwanaku were obsessed with decapitation and with ritual display of severed heads. Grim images of decapitation abound in Tiwanaku art. Many of these feature animal-masked humans carrying sacrificial knives and battle axes resplendent in costumes studded with pendant trophy heads. A class of stone sculptures from Tiwanaku, called *chachapumas*, portrays powerful, puma-masked humans holding a severed head in one hand and a battle axe in the other, as if to capture in stone the horrible, and, one imagines, unforgettable moment of decapitation (Figure 5.22). We discovered one such *chachapuma* at

Figure 5.22   A carved stone chachapuma *holding a trophy head. (Museum für Völkerkunde, Berlin, V A 11906).*

the base of Akapana's ruined western staircase in the same stratigraphic context as the human offerings placed at the structure's foundations (Figure 5.23). This ferocious looking sculpture, carved of dense, black basalt, seems poised in a crouch, ominously displaying in its lap a human trophy head with long tresses of braided hair (Figure 5.24).

Akapana's headless mummy bundles, associated with these lavish displays of trophy heads on ritual drinking cups and on monumental public sculpture, were interred at some time in the early seventh century. Given their state of selective dismemberment and their linkage to images of head taking, these human remains may represent the ancestral bundles of a conquered people. Few acts in the ancient Andean world could have been more intensely charged with the symbolism of domination than scattering the relictual remains of ancestors

Figure 5.23   The basalt sculpture of a chachapuma, *as it was being uncovered at the base of Akapana's western staircase during 1989 excavations.*

and relatives at the foot of the conqueror's principal earth shrine. In the context of Andean ideology, this display of domination was simultaneously a symbolic act of incorporation of the conquered group into the social, cosmological, and political system of Tiwanaku. The conquered group's ancestors were, in a real sense, infused into the sacred essence of the very shrine that was emblematic of Tiwanaku's ethnic and cultural identity. The more profound act of domination here was not the simple taking of enemy heads, but rather the incorporation and assimilation of the conquered group's ethnic identity into the broader "body politic" of Tiwanaku society. Domination here meant quite literally loss of one's head, followed by loss of the ethnic group's autonomous social identity. In addition to evoking the image of a gigantic earth shrine, the sculptures and esoteric offerings

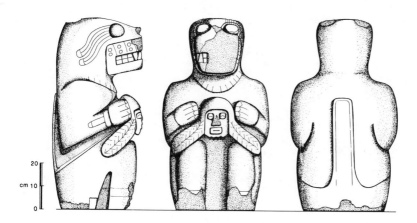

Figure 5.24   Three views of the basalt chachapuma *found at the base of the Akapana. (Drawing courtesy of Javier Escalante, INAR, La Paz, Bolivia).*

arrayed on and around the Akapana constituted a kind of ritual text glorifying the political and ideological power of Tiwanaku society, embodied in the actions of the warrior-priests who were at the apex of the ruling hierarchy.

Puma Punku: Akapana's Twin

Given the principles of dual division and moiety structure that characterized Tiwanaku urban order, much of the architectural and symbolic analysis of the Akapana as a sacred mountain applies with equal force to the Puma Punku (Figure 5.25). As at the Akapana, the architects of Puma Punku installed a system of tremendous internal canals that conducted rainwater from a sunken court on the structure's summit into the interior of the pyramid. Ultimately, this water cascaded out from tunnels driven horizontally into the foundations of the structure. Precisely like Akapana, Puma Punku was designed to collect water and thread it through the structure from one terrace to the next. This terraced platform mound recapitulates, on a smaller scale, the intense symbolic associations inhering in the Akapana. Puma Punku was most likely the principal earth shrine and emblem of the sacred mountain for Tiwanaku's southern moiety division.

Importantly, the distinctive architectural arrangement of a central, stepped-terrace mound in the center of an artificial island-city encoded in the Akapana and Puma Punku complexes reoccurs beyond the

Figure 5.25　The Puma Punku temple at Tiwanaku, exposed in 1978 by the Bolivian archaeologist Gregorio Cordero Mirar-da (INAR). (Photograph by Alan Kolata).

Figure 5.26   View of the civic-ceremonial sector at Lukurmata, a Tiwanaku regional center located on the shores of Lake Titicaca. (Photograph by Alan Kolata).

boundaries of Tiwanaku itself. This concept of urban spatial order, which evoked the place and time of cosmological and ethnic origins and visually related built forms to sacred geography, was a central symbolic expression of Tiwanaku elite culture. This symbolically dense architectural arrangement was extended to regional Tiwanaku capitals such as Lukurmata, Pajchiri, and Khonko Wankané as a self-conscious emblem of Tiwanaku dominion and legitimacy. In each of these regional cities, canals or moats carve the urban landscape into a ceremonial core of temples and elite residences within an island enceinte counterposed against extensive sectors of vernacular architecture. Moreover, at Lukurmata, the most intensively investigated of the Tiwanaku regional cities, the central ceremonial complex organized around a terraced-mound, was furnished with a drainage network similar to that of the Akapana and Puma Punku (Figure 5.26). Here, too, rainwater collecting on the summit of the ceremonial complex was threaded through carved stone drains to the base of the artificially modified rock outcrop on which the complex was constructed. Water from the summit flows into the principal canal demarcating the island-core of the site, and, ultimately, into Lake Titicaca. At Lukurmata, this canal also drains an adjacent sector of raised fields

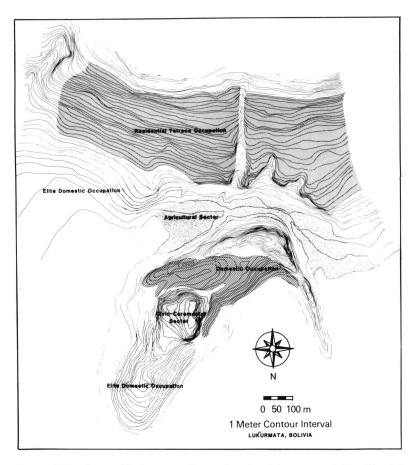

Figure 5.27   Map of Lukurmata illustrating the civic-ceremonial, residential, and agricultural sectors of the city.

(Figure 5.27), unambiguously linking the summit ceremonial complex with agricultural productivity through the connecting thread of flowing water.

Puma Punku itself appears to have been constructed in the Tiwanaku IV phase, most probably between the seventh and eighth centuries A.D. Construction work on the Akapana, on the other hand, began prior to the Tiwanaku IV phase, although a more precise date for initial building activities is not yet clear. This chronological difference represents an intriguing, if somewhat speculative possibility for interpreting potential changes in the function of these two great architectural monuments of Tiwanaku urban civilization.

Figure 5.28   Dog burial found in-situ *in front of a drainage tunnel at the base of Akapana, during 1988 excavations.*

At the time of the early seventh century event that led to the interment of relictual bundles and ritual offerings at the foot of the Akapana, it is clear that the monumental drainage network of the temple that mimicked the alternating surface and subterranean flow of mountain waters was no longer functioning. The dedicatory offerings of artifacts and human and animal remains in shallow pits at the base of the structure would never have been preserved intact, as they were discovered, if this internal drainage system still flowed with accumulated rainwater. In fact, one of the associated dedicatory offerings from this event, a dog burial, was placed directly in front of a tunnel from which the water flowed out of the base of the pyramid (Figure 5.28). This direct juxtaposition indicates beyond much doubt that the great drainage system had ceased to function at some point before the ritual interments on the Akapana, or before circa A.D. 600.

If the Akapana's original symbolic association for the people of Tiwanaku was as an earth shrine linked to sacred mountains as sources of fresh water, how can we interpret this potentially radical change in the function of the temple mound? One possibility, deriving from the pattern of dedicatory offerings, is that at some point in the early seventh century, the intense ethnic and cosmological symbolism of the Akapana was appropriated by the Tiwanaku elite (or perhaps even an individual king) to glorify its position and social standing within Tiwanaku society. Given that the imagery of these ritual offerings are overwhelmingly focused on aggressive, martial themes (the display of trophy heads and the arrangement of relictual bundles lacking skulls and other body parts), we may be witnessing here the aftermath of a particular campaign of military conquest at which the principal temple in the capital city was rededicated to commemorate a transforming event in Tiwanaku history. Such temple rededications, accompanied by a mannered, symbolically rich incorporation of ritual objects, were a common feature of fifteenth- and early sixteenth-century Aztec imperial society in the central basin of Mexico (Broda et al. 1987). Periodic rededications of the Aztec *Templo Mayor* were stimulated by the passing of a designated 52 year cycle in the Aztec ritual calendar, and by extraordinary events in the lives of the reigning monarchs, such as accession to the throne, or the successful conclusion of important military campaigns. If the Akapana offerings reflect a similar act of ritual temple rededication, then the closing of the monumental internal drainage system may reflect a premeditated reconfiguring of the structure's symbolic "text" by the Tiwanaku elite to memorialize an historically momentous event. From a generalized earth shrine and sacred mountain, Akapana at this time may have become a more specific icon commemorating, and further legitimating the right of the Tiwanaku warrior-elites to rule in the city: a massive, brutal, and public expression of self-interested propaganda. Although the old, deeply rooted association of Akapana as a sacred mountain would surely have persisted in the minds of the people of Tiwanaku, the temple rededication imparted a new layer of meaning that more intensely related the qualities and actions of the ruling elites to the ancient earth shrine.

Around the same time that the symbolic associations inhering in the Akapana were being reworked, the Puma Punku complex was being built according to a structural template that replicated the original Akapana design incorporating a monumental, internal drainage system. Although on the Akapana after the early seventh century water no longer seems to have flowed in highly visible, alternating cascades from surface terraces to subterranean chambers, this artful, and symbolically rich mimicking of natural hydrological processes on artificial mountain-pyramids was not lost at Tiwanaku – it simply was transferred to the Puma Punku. It is possible that after A.D. 600, Puma Punku became the general ethnic shrine to earth, mountains, and water at Tiwanaku, while the Akapana was transformed into a more personalized shrine of the lords of Tiwanaku: a monumental paean to, and sacred guarantor of, their right to rule.

Images of Power

Two other related structures at Tiwanaku complete the tableau of
ceremonial architecture in the city core visible on the surface today:
the Semi-subterranean Temple and the Kalasasaya. Both of these
structures are adjacent to the north face of Akapana (Figure 5.29),
and both contain remarkable examples of Tiwanaku's monumental
stone sculpture that add substantially to our understanding of the
meaning and function of these buildings for the people of Tiwanaku.
The Semi-subterranean Temple, as its name implies, is a structure
excavated into the ground to form a rectangular sunken court, constructed of sandstone masonry (Figure 5.30). A monumental staircase on the south side of the structure descends into the temple which
was originally left open to the elements, as was the central, sunken
court on the summit of the Akapana. The Semi-subterranean Temple
at Tiwanaku contains an eclectic assemblage of stone stelae and
sculptures carved in various styles (Figure 5.31), which were carefully
arrayed in subsidiary positions around a centrally located, monumental
axis mundi: the seven-meter tall Bennett stela (Figure 5.32).

The Bennett stela, like other major anthropomorphic monoliths
in the classic Tiwanaku style, represents an elaborately costumed and
crowned human figure pressing a banded *kero*, or drinking cup, against
the chest with one hand and grasping a scepter-like object in the other.
A reasonable argument can be made that this monumental sculpture
visually encoded the principal tenets of Tiwanaku state ideology and
cosmology. The essential agrarian focus of this state ideology is recapitulated in specific images on the sculpture, which Zuidema (1983),
in a provocative interpretation, reconstructs as a representation of a
twelve-month, sideral-lunar agricultural calendar. He suggests that
the doughnut-shaped circles portrayed on the short pants worn by
the anthropomorphic sculpture represent day signs (Figure 5.33a).
Tie-dyed versions of these circles appear on actual textiles preserved
in coastal Tiwanaku tombs, indicating that the costume represented
on the sculpture replicates actual clothing that was worn by humans,
at least on ceremonial occasions. Zuidema interprets the number of
circles on the sculpture which total 177 as reflecting the number of
days in six synodic, or lunar months. Similarly, he suggests that the
sequence of 30 central frontal face and lateral running figures shown
in profile on the low-relief carving of the sculpture correspond to the
30 days of a month.

Several of the figures on the Bennett stela are clearly associated
with flowering plants, most notably the central human figure whose
feet are transformed into plants. The image of a llama with a halter

Figure 5.29   A view of the Semi-subterranean Temple and the Kalasasaya, looking north from the top of Akapana. (Photograph by Wolfgang Schüller).

Figure 5.30 The west wall of the Semi-subterranean Temple (foreground), and the monolithic eastern staircase of the Kalasasaya framing a monumental stone sculpture, the Ponce Monolith. (Photograph by Wolfgang Schüller).

Figure 5.31   One of the carved stone tenon-heads flanking the interior of the Semi-subterranean Temple. (Photograph by Alan Kolata).

Figure 5.32   The Bennett stela as it was being moved from Tiwanaku to the Miraflores Museum in La Paz. (From Posnansky 1945, vol. II: Figure 113).

on either side of this central figure bears numerous representations of distinct flowering plants, both cultivated and wild, that conceptually associates llamas with agriculture and plant life. In particular, the llama figures appear to be draped with a textile that bears an emblem of a banded *kero* with a painted human face from behind which sprouts a maize plant (Figure 5.33b). The association of the *kero* and maize plant immediately brings to mind the ritual drink, *chicha*, or maize beer which was central to indigenous Andean religion and politics. The plant sprouting from the back of the caped llama may represent not a cultivated plant, but the columnar cactus *Trichocereus pachanoi*, a mescaline-bearing cactus that was sought for its hallucinogenic properties. Other images of this columnar cactus appear prominently on the Bennett stela implying that the consumption of hallucinogenic plants was a key instrument for religious and ritual expression among the people of Tiwanaku. We know that the consumption of plants with the capacity to alter consciousness was a common feature of shamanic ceremonies throughout the pre-industrial world. The occurrence of snuff trays, inhalation tubes, and other paraphernalia associated with the consumption of mind-altering substances in Tiwanaku sites makes it clear that this was an important

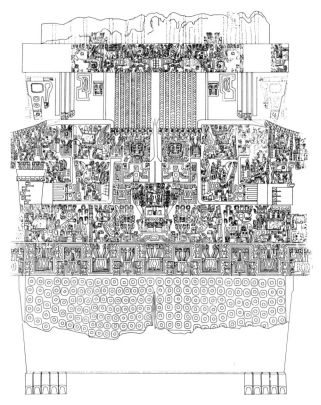

Figure 5.33a   A rollout drawing of the iconography on all four sides of the Bennett stela. (From Posnansky 1945, vol. II: Figure 113a).

Figure 5.33b   Detail of a llama image carved on the Bennett stela.

element of native Tiwanaku religion, worthy of public commemoration on monumental, state art.

The ritual content of the Bennett stela's rich iconography is apparent, linking agriculture, llama husbandry, and calendrics. Zuidema demonstrates that this conceptual linkage reflected social, symbolic, and ecological relationships between pastoralism and agriculture in the high plateau. As he notes: "while the crops are growing, the animals are kept away from the fields, but after harvest they are led into them [to permit llamas to graze on the remaining stubble and thereby through their dung regenerate the fertility of the fields] thus, crops and animals alternate in the same fields" (Zuidema 1983:16).

The Bennett stela, along with other similar monuments at Tiwanaku, was a highly compressed image of esoteric knowledge that turned on the complementary relationships between agriculture and llama husbandry, the two economic pediments of Tiwanaku's political power. The public monuments on which these intense images of ecological and productive complementarity occur also represent idealized portraits of the ruling elite. In fact, the entire message of the cosmically-sanctioned, harmonious, and rhythmic complementarity between farmer and herder reoccurs in standardized images on elements of elite costume, such as tunics, crowns, and sashes, and on symbols of royal authority, such as scepters and staffs of office. Displayed on the greatest sculptural images of Tiwanaku monumental art, this same message was integrated directly into the principal architectural ensembles at Tiwanaku and its secondary administrative centers. The intended meaning of this metaphoric association between images of agropastoral productivity and the representation of royal office, all framed in the context of calendrics, could not be more clear. The elite of Tiwanaku nourish and sustain the common people. Through direct intercession and identity with the divine forces of nature, they will guarantee the agricultural and reproductive success of the nation. The elite were guarantors of reproductive success through ritual intervention with the supernatural forces that affected agropastoral production, but also through manipulation of a pragmatic body of knowledge – an effective agricultural calendar. Furthermore, the elite classes, in effect, harmonized the potentially disruptive competition between farmer and herder by formally synchronizing productive strategies, adjudicating territorial disputes, and redistributing the very different work products of these two occupational pursuits.

If I have decoded the essential meanings integrated in the form and iconography of the Bennett stela, what of the other sculptures arrayed around this central pivot in the Semi-subterranean Temple? It is crucial to note that these sculptures were clearly arranged in a subsidary status position with respect to the Bennett stela. These sculptures are also highly diverse stylistically and some of them were clearly carved many centuries before the Bennett stela itself. At some point, in other words, the architects of the Semi-subterranean Temple assembled an eclectic collection of sculptures that were temporally, stylistically, and most likely ethnically foreign to Tiwanaku. It is likely that these foreign sculptures were sacred emblems of the concentrated spiritual power, or, in Andean terms, *huacas* of distinct ethnic groups. In the process of expanding their hegemony over the Lake Titicaca basin from the fourth century on, the warrior-elite of Tiwanaku ritually appropriated or captured these ancestral *huacas* and incorporated them in subsidary positions within the ceremonial core of their sacred capital city. In so doing, they demonstrated both the ideological and secular superiority of the Tiwanaku state. This process of co-opting local *huacas* in the process of politically incorporating new territories is a familiar one in the native Andean world, replicated in the annals of Inca ethnohistorical accounts. When the Inca subjugated a new territory, the principal *huacas* were brought to Cuzco and housed in a special, central shrine supported by the peoples of the conquered provinces (Rowe 1982:109). The provincial *huacas*, although honored and worshiped in a traditional manner in Cuzco, were, in effect, held hostage to the imposed solar-focused state cults of the Inca. Frequently, as in the case of the powerful lord of the Chimu state deposed by the Inca, the secular authorities of conquered provinces were held in captivity in Cuzco along with their nation's spiritual icons, where they were treated with elaborate royal hospitality that served to underscore their new status as subjects in thrall to their Inca overlords.

The sculptural and architectural assemblage of the Semi-subterranean Temple also conveyed a public, cosmological vision charged with ethnic and political valences, analogous to that described by Paul Wheatley (1971:431–2) for a twelfth-century southeast Asian state:

> examples of capital cities focusing the supernatural power of a kingdom within their enceintes, and therefore symbolizing whole states, are not difficult to find. ... One of the most instructive examples is afforded by the ceremonial and administrative complex of Yashodarapura, laid out by Jayavarman II of Cambodia at the end of the 12th century A.D. The centrally situated temple-mountain, known today as the Bayon, consisted essentially of a central quincunx of towers, representing the five peaks of Mount Meru, axis of the world, surrounded by forty-nine smaller towers, each of which represented a province of the empire. According to Paul Mus's elucidation of the symbolism of this structure, the chapels below the smaller towers housed statues of the apotheosized princes and local gods connected with the provinces of the empire, so

that the Bayon as a whole constituted a pantheon of the personal and religious cults practised in the various parts of the kingdom. By thus assembling them at the sacred axis . . . , the point where it was possible to effect an ontological passage between the worlds so that royal power was continually replenished by divine grace from on high, Jayavarman brought these potentially competitive forces under his control.

The Semi-subterranean Temple and its sculptural ensemble may very well have functioned as Tiwanaku's Bayon, physically embodying the point of fusion of a centralized imperial ideology with multiple regional and ethnic ideological systems.

Immediately to the west of the Semi-subterranean Temple rises the imposing massif of the Kalasasaya. This structure is a large (approximately 130 × 120 meters), rectangular precinct elevated above the ground surface to form a low platform mound. Like Akapana and other platform mounds at Tiwanaku, Kalasasaya was furnished with a central sunken court. Kalasasaya's walls were built of towering, rough-cut sandstone pillars that alternated with sections of smaller, ashlar blocks of high-quality masonry (Ponce 1969). Entry to the Kalasasaya was gained through a monumental staircase that pierces the eastern facade of the structure (Figure 5.30). The undifferentiated, massive facades of this building create a palpable psychological impression of "solidity, strength and overwhelming grandeur" (Oakland 1987:12). Kalasasaya forms a structural unit with the Semi-subterranean Temple. Both structures share canons of architectural design, a formal orientation to the cardinal directions, and an astronomical alignment that marks the vernal and autumnal equinoxes, which are critical temporal markers in the agricultural cycle of the seasons. Specifically, on the morning of the equinoxes, the sun bisects the Semi-subterranean Temple and appears in the center of Kalasasaya's monumental staircase. Kalasasaya was visually linked permanently to the Semi-subterranean Temple through placement of a major stone stela in its central sunken courtyard (Figure 5.34). This sculpture, termed the Ponce stela, was engraved with designs similar in iconographic content to that of the Bennett stela. The Ponce stela faces eastward, gazing through Kalasasaya's monumental gateway toward the Semi-subterranean Temple. It is likely that the Bennett stela was oriented with its face toward the west, as if returning the eternal gaze of its counterpart. These two monolithic sculptures, paired and placed in visual counterpoint along the solar path that divided the urban landscape, one facing east and the other west, may have been intended as representations of the ancestors of Tiwanaku's ruling lineages: in Andean terms, *huacas* par excellence of ethnic identity and continuity.

Figure 5.34   The Ponce Stela, located in the central sunken court of Kalasasaya. (Photograph by Wolfgang Schüller).

The fact that this sculptural ensemble, which evoked the ancient mystique of dynastic ancestors, sits squarely in the middle of Tiwanaku's innermost island enceinte further intensified the spiritual aura that enveloped the city's core. These sculptures brilliantly concentrated the essence of the Tiwanaku elite's political legitimacy, their esoteric knowledge and their moral authority. They were powerful visual statements that overtly linked Tiwanaku's ruling dynasty with the mythic past, with the time of ethnic origins, and with the proper and necessary functioning of the natural world.

Flanking the entry courtyard in the Kalasasaya and facing the central pivot of the Ponce stela were a series of small stone rooms. Although the evidence is indirect, these rooms appear to have been associated with elegant, sculptured stone portrait heads of Tiwanaku males, frequently portrayed chewing coca leaf (Figures 5.35a and 5.35b). These portraits may have been representations of individual Tiwanaku rulers. An intriguing explanation for the use of these small rooms is that they were designed as mausoleums to hold the mummified remains of deceased rulers, or elite lineage ancestors. Ancestor worship and the physical preservation and manipulation of relictual bundles associated with the dead was the fundamental bedrock of indigenous Andean religion, the basis of ritual activity in the ancient social unit of the *ayllu*. We know that similar, although much larger, above-ground burial chambers for the social elite were an important element of the later Aymara kingdoms, and these impressive stone and adobe mortuary towers, known as *chullpas*, are found throughout the old Tiwanaku homeland on the high plateau. Among the Inca elite of Cuzco, ancestor worship took the form of an elaborate cult of the royal mummies which simultaneously fascinated and repelled the Spanish chroniclers like Bernabé Cobo who vividly recorded this key element of indigenous spirituality:

[The Inca] had the law and custom that when one of their rulers died, they embalmed him and wrapped him in many fine garments. They allotted these lords all the service that they had in life, so that their mummy-bundles might be served in death as if they were still alive . . .

It was [customary for the dead rulers to visit one another, and they had great dances and revelries. Sometimes the dead went to the houses of the living, and sometimes the living visited them.

Royal relatives of the deceased] brought [the mummies], lavishly escorted, to all their most important ceremonies. They sat them all down in the plaza in a row, in order of seniority, and the servants who looked after them ate and drank there . . . In front of the mummies they also placed large vessels like pitchers, called vilques, made of gold and silver. They filled these vessels with maize beer and toasted the

Figure 5.35a-b   Two sculptured stone portrait heads of the Tiwanaku elite, depicted chewing coca. (Museum für Völkerkunde, Berlin, no catalogue numbers available. Photograph by Alan Kolata).

dead with it, after first showing it to them. The dead toasted one another, and they drank to the living . . . this was done by their ministers in their names. When the vilques were full, they poured them over a circular stone set up as an idol in the middle of the plaza. There was a small channel around the stone, and the beer ran off through drains and hidden pipes. (Cobo [1653] cited in Conrad and Demarest 1984:114)

This lurid spectacle of the descendants of dead kings ministering to their ancestors' elaborately costumed, dessicated corpses with offerings of food, drinks, and toasts in the plazas of Cuzco obscures the subtle political and religious nuances embedded in the cult of the royal mummies. Although grounded in the pan–Andean religious practice of ancestor worship, this elite cult was transformed into something more than the simple veneration of a dead lineage ancestor. The elaborate feasting of the dead royals was organized around and intended as ceremonies of agricultural fertility: "when there was need for water for the cultivated fields, they usually brought out [the dead king's] body, richly dressed, with his face covered, carrying it in a procession through the fields and punas, and they were convinced that this was largely responsible for bringing rain" (Cobo [1653] 1979:125). Dead kings were frequently addressed in the protocols of public toasts as Illapa, the weather deity who personified the atmospheric forces of wind, rain, hail, lightning, and thunder: all of those meteorological phenomena responsible for the growth or destruction of agricultural crops.

The public display of the royal mummies arranged in order of seniority in the principal plazas of Cuzco during state occasions was a graphic affirmation of the legitimacy of Inca dynastic rule. On these occasions, the reigning king would participate in ceremonial processionals throughout Cuzco quite literally in conjunction with the complete line of his royal ancestors, who were physically represented by their richly adorned, relictual bundles. Who could contest the legitimacy of the Inca when the entire dynasty, the distilled history of their ruling mandate, was constantly visible and present to the nation? By these ritual actions, the deceased monarchs and the living emperor symbolically became one: embodiments of legitimate power, emblems of agricultural fertility and abundance, and powerful icons of national identity.

The mummy bundles of the Inca rulers were kept in a number of places including the principal temple of Qoricancha where elaborate niches most probably held these and other relictual bundles. We lack similar ethnohistorical accounts of mortuary rituals and practice for Tiwanaku to definitively associate the Kalasasaya structures with such behavior. We must rely on archaeological evidence for our interpretations. In the case of the structures designed into Kalasasaya's interior courtyard that evidence is largely negative: the rooms themselves were long ago emptied of their contents. However, we can only conjecture from their distinctive form and architectural context that they at one time held objects of high cultural value. Objects that were precious and designed to be periodically removed and displayed. Relictual bundles of ancestors, among other objects of prestige and power, fit this description well.

The association of the Kalasasaya temple with the Tiwanaku elite, with the elite's lineage ancestors, and with agricultural ritual in which the elite were the principal intercessors between the natural and supernatural worlds finds additional support in the iconographic record of another sculpture within this temple: the Gateway of the Sun (see Figure 1.4 p. 17). Perhaps the most famous stone sculpture in the ancient Andean world, the Gateway of the Sun, was discovered in the northwest corner of the Kalasasaya, although, as indicated previously, its original location may have been the Puma Punku temple mound. The central figure of the Gateway of the Sun at Tiwanaku represented a celestial high god that personified various elements of natural forces intimately associated with the productive potential of *altiplano* ecology: the sun, wind, rain, hail – in brief, a personification of atmospherics that most directly affect agricultural production in either a positive or negative aspect (Demarest 1981). This celestial high god was most likely an ancient representation of Thunupa, the Aymara weather god (equivalent of the Quechua Illapa), manifested majestically in the lightning and thunder that rips violently across the high plateau during the rainy season. This weather deity is portrayed standing on a triple-terraced, stepped pyramid, perhaps even the Puma Punku itself, holding a sling in one hand and an atlatl (spear-thrower) in the other. The uppermost frieze of the sculpture depicts not only the forceful, projecting image of Thunupa displayed in full battle regalia, but also 11 other frontal faces, each encompassed by a solar mask virtually identical with that of Thunupa, and 30 running, or kneeling masked figures shown in profile oriented toward the central figure. These 30 subsidiary figures are arranged in a symmetrical array, each side consisting of three rows of five figures each. This distribution of figures was interpreted by Posnansky (1945) as a representation of a calendar in which each of the 12 solar-masked figures represented one month in a solar year. Zuidema (1983) interprets the iconography of the gateway in a similar fashion, although he assigns the names of the various months of the Christian calendar to different positions than Posnansky. Zuidema suggests that the solar-masked faces stand either for the sun in each of the 12 months of the solar year, or for full moons in each of these months. In this interpretation, the 30 running profile figures refer to the days of each (synodic or solar) month.

However one reconstructs the precise structure of the calendrical information embedded in the complex iconography of the Gateway of the Sun, it is apparent that this monument, along with the Bennett and Ponce stelae, distill the essence of the Tiwanaku elite's esoteric knowledge, a knowledge that was intimately linked to their key role in sustaining agricultural production. These sculptures clearly had multiple meanings and uses, and only a select group of elite understood them all. They were simultaneously intensely sacred objects, studded with the images of gods, mythical beasts, and mystical symbols, monumental representations of the dynastic ancestors of the lords of Tiwanaku, and clever repositories of esoteric, yet pragmatic knowledge, like libraries of agricultural lore and practice etched in stone.

The Palaces of the Lords

If the moat-encircled core of Tiwanaku, with its splendid temple complexes, exotic ritual offerings, and monumental sculptural ensembles, was the religious focus of the city, a place for worship embued with the essence of spirituality, it was also a place for living. Given the highly charged religious and political significance of Tiwanaku's civic-ceremonial core, it is not surprising that the right of residence within this sacred precinct was apparently restricted to the elite lineages of highest status. Intensive archaeological investigations in one residential and ceremonial complex, the Putuni, offers fascinating and detailed insight into the daily life of the Tiwanaku elite: the set of royal lineages accustomed to wielding power both secular and sacred.

In many respects, the Putuni is an architectural complex with uncommon, if not entirely unique structural features at Tiwanaku (Figure 5.36a). Early in this century, George Courty, one of the principals of a French mission to the site that conducted excavations in the area, commented that the architecture of Putuni was different from all the rest at Tiwanaku (Créqui-Monfort 1906). He noted that all other structures in Tiwanaku are distinctly above or below ground. Putuni, on the other hand, combines elements evocative of both elevated and subterranean architectural spaces. The structure itself consists of an elevated platform approximately fifty meters on a side surrounding an open, partially sunken interior courtyard. On the east side of the complex, the French mission uncovered a spectacular painted, polychrome stone staircase that originally descended into the central, sunken courtyard. (This staircase, in the destructive, acquisitive ethic of the times, was promptly dismantled for shipment to Paris, where it undoubtedly remains today packed in excelsior-stuffed wooden crates, mislaid somewhere along the labyrinthine back-corridors of the Musée de l'Homme.) The only extant access to the elevated

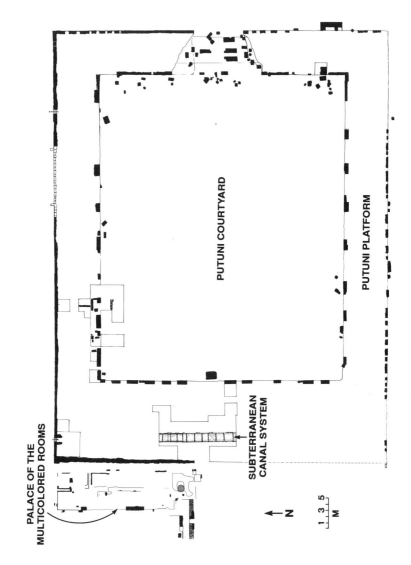

PALACE OF THE
MULTICOLORED ROOMS

PUTUNI COURTYARD

PUTUNI PLATFORM

SUBTERRANEAN
CANAL SYSTEM

N

1 3 5
M

Figure 5.36a   Map of the Putuni complex.

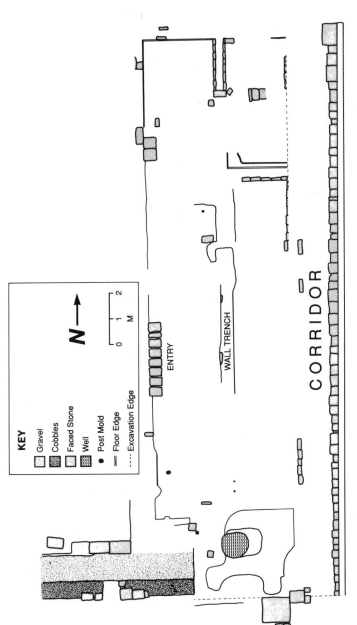

KEY

- ⬜ Gravel
- ▨ Cobbles
- ⬜ Faced Stone
- ▦ Well
- ● Post Mold
- ▬ Floor Edge
- ---- Excavation Edge

N →

0 1 2
M

ENTRY

WALL TRENCH

CORRIDOR

Figure 5.36b   Map of the Palace of the Multicolored Rooms within the Putuni complex.

platform surrounding the courtyard is an unprepossessing set of stone stairs tucked into the northwest corner of the structure. The top of the platform was most likely finished with carefully dressed paving stones, as were other structures in the Putuni complex. However, these paving stones were removed in looting and quarrying operations that have been ongoing in Tiwanaku over the past five centuries. The design of Putuni would permit large numbers of people to gather in the central courtyard, while a relatively few individuals were elevated above them, standing along the top of the platform.

Systematic excavations in the Putuni undertaken by my research team reveal some provocative new clues about the function and meaning of this special architectural complex. Perhaps the most telling discovery about the Putuni is that it was not an isolated, single-purpose structure, as previous investigators have assumed. Rather, the Putuni platform-and-courtyard complex represents the central focus of an ensemble of buildings that integrated intimate, private living quarters with open spaces designed for large, public convocations. During the 1989 field season, we discovered the elite residential component of this ensemble in the area immediately adjacent to the Putuni platform. Here we excavated the partially preserved remains of an elegant, generously proportioned building. This structure, which we have called the Palace of the Multicolored Rooms (Figure 5.36b), was constructed of stuccoed, painted adobe laid on foundations fashioned from beautifully cut stone blocks. The foundation stones were sunk into wall trenches excavated into the ground to accommodate the overlying structure. Internal wall trenches and alignments of foundation stones suggest that the floor plan of the palace incorporated five interior rooms. The original entrance to the palace, now utterly destroyed by centuries of unrelenting grave and stone robbing, was a truly regal gateway, graced by a monumental stone architrave that displayed in low-relief carving two rampant pumas, ritually costumed and crowned (Figure 5.37). The floor of the palace was a distinctive surface of dense, hard-packed red clay. Clumps of charred grasses pressed into the clay floor indicate that, while occupied, the palace supported a thatched roof. At the time of abandonment of the palace, or shortly thereafter, this thatch burned and collapsed inward where fragments from the old roof were incorporated into the floor.

The red clay forming the floor extends under the east wall of the palace into the Putuni platform and is the same material that was used to surface the interior courtyard of the Putuni. It is clear from these structural relationships that the Palace of the Multicolored Rooms and the adjacent Putuni platform and courtyard complex were constructed simultaneously during a major episode of urban renewal at

Figure 5.37   A stone architrave, with opposed pumas carved in low relief. Fragments of an identical architrave were discovered in excavations in the principal entry to the Palace of the Multicolored Rooms in 1990. (Museum für Völkerkunde, Berlin, VA 10883; Photograph by Alan Kolata).

Tiwanaku. Both the Putuni palace and the temple platform were built over earlier, domestic structures that were purposely razed to accommodate the new building scheme. Radiocarbon dates on charcoal samples taken directly from the floor of the palace indicate that this episode of urban renewal took place at some point between A.D. 780 and 900, or in the Tiwanaku V period.

The Palace of the Multicolored Rooms derives its name from its brilliantly painted walls. Chips of spectacularly hued paints littered the palace floor. The colors of these mineral-based pigments include rich malachite green, deep cobalt blue, and an electric red-orange extracted from cinnabar. The distribution of paint chips recovered from the palace floor suggest that some rooms were painted primarily in monochrome, while others were embellished with multiple colors. Given the tremendous quantity of pigment chips incorporated into the debris excavated along the central axis of the palace, it appears that the principal internal supporting wall was entirely painted. Because the original adobe walls of the palace are not preserved above the foundation stones, any evidence of figural drawings or painted murals, similar to the iconographically rich engravings on Tiwanaku stone sculpture, is now long destroyed. A rare ceramic representation of a Tiwanaku structure confirms that some buildings were indeed painted with elaborate representations of felines and other figures (Figure 5.38). Although any complete murals that might have animated the palace walls are now lost to us, individual adobe bricks with adhering fragments of pigment preserve a record of the painting technique. The process began with a thin coat of white plaster that provided a clean,

Figure 5.38   A ceramic representation of a Tiwanaku house. Note the mural painted above the entrance to this circular, domed structure. (Museo Nacional de Arqueología, La Paz, Bolivia).

uniform substrate. Normally, one or two coats of intensely colored paint were then applied over this stucco-like base. But some brick fragments recovered from the ruins of the palace had preserved faces with from six to fifteen layers of paint. Frequently, these multiple paint layers were of a single hue applied again and again to the same surface suggesting that particular colors carried important symbolic or decorative connotations. Although no paintbrushes or other instruments for applying the paint have been found in excavations to date, several different kinds of vessels with crushed, dry pigments were recovered. These paint receptacles included ceramic cups, translucent stone jars (one containing a brilliant cinnabar-based red pigment), silver tubes packed with cobalt blue pigment, and flat pieces of sandstone with multiple pigments adhering to the surface suggesting that these objects served as palettes.

Although densely painted, and clearly designed as an architectural backdrop for the display of wealth and power, the essential domestic or residential character of the Palace of the Multicolored Rooms is readily apparent. Our excavations uncovered facilities designed specifically for routine household maintenance, particularly within a major palace kitchen complex. This complex included pits with embedded ceramic vessels appropriate for storing food and drink, hearths for cooking meals, and wells, extending as much as four meters deep,

Figure 5.39   Monumental sandstone and andesite drainage canals underneath the Putuni complex.

that provided easy access to fresh water for drinking, cooking, and preparing fermented drinks, such as maize and *quinoa chicha*.

In addition, the palace, and particularly its kitchen complex, was served by an elaborate waste removal system of enclosed stone canals connected into the deeply buried drainage lines that undergird the civic-ceremonial core of the city. In the Putuni area, the main trunk line of this sewer system is truly a marvel of hydraulic engineering. The subterranean canal, measuring some ninety centimeters wide and one meter from base to cap, was built with precision-cut, closely fitted sandstone and andesite blocks (Figure 5.39). The entire sewer line was then packed in a thick cap of pure, red clay, effectively sealing the structure. Excavations beneath the Putuni platform uncovered two deep tunnels capped with stone slabs that gave access to the buried trunk line near critical junctions suggesting that routine maintenance procedures were integrated into the design of the sewer system. Waste water in this remarkable system ran on a continuous two percent grade until discharging into the Tiwanaku River.

The palace may also have been supplied with fresh, running water through a system of totally enclosed, surface canals that tapped into springs which still produce today on the southern outskirts of the ancient city. Unlike most other pre-industrial cities, Tiwanaku, or rather Tiwanaku's elite neighborhoods, could boast of a secure and hygenic water system that segregated wastewater from freshwater supply. The sophisticated design skills of Tiwanaku's hydraulic engineers enabled a level of hygiene and luxuriousness for at least some of the city's residents that remains unmatched in the same rural areas of the *altiplano* today, and even in some of the *barrios* of modern Latin American cities.

The Palace of the Multicolored Rooms is an intriguing structure that offers glimpses into the opulent, and ritually charged life-style of the Tiwanaku elite. Power, ritual, and spirituality interpenetrated every aspect of life among the elite. The rich, glowing colors painted on the palace walls and the elaborately carved stone entrance were raw displays of accumulated wealth and status, tangible reminders to the people of Tiwanaku of the secular power vested in their rulers. At the same time, this display of wealth served a more esoteric, religious purpose. In many respects, the Palace of the Multicolored Rooms was constructed with an eye to ratifying the role of the elite as intermediaries with the supernatural forces of nature that reflected the indigenous concept of the divine. The palace and adjacent Putuni temple complex are located squarely within the city center, inside the concentrated, sacred confines of Tiwanaku's moat. The palace was physically situated near the center of Tiwanaku's metaphorical island, associated symbolically with the creation of humankind, and with the origins of time and of civilization. In essence, the palace occupants lived in the space and time of the sacred.

The intentional linkage of this elite dwelling with notions of the sacred was further intensified by a series of dedicatory offerings that were deposited in the foundations of the structure. Our excavations encountered a hierarchical series of ritual offerings that consisted of perhaps the most profoundly personal, emotionally powerful kind: human dedicatory burials. The most important of these dedicatory burials were shaft-and-chamber tombs sunk into the four corners of the structure at the time of construction of the palace. Only the northeast and southeast corner tombs were sufficiently preserved to recover details of tomb architecture and contents.

The northeast corner shaft-and-chamber tomb was completely intact, and its rich contents evoke well the wealth and ritual status of the palace occupants. To judge from dress and tomb offerings, the burial was that of an elite individual, most probably a female. The burial itself was located at the base of the shaft section of the tomb with a slightly raised side chamber serving as a repository for a textile-wrapped bundle of grave goods. The skeleton was in a seated position facing north with arms and legs tightly flexed against the body, a classic burial position in the Andes that results from placing the corpse

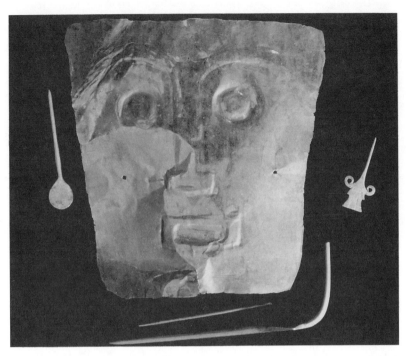

Figure 5.40   Repoussé miniature gold mask from the Putuni shaft-and-chamber tomb. (Photograph by Wolfgang Schüller).

in an egg-shaped mummy bundle. Although long decayed from the corrosive effects of high groundwater characteristic of the Tiwanaku region, remnant fabric impressions and richly organic, blackened soil surrounding the skeletal remains indicates that this individual was once tightly wrapped in just such a textile bundle. The most spectacular grave goods were associated directly with the skeleton. At the time of burial, four copper bracelets were placed on the corpse's right arm. A stunning collar fashioned from hundreds of tubular beads, delicately crafted in a rich variety of luxurious materials including purple lapis lazuli, cobalt-blue sodalite, sky-blue turquoise, coral-colored stone, and cream-colored bone, hung pendant from the neck. A miniature gold mask with a repoussé image of a human face was discovered lying at the feet of the skeleton (Figure 5.40). This stylized gold mask has tiny perforations along its perimeter, suggesting that it was originally sewn to fabric, most likely as an element of costume. Along with this gold mask, an eclectic assemblage of grave offerings was found distributed around the original mummy bundle. These included clusters

Figure 5.41   Copper disc mirror with a lead flask adhered to its surface, and various metal implements from the Putuni shaft-and-chamber tomb. (Photograph by Wolfgang Schüller).

of exotic minerals, slender bone awls and bone tubes, one containing yellow pigment, a thin andesite scraper, and a red, globular ceramic vessel inside of which was placed a collection of beautiful grayish-black obsidian chips. The small side chamber of the tomb to the north of the burial contained its own set of grave goods that were apparently wrapped in a textile bundle fastened with long, copper pins. The centerpiece of this bundle was a perfectly preserved copper disc that most likely served as a mirror, although, like the gold mask, it may have been incorporated as an element of costume since it too was perforated. Adhering to the surface of this disc was an elegant, long-necked flask fabricated from lead, a rare, if not unprecedented use of this material at Tiwanaku (Figure 5.41). Accompanying the lead bottle was a long-necked companion piece of polished red ceramic. Scattered around these central pieces in the side chamber were a series of smaller metal and bone objects, including gold and copper pins, bone tubes and needles, a copper spatula, a sandstone pigment palette, and lumps of white and yellow minerals. The precise significance of these various grave offerings remains elusive, although it is not difficult to propose that the side chamber collection, in particular, represents items related to personal adornment, a kind of toiletry kit of the deceased.

The shaft-and-chamber tomb at the southeast corner of the palace contained fewer grave goods than the northeast corner tomb, although in some ways this dedicatory interment is more interesting and evocative. This tomb contained two individuals, one of which was an adult in a seated, flexed position similar to that of the northeast corner mummy bundle. Underneath the skull of the adult was a second burial: a complete skeleton of an infant laid prone. Accompanying this double burial was a silver pin and a pair of deer antlers that were placed near the adult's skull. Antlers occur in Tiwanaku ceramic iconography as elements of headdresses worn by costumed, masked figures in processions. Frequently, these masks portray snarling felines with imposing fangs, and are associated with scenes of decapitation and dismemberment. The individuals wearing these elaborate costumes may represent ritual warriors. It is also possible, although equally speculative, to suggest that the persons depicted wearing these headdresses were ritual practitioners, or shamans, cloaked in deer costumes. We know that this sort of shamanic connection between humans and deer was a common feature of native American religions, and the clear ceremonial context of the cavorting, costumed, and antler-bedecked figures portrayed on these ceramics implies a similar association among the people of Tiwanaku. If, in fact, the adult occupant of this shaft-and-chamber tomb was a shaman or priest, the sacred character of the Palace of the Multicolored Rooms was even further underscored when this individual was interred at the time of construction. In the absence of associated grave goods, the significance of the infant's inclusion in this dedicatory burial remains enigmatic.

The other two shaft-and-chamber tombs at the northwest and southwest corners of the palace are not preserved, although we do have clear evidence of massive looting in these areas confirming their existence. A fifth shaft-and-chamber tomb, also heavily sacked, was placed under the monumental west gateway to the palace. All that remained of the contents from this tomb were some scattered pieces of human bone. The distribution of these tombs forms a distinct, and clearly premeditated pattern in the palace, one at each corner of the palace and one beneath the principal entrance, implying that at the time of construction a major effort was made to sanctify, or ritually charge the structure with these dedicatory burials of humans.

Another kind of burial was associated with the construction of the Palace of the Multicolored Rooms. At the time the palace was built, its architects razed earlier structures to accommodate the new Putuni palace-temple complex. The rubble from previous construction was leveled through an ambitious cut-and-fill operation. A layer of coarse gravel was then deposited over this construction fill. Finally, the continuous red clay floor characteristic of the Tiwanaku V period Putuni complex was laid down as the base for new walls. In the course of establishing the foundations for the palace, both complete and partial human burials were incorporated into the razed debris immediately below the sub-floor gravel layer. Frequently during excavations in the southern sector of the palace, these rather melancholy burials were found pushed into the beds of old, abandoned drainage canals that once served earlier structures. The context of these burials makes it clear that they, along with their more formal shaft-and-chamber tomb counterparts, represent a single episode related to the time of construction of the palace. Unlike the elaborate shaft-and-chamber tombs, however, these sub-floor burials contained no associated grave goods and were often found mixed indifferently with the bones of llama and alpaca. The numerous partial burials of humans and llamas found just underneath the red clay floor of the palace constitute a kind of foundation of bones. It is equally clear that these sub-floor burials do not represent accidental inclusions from the demolition process that created the palace's foundations. Although lacking grave goods, a number of these burials were carefully placed in old canals, and in one such instance nearly complete skeletons of a male-female couple were encountered locked in a tight embrace. Most of the sub-floor burials were not complete, but rather body parts. But these body parts were invariably articulated (skull to spinal cord, pelvis to leg bones, wrist and hand to arm bones, and the like), indicating that flesh was still on the bones when these partial burials were deposited in the structure's foundations.

The construction of the Palace of the Multicolored Rooms was clearly more than a pragmatic effort to develop luxury housing for the Tiwanaku elite. The process of construction was intertwined with rituals of consecration, including the careful placement of human dedicatory burials, that transformed an otherwise prosaic dwelling into a profoundly sacred space. In a sense, the Palace of the Multicolored Rooms was simultaneously an ordinary dwelling for satisfying the daily needs of its extraordinary occupants, and a ritually charged space for expressing the intimate connection of the palace occupants to the sacred. If one of the primary roles of the Tiwanaku elite was to act as intermediaries between the people of Tiwanaku and the supernatural forces of nature, it is not surprising that their palaces were sanctified in this manner. Nor is it unusual that the private apartments of these elite were structurally merged with larger public spaces that could accommodate congregations. In a real sense, Tiwanaku royalty did

Figure 5.42   One of the room-like niches located on the perimeter of the Putuni platform.

not simply intercede from time to time with the forces of nature, they *lived* the role of divine intermediaries, and their special residences reflected that essential fact.

Two additional architectural elements of the Putuni palace-temple complex underscore this intimate nexus between the private lives and public roles of the Tiwanaku elite. Within the interior courtyard of the Putuni are a series of room-like niches set back into the perimeter of the platform (Figure 5.42). Our excavations cleared three of these niches, which averaged approximately three square meters in area, and indicated that at least seven or eight originally existed within the Putuni. The niches were fashioned from cut stone blocks, including hard black andesites, some of which had been recycled from earlier constructions. The niches had entrances accessible only from the interior courtyard. One of the niches on the northern side of the platform preserved elements of what had clearly been a sliding stone door. As we have seen, small rooms with sliding doors were characteristic features of the temple complex at the pre–Tiwanaku site of Chiripa, and may represent a kind of convention for ceremonial architecture in the region. This elaborate sliding door feature and the relatively small size of the structures suggest that precious objects of some sort were stored within the niches and periodically brought out for display. These niches may have been intended as repositories for sumptuary goods associated with the Tiwanaku elite, or perhaps for objects intended for use in public ceremonies such as elements of costume, or other ritual regalia. Alternatively, like the stone rooms flanking the courtyard of the Kalasasaya temple, these niches may have served as mausoleums for the mummy bundles of the elite who once lived in the Palace of the Multicolored Rooms.

A possible mortuary function for these niches in the interior courtyard is strengthened by a second, previously unrecognized feature of the Putuni that was uncovered in excavations in 1990. The Putuni platform had appeared on existing maps as a simple rectangle. However, our new excavations reveal that, in fact, the southwest corner of the platform projects farther west to form a substantial, eight-meter-wide extension. This southwest platform extension fits perfectly around the southern wall of the Palace of the Multicolored Rooms. The exterior retaining wall of the Putuni platform at this juncture is particularly impressive. The Putuni architects clearly selected the largest and most finely cut andesite blocks to erect this section of the platform. Regular, imposing black megaliths of the platform extension that were sunk into deep trenches to properly seat the foundations form an impressive facade. The spaces between the larger megaliths were fitted with smaller black and gray andesite and red sandstone blocks. Many of the smaller blocks show evidence of being reused (not surprising in a relatively late, Tiwanaku V period complex within this architecturally complex city), but they are all beautifully cut and retouched to form a tight and visually interesting fit. Posnansky (1945: Figure 144) illustrates a magnificently executed bas-relief stone carving of a puma head that was reputed to come from this same area of the Putuni platform (see Figure 5.8). The deep, inset eyes of the sculpture suggest that significant features of the bas-relief design were brought into sharp relief with inlays of precious metals or mineral and shell mosaics that would have glittered in the intense *altiplano* sun or more subtly glowed in the evening under the illumination of torches fashioned from resinous shrubs. This carving may have been one of several, virtually identical ornamental blocks that graced the platform's retaining walls, creating a monumental, repetitive facade of puma heads, emblematic, perhaps, of kingly authority and regal power.

What motivated the architects of this complex to embellish the Putuni platform at this point with such lavish and labor intensive displays of structural and sculptural finesse? The solution to this puzzle lies in the way this section of the platform was used by the Tiwanaku elite. Our excavations reveal beyond much doubt that the platform projection served as a high status necropolis. Here we encountered dozens of cylindrical shaft tombs, many of which had been thoroughly looted for their precious contents. Despite the systematic removal of the grave contents, enough material that had accompanied the dead remained scattered in the disturbed fill of these tombs to establish that this burial ground was once a sumptuous, and evidently, coveted final resting place. Fragments of unusual and exotic polychrome ceramic vessels were found in both the tombs and in the fill of the platform itself, as if to sanctify the burial grounds. Some of these vessels were imported from as far away as Potosí in southern Bolivia, the Cochabamba Valley well to the southeast of the *altiplano* and the *yungas* regions of the sub-tropical Amazonian drainage. It would seem the Tiwanaku elite took to the grave precious, exotic items imported from distant lands that they had acquired in their lifetime.

From all of the foregoing evidence of diverse dedicatory and primary human burials in the palace-temple complex of Putuni, we glimpse an essential truth about the conduct and meaning of private life for the Tiwanaku elite. Their central role as interlocuters with the divine, and more precisely with what Godelier (1978:767) called the "invisible realities and forces controlling . . . the reproduction of the universe and of life," demanded that they manipulate mystical symbols that linked them publicly with the realm of the supernatural. In the context of the ancient Andean world, mystical communication with the divine was achieved through the dead, through the long chain of deceased ancestors whose actions and qualities ineluctably merged with the heroic, legendary time of human origins. The dead, and most powerfully, the lineage ancestors, were the prime conduit into the realm of the supernatural. Necrolatry, or the worship and propitiation of the dead, was the sacred obligation of the living, as well as the most powerful tool for gaining access to the invisible realities and forces that controlled and ensured the continuity of the world. In this world, it is not suprising to find that the living resided cheek-by-jowl with the dead and to discover that the palaces of the elite merged residential, ceremonial, and necropolis functions. As is evident from the archaeology of the Putuni complex, the Tiwanaku elite constructed and deployed symbols emblematic of their mystical union with the divine.

The mortuary aspect of the Putuni complex seems to have been one that was established early in the history of the city. Evidence from excavations beneath the floor of the Palace of the Multicolored Rooms and the adjacent Putuni platform suggests the presence of elite tombs that date from at least 200 B.C. on. In the period immediately prior to the paroxysm of urban renewal that witnessed the construction of the Palace of the Multicolored Rooms and the Putuni temple around

A.D. 800, this area was already functioning as an elite residence with an adjacent burial platform. However, in this earlier period (c. A.D. 400–800), the area occupied by the later Tiwanaku V palace and temple complex was evidently more residential in character. Excavations beneath the floor of the Putuni platform's interior courtyard encountered a complicated series of wall foundations, hearths, storage and refuse pits, and residential debris. Similarly, the area beneath the floor of the palace's southernmost wing revealed a series of well-constructed hearths integrated into a rather large and formal kitchen with food preparation and cooking areas. This communal kitchen was clearly designed to service a number of adjacent living quarters. The kitchen was segregated from a burial platform immediately to the south by a massive wall, although a narrow doorway offered access from the kitchen area of the residences into the area of the platform. This mortuary structure with elite shaft tombs was later enlarged and transformed after A.D. 800 into the Putuni temple's platform extension.

The foundations of the major wall discovered underneath the Palace of the Multicolored Rooms continued westward for over 30 meters. Other segments of identical walls are found throughout the civic-ceremonial core of Tiwanaku indicating that in the Tiwanaku IV period elite residential quarters were organized into distinct *barrios*, or neighborhoods, that were insulated from public view by massive adobe walls set on cobblestone foundations. Residential and service areas, such as communal kitchens, were clustered within the large compounds created by the *barrio* walls. These massive walls, with only a few narrow entrances, reduced easy access to the elite residences within and afforded a substantial measure of security and privacy to their residents.

During Tiwanaku V phase urban renewal, the *barrio* walls were razed to accommodate construction of the Putuni temple and its adjacent palace complex. A similar process of leveling the Tiwanaku IV phase *barrio* walls to accommodate new construction seems to have occurred in other areas of Tiwanaku's civic-ceremonial core. This dramatic reconfiguration of the urban landscape resulted in a complete integration of ceremonial and elite residential areas. The leveling of the Tiwanaku IV phase *barrio* walls and the residences within permitted a significant redesign of the city. Large expanses of land within the moated sanctuary of the city center that were previously given over to elite residences were transformed into elegant temple complexes with fewer, and more formal palatial residences adjacent to them.

While the center was being reshaped, outside of the inner civic-ceremonial core, the city witnessed a dramatic expansion in residential construction. The boom in construction in what was once the

Figure 5.43   Stone foundations of a Tiwanaku V period residence in the Akapana East sector, outside of Tiwanaku's civic-ceremonial core.

peripheral areas of the city resulted in a proliferation of dwellings of a different sort from that represented by the palatial residences of the city core. These residences were much smaller and less elaborate than structures like the Palace of the Multicolored Rooms. Rather than fine, ashlar masonry foundations, these more modest dwellings were built on river cobbles with adobe walls and thatched roofs (Figure 5.43). They exhibit none of the impressive architectural ornamentation of the central palaces. There is no evidence for monumental, carved stone gateways or polychromed walls. Although many of these structures were equipped with deep, fresh water wells and small floor drains for conducting away wastewater, they were not tied into the impressive, subterranean sewer lines of the city center. Moreover, unlike the palaces, the vernacular architecture outside the moated precinct was not designed to be juxtaposed, or integrated with ceremonial structures, or large, public plazas. Rather, we find repetitive ranks of similar structures that clearly served a residential function, almost like blocks of apartments. All of these buildings featured cooking hearths, storage pits, wells, and small interior and exterior patios that were frequently the site of domestic and small-scale craft activities such as weaving and the production of stone tools.

Who might have been the residents of this kind of architecture? It is tempting to conclude from the obvious differences in the quality and context of this architecture when compared with the palatial residences of the center that the occupants of these structures formed some kind of lower class within the city. This may, in fact, be true. But other elements of these dwellings indicate that the residents were not entirely without privilege and access to wealth in Tiwanaku society. They did not, in other words, form the lowest stratum of Tiwanaku's hierarchical social world. For one, although not of the same quality and scale as the city's palaces, these structures were well constructed of stone, adobe, and thatch, and they were supplied with rudimentary, but effective cooking and sanitary facilities. Perhaps more telling, our excavations of domestic structures outside of the moated core revealed that they took the identical cardinal orientation of the ceremonial and elite residential architecture in the city center. This consistent structural alignment to the cardinal directions suggests that some kind of corporate or state planning was involved in the construction of these buildings.

Objects once used by the occupants of these dwellings in daily life provide other clues to their relatively high position in the social hierarchy. Each of the houses excavated to date contained significant numbers of metal artifacts, principally copper lamina and plaques, pins, nails, and awls. Most of these items were intended as decorative and symbolic elements to be sewn into clothing. Costume was one of the principal public markers of ethnic and class status in the ancient Andean world, and the rich, metal-encrusted clothing worn by the people of Tiwanaku was no exception. In general, metal objects were relatively scarce and were the product of labor-intensive processes of production. As a consequence, they were a commodity that commanded high status. Their use in Tiwanaku society, as was the case with the Inca state, may have been restricted to, or at least more prevalent among the political and social elite, and some classes of precious metal objects regulated by sumptuary laws.

In addition to metals, substantial quantities of cut and polished bone, malachite, turquoise, sodalite, and lapis lazuli beads, along with beautiful, pyroengraved llama bones with elaborate iconography were encountered in these houses (Figure 5.44). These objects, of course, are not utilitarian, but rather were associated with personal adornment and the display of wealth. Some of the pyroengraved bones were fashioned into snuff trays and tubes for the ritual consumption of hallucinogenic drugs such as the powdered seeds of *Anadenanthera*, or *wilka* as it is called by Quechua-speaking natives of the Andes. Other such engraved bone tubes were used as flutes. A striking find of a terra

Figure 5.44 A pyroengraved llama bone recovered during the excavation of a domestic structure in the Akapana East sector of Tiwanaku. (Drawing courtesy of John Janusek).

cotta ring from one of these houses strengthens the inference that the residents in this sector of the city, although perhaps not of the highest social stratum, were nevertheless considerably wealthier and of higher status than the urban commoners and rural folk who constituted the bulk of Tiwanaku's population. This piece carries an embossed, stylized representation of a masked human wearing an elaborate crown. The intaglio design makes it clear that the ring functioned as a signet device for marking, or sealing objects as the property of the owner (Figure 5.45). Such signet rings are rare in Tiwanaku, suggesting that they were the property of a restricted class of people. They may have belonged to elite of a rank immediately below that of the royal lineages who were charged with conducting some of the day-to-day affairs of the state.

That the residents of these structures performed some kind of public role in Tiwanaku society is further substantiated by another class of objects uncovered consistently in our excavations. All of these houses possessed a high proportion of fine, polychrome ceramic vessels in their domestic repertoire. These highly polished, strikingly beautiful vessels

Figure 5.45   Terracotta signet ring from one of Tiwanaku's residential structures in the Akapana East sector of Tiwanaku.

were used exclusively as serving dishes for food or drink: the roster of these vessels includes fine basins, bowls, and drinking cups, or *keros*. In fact, some of the drinking cups found in these houses are of only marginally inferior quality to those recovered from the ritual *kero* smashed on the Akapana. The presence of fancy serving ware and elegant drinking cups strongly implies that the occupants of these "peripheral" houses, like their superiors who lived in the central palaces of the city, were obliged to engage in feasting, and in ritual hospitality, among themselves, and perhaps with guests of equivalent status from outside the city. Public feasting embued with an ethic of conspicuous, ritualized generosity was the essential social etiquette that kept the wheels of politics and commerce moving in the ancient Andean world. In some sense, the relationship between city and countryside was fostered and tightly interwoven through the mechanism of reciprocal hospitality between rural and urban elites. The politics of the native Andean world demanded face-to-face contact, and a sense of broad public participation. Elaborate public feasts and bouts of prodigious drinking were the standard forum for formalizing and expressing social ties among equals, as well as with one's social inferiors. Without these feasts, drinking bouts, and displays of reciprocal hospitality sponsored by the political elite, few public works would have been accomplished. What seems an inefficient, even outrageously wasteful, deployment of time and resources, was, in fact, an essential political tool of the ruling elite. To be generous in food and drink was to give public evidence of a special capacity to provide for your constituency, and therefore affirm your capacity to govern well.

All of this evidence – the planned and cardinally aligned apartments, the relatively high structural quality of the dwellings, and the diversity and function of the artifacts found within them – points to the conclusion that the Tiwanaku V period houses outside the moated precinct of the city center accommodated a class of people in Tiwanaku's social hierarchy that was lower in prestige and access to wealth than the ruling lineages, but considerably higher in social and economic position than the rural commoners. The precise relationship between these people and the noble households that resided in the central palaces is difficult to assess from the archaeological evidence alone. It is possible that the residents of the houses toward the periphery of the city were members of junior lineages of the ruling nobility. If analogies from the Inca state are appropriate, this class of people who were intermediate in status and wealth may have had some collateral, or even fictive kinship relationship with the ruling lineages, and functioned within the government as members of Tiwanaku's rudimentary state bureaucracy.

The social life of Tiwanaku as a city entailed not only the performance of religious and political duties by the elite (and near elite), but also involved other activities that produced tangible commodities, some of which intersected substantially with the political and religious roles of Tiwanaku's inhabitants. Most of the households in Tiwanaku were engaged to one degree or another in the production of textiles and basic kits of bone, obsidian, basalt, and chert tools for their own use. Yet some of this household craft production took a more clearly ceremonial and elite tack. The discovery of fragmentary gold and silver laminae, exhausted obsidian cores, and microchips of turquoise and sodalite in the main sewer trunk line beneath the Putuni palace-temple complex implies that certain crafts were practiced even within the highest status households at Tiwanaku. These fragmentary remains are clearly the by-products of larger-scale craft production that were disposed of in the most convenient (and rather modern) fashion of flushing them down the drain.

Who the actual artisans of these luxury crafts were remains unclear. We can readily imagine two plausible scenarios. The elite may have retained gifted artisans to craft the luxury items that were emblematic of and essential to the performance of their regal and priestly duties. Specialized artisans were in great demand and given unusual privileges by other kingly courts of the native Andean world, most notably in the Inca empire and the Kingdom of Chimor on the Peruvian north coast. Similarly, in another part of the ancient Americas, lineages of particularly adept craftsmen, especially featherworkers and lapidaries, were given exceptional political autonomy, social status, and economic opportunities by the Aztec kings of central Mexico (Berdan 1982:28–9) in exchange for exclusive access to their products. That some artisans of particularly fine, or specialized objects, such as textiles, gold, silver, and lapidary work, were retainers to Tiwanaku ruling lineages is certainly a strong possibility. Alternatively, the scions of Tiwanaku's ruling lineages themselves may have been obligated to learn an elite craft as a part of their training. It is certainly not an alien, or unprecedented concept for a pre-industrial king, his immediate family, and his courtiers to also have been artisans, crafting, as one of their obligations and prerogatives, the symbols of their own spiritual and secular power.

Specialized craft production of a more utilitarian stripe also went on within the confines of Tiwanaku's urban ambit. Apart from the generalized household production of ordinary textiles and tool kits for home consumption, our excavations on the far eastern periphery of the city uncovered the site of a massive ceramic workshop (Figure 5.46). This site, which carries the contemporary name of Chijijawira, was ideally situated for its purpose. Chijijawira is elevated astride an artificially modified natural ridge adjacent to the easternmost canal, or moat that defines Tiwanaku's city limits. This location takes maximum advantage of two important resources for the production of ceramics (or, for that matter, any mass-produced objects): water and a source of energy. The virtually constant wind that blows, at times with gale force, from the southwest ensured that the kilns elevated on the Chijijawira ridge had sufficient draw and ventilation to achieve the high temperatures necessary for firing ceramics. Water, of course, drawn from the adjacent canal was essential for processing and manipulating the clay that was the raw material for the finished products. The location of a ceramic industry on the margins of the city is not surprising. Because Tiwanaku was a regal city, and one which carried intense religious meaning, one would not expect to find the nitty-gritty of mass production lapping against the walls of the temples and palaces within the inner *sanctum sanctorum*. Repeated firings of ceramics required enormous quantities of fuel, principally animal dung, and generated considerable quantities of smoke and ash. Pre-industrial cities were not immune to the problems of environmental contamination. Chijijawira's siting on the urban periphery mitigated these potential hazards. Huge numbers of the tools, materials, and by-products from ceramic production were recovered during excavation. Material

Figure 5.46 View of excavations in a midden associated with the massive Chijijawira ceramic workshop on the far eastern periphery of Tiwanaku. (Photograph by Wolfgang Schüller).

remains from all stages in the production of pottery vessels were encountered at Chijijawira: mica and pyrite amendments for composing the raw clay; mortars for processing minerals, clay, and pigments; ceramic and bone polishers for burnishing the vessels; molds for ceramic figurines; warped and partially melted vessels dumped as wastage from poor-quality firings; partially vitrified adobe bricks from firing pits; and, above all, tons of burnt clay, earth, bones, and dung.

From the ceramic inventory recovered in the Chijijawira excavations, we know that this workshop produced all classes and grades of vessels for the city: plain and decorated, utilitarian and ceremonial wares. We know, as well, that the specialized potters who worked on the Chijijawira ridge also lived there. Domestic debris, such as small stone tools, plant remains, and fish and animal bones, is liberally interspersed with the remnants of ceramic production. An infant burial with ceramic offerings was also uncovered, implying directly some kind of residential permanence, and further strengthening the conclusion that the potters of Chijijawira lived and worked on the periphery of the city, constituting a distinct *barrio*, or neighborhood inhabited by people pursuing this specialized trade. Given that these potters lived in relatively close proximity to the city center (although relegated to the margins) and that they benefited from one of the great public works of the city (the easternmost canal), it seems likely that they served the interests of Tiwanaku's elite, providing some of the ceremonial and secular vessels that were essential for everyday life in Tiwanaku.

Other specialized craft neighborhoods undoubtedly exist within the city, waiting to be exhumed from under the burden of sediment that has entombed Tiwanaku over the centuries since its abandonment. Tantalizing surface evidence suggests that a major basalt stoneworks is to be found on the eastern side of the city not far from Chijijawira, and to the northwest of the Putuni complex, a mound densely littered with fragments of lapis lazuli, turquoise, sodalite, and other colored minerals argues for a fine lapidary workshop not far beneath the surface. We must wait for future excavations to reveal the complete spectrum of industrial and artisanal workshops within Tiwanaku's urban environment. But, for the moment at least, we can be confident that these workshops did, in fact, exist and were an important element of urban life and of Tiwanaku's day-to-day social and economic transactions.

Tiwanaku's Social Map

If we reflect carefully on the nature of the social identities, occupations, and activities in Tiwanaku, we come to an unusual conclusion. Viewed from the perspective of the contemporary western eye, Tiwanaku would have been foreign in the extreme, not conforming to standard conceptions of what a city, even a premodern city, "ought" to look like. Unlike other great cities of antiquity in Europe and the Near East, Tiwanaku's *raison d'être* had little to do with commercial, or merchantile activities. Western perceptions of ancient cities invariably conjure images of jostling crowds snaking through narrow cobbled lanes, spilling out of markets and bazaars, churning up clouds of dust in the frenzy to buy, sell, and barter. Bedraggled street vendors hawking cheap trinkets; sharp-eyed, tight-fisted merchants hunkered down over piles of precious rugs, spices, and other exotica newly arrived by caravan; potters and jewelers; leather workers and carpenters; stone masons and artisans; bakers, butchers, and tallow makers; porters, jugglers, clowns, prostitutes, and thieves plying their trade in workshops, public squares, and back alleys all are familiar characters in this perception of the archaic city. The heart and soul of this image revolves around trade, commerce, and the daily life of the marketplace, and the notion that a city was a place of meeting and of melding for many different kinds of people. From this perspective, all "real cities" require a central market, or better yet many markets big and small to keep the economic life's blood of the place flowing. Through trade and exchange, through buying and selling of every imaginable kind the city was made and remade. People from the countryside migrated to the city to escape the grinding, invariant rhythms of farms and fields, to exploit new economic opportunities, to set up shop, to settle in, to become entrepreneurs.

But this familiar image, so central to western conceptions of urban life, does not fit Tiwanaku. Tiwanaku, like other native Andean cities, had no markets. There was no flourishing merchant class. There were no free artisans and craftsmen organized in guilds who could exert independent pressure and political checks on the decisions of municipal authorities. There were no commercial transactions in the modern sense of disinterested buyers and sellers brought together in a marketplace. There was no broad-based, public participation in the political life of the city as we see, or at least imagine as an ideal, in the archetypical city of classical antiquity, the *polis* of Greece, exemplar of urban "democracy." Moral, political, and military authority in Tiwanaku flowed from the ruling lineages, and from their coterie of kin, fictive kin, retainers, and camp followers. Tiwanaku, to a greater degree than urban centers in other parts of the pre-industrial world, was an autocratic city, built for and dominated by a native aristocracy. In this sense, Tiwanaku was truly a patrician city; a place for symbolically concentrating the political and religious authority of the elite. Although not entirely absent, in comparison with the ancient cities of the western world, Tiwanaku boasted little in the way of pluralism and social heterogeneity.

The social map of Tiwanaku was not a riotous mosaic of many peoples anonymously and independently pursuing their livelihoods, moving into and out of the city as employment opportunities waxed and waned. Rather, in Tiwanaku, there was a singularity of purpose and a higher degree of social control. The true *raison d'être* of the city turned on servicing the aristocratic lineages and their entourages. The city was an extension of the elite households, and a public expression of their religious and secular authority. Its residents were attached one way or another to the economic, political, and social needs of the princely households. Tiwanaku's public architectural ensembles reflected and sustained that singularity of purpose. If there was a visual and cultural focus to the city, it was not a central market or caravansary, but rather the symbolic mountain-temples of Akapana and Puma Punku, the distilled essence of elite ideology. The religious and political mystique of the elite, wielded in premeditated self-interest, shaped the city, not the invisible hand of the marketplace.

Focused as they were on the needs and politics of the aristocracy, the cities created by the people of Tiwanaku were small by modern standards. Tiwanaku itself, despite being the capital of a predatory state, approached a peak population of thirty to forty thousand. Secondary cities such as Lukurmata, Pajchiri, and Khonko Wankané probably never reached 10,000 inhabitants. In contrast, the hinterlands herded by the urban nuclei were thickly settled by rural commoners, fishers, farmers, and herders. Unlike the pre-industrial metropolises of Europe and Asia, which were irrepressible magnets for the surrounding countryfolk, there was little economic or social incentive or, perhaps more precisely, opportunity to migrate to Tiwanaku's cities. Right of residence in Tiwanaku's regal-ritual cities was tied to some kind of relationship with the patrician lineages, either as kin, fictive fin, or as retainers. The inherent structural limitations of this kind of patron-client relationship, which demands a greater measure of face-to-face contact, limited the scale and diversity of social relations in Tiwanaku's cities. Lacking the natural democracy and entrepreneurial opportunity that comes with a market, Tiwanaku was essentially a "company town" catering to the twin, interpenetrating businesses of state religion and politics. Urban economic activity and policy, such as it was, was stimulated and controlled by the aristocratic households. The artisans on the periphery of Tiwanaku were not producing pottery and lapidary work for sale in an urban market. They were not completely free economic actors. Rather, they were bound in a web of social relations with their elite patrons and with their own *ayllu*'s members and trading partners. In exchange for their clients' skilled labor, the Tiwanaku nobility provided both raw materials for the craft and artisanal pieces they wished to commission and, most likely, for the full-time craft specialists, their basic subsistence. The daily sustenance of these retainers and the junior lineages of the nobility were satisfied in exchange for their labor service, whether this was in the form of crafting precious objects or participating in the governance of the state. In the absence of money, a substantial quotient of the circulation of basic commodities in Tiwanaku took place as informal barter among families and close associates – that is, at the level of the *ayllu*. The daily economic life of the *ayllu* was fueled by these kinds of direct, reciprocal relationships. But this form of intensely interpersonal exchange is radically different from that accomplished in an impersonal market. The point of direct, reciprocal exchange between patrons and clients, or between *ayllu* members, was not simply to effect a transfer of goods and services, although this was the overt purpose of the exchange. It was also, and perhaps more importantly, to build, express, and sustain a network of social relations. Mutual labor exchange and interpersonal relationships were the life's blood of Tiwanaku's economy.

But the lack of a market and Western-style commercial transactions, a tendency toward social homogeneity, political domination by eminent households, and relatively small population does not mean that Tiwanaku was an entirely closed, static community. The regal-ritual status of Tiwanaku, and the mystique that inhered in the city because of its legendary role in native cosmology, ensured that it became an important pilgrimage center. The awe-inspiring natural setting of the city and its remarkable human-created ensemble of temples drew people to Tiwanaku. Country folk from the surrounding areas and from farther afield came to the city for important public ceremonies, to participate directly in the state cults, and perhaps to bury their mummified ancestors in the city's sacred ground. This periodic, temporary influx of pilgrims, who spoke a variety of dialects and practiced distinct customs, brought a certain dynamism to the texture of daily life in the city. The flow of foreigners and foreign ideas and beliefs to and from the city was intensified by Tiwanaku's role as a principal nexus in the llama caravan trade that extended across the south-central Andes and by its military adventures and conquests.

In overview, recent archaeological research strengthens Ponce's (1972) basic concept of Tiwanaku society as stratified, at a minimum, into three social classes: a governing group of lineages composed of warrior-elite who held political and religious offices; a "middle class" of artisans who worked as retainers of the ruling lineages; and a commoner class of farmers, herders, and fishers who were the sustaining force for Tiwanaku's economic system. There were a variety of status gradations within each of these general classes. More subtle distinctions were undoubtedly made, for instance, between lineal and collateral, or senior and junior kin descendants of the ruling households so that there were "high" and "low" nobility. Similarly, the craft *barrios* were probably status-stratified in terms of occupational specialization. But, without primary textual evidence, the specific nature of these finer social distinctions remain inaccessible.

The rural commoners, the agriculturalists and herders, who lived and worked in the hinterlands surrounding Tiwanaku's urban centers provided the surplus product that underwrote the complex system of public works that came to characterize Tiwanaku civilization. These public works included audacious projects for reclaiming vast tracts of rural land that were incorporated into the Tiwanaku economic system as dedicated agricultural estates under the direct control of Tiwanaku's ruling lineages (Kolata 1991). It was from these remarkably productive estates that wealth in the form of agricultural surplus flowed back into Tiwanaku's urban society, providing the economic bedrock for the political power of the aristocratic lineages, and for unparalleled achievements in the esoteric realm of religious and political architecture and art. In a real sense, the urban and rural milieus were intimately interconnected in the process of creating Tiwanaku civilization. Perhaps the greatest enduring testament to the ingenuity and power of Tiwanaku civilization was the manner in which it reshaped entire natural landscapes for the benefit of its populations. Tiwanaku's harnessing of the natural environment found intense symbolic expression and recapitulation in the artificial, built environment of its cities. The sophisticated agrarian technology and the manner in which the people of Tiwanaku organized their agricultural landscapes forms the subject of the following chapter.

6

Metropole and Hinterland

The economic system that underwrote the remarkable wealth and productivity of the people of Tiwanaku was intimately related to the environmental matrix in which that society was embedded. The diverse physical landscapes and resource endowments of the south-central Andes provided a broad spectrum of natural resources that was potentially exploitable by indigenous cultures of the region. However, it was the cultural choices made by the people of Tiwanaku concerning the kinds of natural resources that were to be exploited, the intensity with which human and natural resources were harnessed for the benefit of populations, and the form of the organization of economic production that are of interest here. Reconstructing the nature of these choices and exploring their implications for the structure of Tiwanaku society draws us into the realm of that ancient society's political economy. If we are to understand the world that the people of Tiwanaku created for themselves, we must seek to reconstruct the underlying web of social, political, and economic relationships that shaped their lives.

Because Tiwanaku was a non-literate society, we have no detailed accounts of how its economy was organized. No library of bureaucratic documents with official records of production and exchange, occupational specializations, population censuses, and talleys of taxation exist. So we are thrown back onto the resources of the archaeological record to reconstruct the essential fabric of Tiwanaku's economic life. We cannot expect that a systematic and objectively accurate account of Tiwanaku political economy will ever be recovered from the shattered, physical remains of this society now long extinct. Nevertheless, in terms of the archaeological record available to us today, we can perceive, however imprecisely and obscured by the inevitable loss of cultural memory, at least the broad outlines of the stratagems that

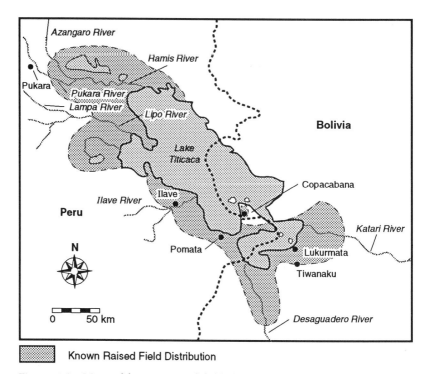

*Figure 6.1   Map of known raised-field distribution around Lake Titicaca.
(Based on Erickson 1988: Figure 2; and Kolata 1991).*

the elite classes of Tiwanaku pursued in extending their hegemony throughout the Titicaca basin. Here I will concentrate on the Tiwanaku elite's economic and social organization of the intensely rich, productive core of their society: the agricultural and high pasture lands encircling Lake Titicaca (Figure 6.1). In particular, I will focus attention on the area I refer to as the metropolitan district of the Tiwanaku heartland (Figure 6.2). This area formed the immediate sustaining hinterland of the Tiwanaku state, and consisted of a series of interlinked, densely nucleated urban settlements, such as Tiwanaku, Lukurmata, Pajchiri, and Khonko Wankané among others, set within a constellation of smaller, dispersed rural settlements. In order to understand the organizational scheme through which the elite of Tiwanaku structured the economic landscape of this sustaining heartland, we must examine the character and disposition of archaeological sites from the frame of reference of these two distinct social realities: the cosmopolitan and the rural.

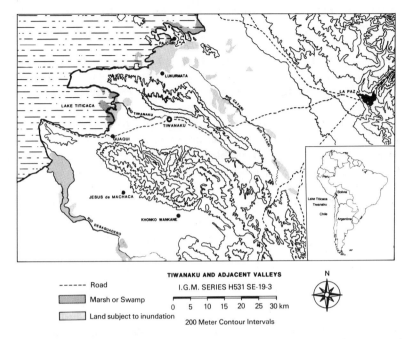

Figure 6.2   Map of Tiwanaku and adjacent valleys, illustrating the principal urban settlements of Tiwanaku, Lukurmata, Pajchiri, and Khonko Wankané, as well as the location and general topographic and hydrological features of the subbasins of the Río Tiwanaku, the Río Catari, and portions of the Machaca-Desaguadero region. (Based on Kolata 1991: Figure 1).

Local Environment

Before beginning this exploration of the principal elements of Tiwanaku's political economy, we must gain a finer-grained understanding of the natural environment that formed the underlying physical pediment for the city of Tiwanaku and its immediate rural hinterland. It was the interlinked potential of this heartland of city and hinterland that was initially responsible for creating and sustaining the astonishing economic engine that propelled Tiwanaku within the course of a few centuries from an unprepossessing *altiplano* village to the capital of an expansive, predatory state.

At first glance, the windswept, frost-plagued plains of the Bolivian high plateau do not evoke an image of agrarian utopia. The Western mind almost unconsciously associates notions of fertility and abundance with warm lands and tropical climates. We see agricultural paradise in the rich, irrigated bottomlands of the great rivers of antiquity:

in the Nile delta of pharaonic Egypt, in the sinuous paths taken by the Tigris and Euphrates rivers tapped by the royal dynasties of Sumer, in the organic, sediment-laden, turbulent flow of the sacred Ganges and Indus rivers exploited by the Harrapan civilization. Perhaps from lack of familiarity alone, we are not accustomed to perceive the cold, sere landscapes of the Andean *altiplano* as an environment of equivalent economic value.

Even the nearly universal, visceral response to the severe beauty and inhuman scale of the *altiplano* distances the casual observer from an appreciation of its remarkable ecological and economic potential. Without question, the Andean *altiplano* is different in scale and in kind from other hearths of civilization. It was no "Fertile Crescent" in the common sense of that term. Nowhere else in the ancient world do we find enormous, densely populated cities set at such high altitude (3,800–4,000 masl). Nowhere else did an agriculturally based civilization have to cope with the constant threat of famine triggered by chronic frosts, periodic droughts, and occasional catastrophic inundations from the cold, brackish waters of an interior sea like Lake Titicaca.

There is little question that the environmental conditions of the Andean *altiplano* set certain biological constraints on agricultural production and generate exceptional risks for the small farmer. The *altiplano* climate alternates dramatically between wet (November–March) and dry (April–October) seasons, but this normal cycle is frequently distorted by droughts or extended rainy seasons that can destroy seedlings and maturing crops. Remarkable variation in diurnal temperatures creates the potential for killing frosts virtually throughout the entire agricultural cycle. Sporadic hailstorms and ferocious *altiplano* windstorms that strip topsoil and generate choking dust bowl conditions complicate the already hard life of a small farmer on the high plateau. Today's *altiplano* farmer constantly walks the thin edge between disaster and survival. Even in the most favorable ecological niches along the edges of Lake Titicaca, the *altiplano* experiences almost total crop failure on an average of once every five years (Weil 1974:54). Given these difficult conditions, contemporary, Western-trained agronomists in Bolivia and Peru, charged with the responsibility of recommending programs of agricultural development, dismiss the *altiplano* as a marginal environment and look rather to the warm, sub-tropical lands of the Pacific coast or to the heavily forested Amazon watershed to locate their projects.

Despite these rather daunting environmental conditions and apparent physical constraints to effective agricultural production, there remains an exquisite irony and a paradox here that stems from a persistent cultural and ecological misperception of the *altiplano*'s true economic potential. The irony is that for over 3,000 years, and, to a somewhat lesser degree even until today, the *altiplano* has been Bolivia's principal center of aggregate population and agricultural production. Yet its daunting scale and its indigenous character remove it from the political process of development in that modern nation state. The paradox of this misperception is that in antiquity the *altiplano* supported human populations substantially larger than it does today, in some instances 20 or 30 times larger. To untangle the conundrum of why indigenous peoples in the prehispanic past were significantly better off than their contemporary counterparts, we must reassess the ecological potential of the high plateau and understand the technologies and organizational schemes of agricultural production in a cultural tradition now lost to us. In doing so, we will have come a long way toward grasping the essence of the world inhabited by the people of Tiwanaku. We may also come away with a deeper appreciation of the tenacity and ingenuity with which the indigenous peoples of the Andes adapted to their intensely beautiful, yet demanding environment over the course of millennia.

Tiwanaku's Local Economy

The heartland of Tiwanaku's metropolitan district lies in a series of three enormous valleys hemmed in on the east by the majestic, glacier-encrusted Cordillera Real and bounded on the west by a long north-south trending mountain chain of volcanic origin that delimits the modern frontier between Bolivia and Chile. Each of these valleys, defined geologically as separate hydrological units referred to as the Catari, Tiwanaku, and Machaca sub-basins, border on the shores of Lake Titicaca (Figure 6.2). The uninitiated traveler might imagine the Bolivian *altiplano* to be a uniform, featureless plateau, rolling on dully and endlessly to the horizon. This common image distorts ecological reality. These three valleys of the *altiplano*, which became the setting for the emergence of Tiwanaku as an urban civilization, are morphologically complex and highly variegated in terms of topography, soils, vegetation, and sources of water. They are a patchwork quilt of physical forms and textures.

Each of these valleys presents a complicated landscape of mountains and plains, rivers and streams, *quebradas* and lake terraces. Ancient mountain slopes deeply incised by flowing surface water carry enormous charges of sediment to the land below. Extensive alluvial fans and plains were formed in the past 15,000 years from the clay, sand,

and gravel products of incessant erosion from these surrounding mountain chains. The broad littoral and near-shore zone of Lake Titicaca presents an entirely different environmental aspect. Muddy, organic soils, marshes, and stony beaches form a rich wetlands teeming with wildlife and aquatic plants. High, arid pockets of pastureland above 4,100 masl crown this geological layer cake of local ecological diversity. Each of these zones with differing natural attributes and economic potential contributed to the development of Tiwanaku's urban civilization.

The local economy of Tiwanaku's metropolitan district revolved around three principal, intimately related systems of production: intensive agriculture, extensive llama and alpaca pastoralism, and exploitation of Lake Titicaca. Each of these three systems of production was associated with a particular environmental zone, and involved distinct forms of activities and organization. Each of these systems of production also entailed different intensities of central government investment in labor recruitment and management.

Perhaps the most important of these three basic forms of economic production, and the one that manifests the most intense degree of state involvement in planning and mobilization of human labor was Tiwanaku's remarkable system of intensive, raised field agriculture together with a supporting infrastructure of hydraulic technology: dikes, aqueducts, causeways, and canals. The history of the reclamation of natural wetlands for intensive agricultural production by the Tiwanaku state is, in a sense, emblematic of the larger social history of the people of Tiwanaku. The emergence, floresence, and ultimate collapse of intensive raised field agriculture in the Lake Titicaca region virtually recapitulates the trajectory of Tiwanaku state expansion and decline. We can see clearly a general relationship between the capacity to create and sustain a substantial surplus of agricultural production and the institutionalization of political power in the hands of the Tiwanaku elite classes. The fundamental basis of power for the elite of Tiwanaku society was control over a secure, sustainable fund of agricultural products which was then employed to finance other local and foreign ventures: construction of monumental temples and palaces, subsidies for artisan retainers, wars of conquest and territorial expansion, or reinvestment in the agricultural landscape. In the world of Tiwanaku, agriculture was power. The elite of that world was supremely sensitive to this equation. The first step toward understanding the political economy of Tiwanaku society is to capture the complex relationships that underwrote the technology and organization of agricultural production on the broad littoral and alluvial plains of Tiwanaku's metropolitan district.

The Technology of Raised Field Agriculture

Systems of raised field agriculture, if not quite ubiquitous in the ancient Americas, are nevertheless broadly distributed throughout Central and South America, and, to a lesser degree, in North America as well. This type of paleohydraulic system occurs in different climatic regions ranging from the humid tropics of the South American lowlands to the middle latitude, temperate zones of the upper midwest in the United States. In certain ecological contexts, such as in perennially inundated, marshy landscapes, the primary function of raised fields is to promote drainage and lower local water tables to reduce the potentially disastrous conditions of root rot. In other settings, raised fields mitigate the hazard of killing frosts. Still other systems of raised fields appear to promote the conservation of water and the recycling of essential nutrients. An analogous type of cultivation system occurred in Great Britain and Ireland as early as the Neolithic period, and was used in some form into the nineteenth century A.D. Here raised fields are referred to as "ridge and furrow" fields or "lazy beds." As these examples suggest, raised field technology appears in various guises virtually throughout the world in the tropics and temperate middle latitudes. This wide geographic variation in raised field technology is matched by high diversity in shape and function. The raised field complexes of the circum–Lake Titicaca region in Peru and Bolivia, which are of principal concern to us, represent the largest, virtually continuous expanse of this cultivation system in the world. This specialized, intensive form of agricultural production was the cornerstone of Tiwanaku's agrarian economy.

Morphology and Structure

The raised fields of the Titicaca basin are essentially large, elevated planting platforms ranging from 5 to 10 meters wide and up to 200 meters long. Within a given segment of a raised field system, approximately 30 to 60 percent of the area of a segment is given over to the planting surface itself (Figure 6.3). The remaining portion is occupied by intervening canals that derive their water from local rivers, natural springs, or percolating groundwater. At times, the flow of water from natural sources that fed raised field systems was enhanced and regulated by massive hydraulic projects designed by the agro-engineers of Tiwanaku: dikes, aqueducts, primary canals and canalized springs, *quebradas*, and rivers (Ortloff and Kolata 1989).

The basic principles and technology of constructing raised fields are simple (Figure 6.4). Tiwanaku raised fields consisted of elevated

LAKAYA I: RAISED FIELD SYSTEM

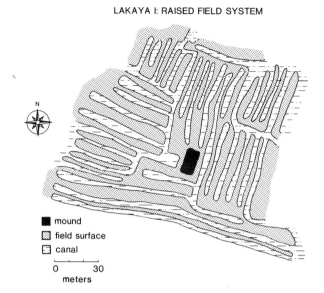

Figure 6.3　A plan of a representative segment of a raised field system from the Lakaya sector of the Pampa Koani. (Based on Kolata 1991: Figure 2).

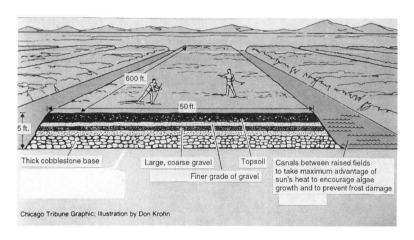

Figure 6.4　Internal structure of a raised field. (Based on Chicago Tribune Sunday Magazine, November 23, 1986:13).

platforms of earth which functioned as the planting surface paired with adjacent ditches or canals. The tools required to build these fields included wooden digging sticks, usually equipped with hard stone, or more rarely, metal bits, and foot plows to cut sod and break up soil. Baskets or folded textile bundles served to transport earth to the construction site. The foot plow, referred to in Quechua as the *chaquitaklla*, was the principal agricultural tool of the Inca, and little-altered variants of this basic tool remain in use today in rural agrarian communities throughout the Andean *altiplano* (Figure 6.5). Field systems were layed out by first designing and cutting the canals adjacent to the planting platform. Teams of workers would cut and turn the sod from the base of the intended platform to establish an appropriate foundation for the raised field and then mound the earth cut from the canals into the center to form the actual elevated planting platform.

The construction of the elevated planting bed was one of the keys to the technological effectiveness of this cultivation system. By cutting and turning the surface sod and its underlying earth and mounding this material into an elevated bed the ancient farmers of Tiwanaku were transforming and enhancing the soil structure of their agricultural fields. The process of constructing a raised field resulted in earth that was loose and well aerated with the capacity to capture both water and air in micropores within the soil. This property of non-compacted, aerated soil structure increases the ability of growing plants to retain water and absorb essential, water soluble nutrients. Thorough tilling of the soil on the elevated planting platform provided an excellent bed for germinating seeds and allowed development of a vigorous root system that was essential for healthy, mature crops. Moreover, a loose, well-tilled soil structure permitted Tiwanaku farmers to plant their crops in more closely packed, denser rows resulting in higher yields. In addition to generating higher yields, close packing of plants also reduced the otherwise formidable competition from the tough, weedy plants native to the *altiplano*.

Throughout the agricultural cycle, the farmers of Tiwanaku would maintain planted fields by weeding them by hand or by hoeing with their essential, all-purpose agricultural tool: the wooden digging stick with a hafted, basalt hoe-blade. Weeds extracted from the fields were mulched, or directly worked into the soil where they would decompose slowly, adding needed nutrients to the fields. Other forms of fertilizer were also available to Tiwanaku farmers. For centuries, indigenous farmers in the Andean highlands have brought their livestock down from remote *puna* pastures during the long, dry months of winter to graze in fallow and on the stubble of recently harvested fields. The

Figure 6.5   Illustration by Guaman Poma de Ayala of native farmers using the chakitaklla, *or traditional Andean foot plow.*

dung of llama and alpaca became an invaluable source of natural fertilizer in these agro-pastoral societies. In this fashion, the pastoral and agricultural economies were meshed in a mutually beneficial, regular rhythm of seasonal activities that overlapped and reinforced each other, promoting a stable cycle of production.

One of the most important and abundant sources of locally available fertilizer was the rich, organic, nutrient-laden sediments that developed in the canals adjacent to the raised fields' planting platform. Recent experimental work in restored Tiwanaku raised fields indicated that the canals surrounding the raised fields were rapidly colonized by a diverse range of aquatic plants, but most importantly by communities of nitrogen-fixing organisms such as the plant *Azolla*, and by certain free-living, blue-green algae. These plants were harvested directly from the surface of the water and incorporated into the planting bed immediately before sowing, or their decayed products were dredged from the muddy sediments of the canals and redistributed over the surface of the field. The high nutritive content of these decomposed aquatic plants, and their capacity to fix atmospheric nitrogen, greatly ameliorated the nutrient deficit that characterizes most *altiplano* soils.

We know from careful excavations in the agricultural sector at the site of Lukurmata that Tiwanaku farmers did in fact periodically clean out the sediments from canals between raised fields. These nitrogen-rich sediments were then used to resurface and revitalize the planting platforms of the raised field system. Excavations in similar buried field segments in the Pampa Koani zone near Lukurmata revealed, after careful sieving of sediments, that substantial quantities of fish bones and scales were mixed in with the agricultural topsoil. This discovery hints at another form of natural fertilizer employed by Tiwanaku farmers: remains of fish spread over the field surface and left to decay. Spanish chroniclers of the sixteenth century such as Cieza de León and Cristóbal de Molina reported that small, whole fish such as anchovy or heads of fishes were frequently planted alongside maize seeds by indigenous farmers on the coast of Peru. This was certainly a pattern that extended back into the period of Inca domination. The use of fish rich in natural oils as fertilizer was apparently a common practice in the prehispanic Andean world wherever sufficient quantities were available. Communities of small, gregarious fish quickly colonized the canals of Tiwanaku raised fields adjacent to Lake Titicaca that we have rehabilitated. Along with the archaeological evidence for fish remains in agricultural top soils, the proximity and ready availability of small fish in the field canals confirms that Tiwanaku farmers assiduously exploited this rich source of natural fertilizer to maintain and enhance the fertility of their raised fields. Furthermore, the evidence for a sub-community of fishers within the urban boundaries of Lukurmata also raises the possibility that groups of people who specialized in the exploitation of Lake Titicaca were formally integrated into the agrarian economy as procurers of an essential resource (natural fertilizer), much like the occupationally specialized pastoralists. Each of the three fundamental categories of actors in the Tiwanaku local economy, agriculturalists, pastoralists, and fishers, pursued independent courses of economic activity which were nonetheless integrated conceptually, symbolically, temporally, spatially, and pragmatically.

Heat Conservation

Apart from their capacity to sustain aquatic plants and animals that could be exploited as forms of natural fertilizer, the canals between fields played a second, vital role in maintaining the productivity of raised fields in the specific environmental context of the Andean high plateau. Perhaps the greatest risk that *altiplano* farmers face on a daily basis during the growing season is the potential for devastation wrought by killing frosts. Recognizing the severity of chronic frost hazard and the subsequent cost to human productivity and self-sufficiency, several international development agencies working in the *altiplano* today have constructed solar greenhouses, called *invernaderos* by local farmers, consisting of aluminum or wooden frameworks covered by polyethelene sheeting. These simple greenhouses have proved stunningly successful in harnessing the intense solar radiation of the high plateau and providing a protected, enclosed environment that conserves both heat and humidity. Nevertheless, despite their success on a small-scale, the drawbacks of the *invernadero* are plain to see. They are too costly for the average farmer in rural Bolivia and Peru and cannot be readily adopted by peasant families without heavy subsidies. Furthermore, their applicability is limited in scale because of high cost and the technological inability to enclose huge expanses of land. To date, these small greenhouses have been used to grow selected cash crops such as green vegetables, tomatoes, and herbs for urban markets. *Invernaderos* cannot be constructed on a scale large enough to grow significant quantities of essential staple crops such as potatoes, *quinoa*, broad beans, and winter wheat. The transfer of modern Western technologies of hot house vegetable production to the *altiplano* has done little to alleviate chronic problems of inadequate food supply.

Ironically, over 2,500 years ago, in the process of developing the raised field system of cultivation, the people of Tiwanaku and their counterparts around the shores of Lake Titicaca solved the problem of utilizing solar energy on a large scale to stabilize and enhance crop production in the *altiplano*. In experiments undertaken in restored Tiwanaku raised fields, my research collaborators and I examined the specific heat storage pathways and potentials within these systems. The results of this experimental work, based on both a computer

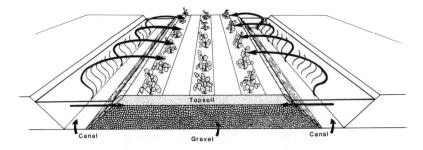

Figure 6.6   Vectors of heat storage and transfer in Tiwanaku raised fields in the Titicaca Basin. (From Kolata 1991: Figure 3).

model of the thermal properties of raised fields over a 24-hour period during the *altiplano* growing season and on direct empirical observations, demonstrate dramatically that the design of raised field systems absorbs heat from solar radiation efficiently, promotes heat conservation, and functions effectively to protect both seedlings and maturing plants from frost damage during sub-freezing *altiplano* nights (Kolata and Ortloff 1989). The canals surrounding the raised fields are the key to this frost mitigation effect.

The controlling factor in the ability of a given physical medium, such as stone, clay, soil, or water, to regulate and transfer heat is a property referred to as thermal diffusivity. In general, the lower the thermal diffusivity value, the more heat storage effect occurs in a given medium. Both water and soil containing substantial moisture have low thermal diffusivity values, and consequently the capacity to readily retain and transfer heat. In effect, the canals surrounding raised fields functioned as gigantic solar collectors and heat sumps, absorbing the energy of intense solar radiation during the day and transferring this stored heat into and around the planting platforms of the fields at night (Figure 6.6). The ability of the canals to capture and store heat from solar energy was impressive. During peak periods of solar radiation in the early afternoon, we recorded canal water temperatures that exceeded ambient air temperatures by as much as 10 to 20°F. As air temperatures gradually fall in late afternoon and early evening when the sun begins to drop behind the surrounding mountains, we observed two mechanisms of heat transfer in the raised field system. First, the stored heat in the canals radiated upward elevating local ambient temperature. Second, the water in the canals also transferred heat through the side walls of the planting platforms into the soil. That is, the warm water of the canals was drawn laterally through

Figure 6.7   Raised planting platforms at Lakaya, with water-filled canals on either side.

capillary action into the planting platform around the area of root development of the crops (Figure 6.7). The effect of these two distinct vectors of heat transfer was to create a "heat envelope" that protects both sub-surface developing root systems and the vulnerable, fresh foliage of maturing plants from the ravages of a hard freeze.

Experiments in Raised Field Rehabilitation

Over the past several agricultural seasons, we obtained graphic confirmation of these heat conservation effects in our experimentally rehabilitated raised fields. The most dramatic event occurred in 1988. That year, four hectares of ancient Tiwanaku raised fields were experimentally reconstructed near the village of Lakaya, situated on the southern shores of Lake Titicaca some ten kilometers north of Tiwanaku itself (Figure 6.8). These well-preserved Tiwanaku raised fields were reconstructed by Aymara from local communities around Lakaya and planted in potato, *quinoa*, cañiwa, and a variety of European crops including winter wheat, barley, and oats. On the nights of February 28–29, 1988, the Bolivian *altiplano* suffered a killing frost with temperatures in the Lakaya sector dropping to 12°F

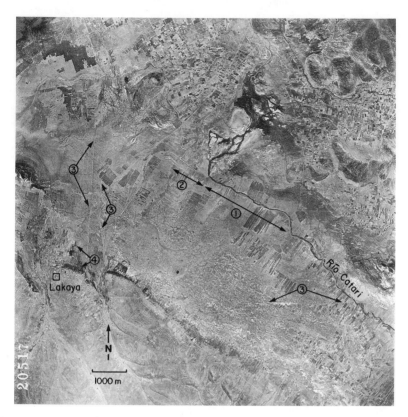

Figure 6.8 Aerial photograph of the southern portions of the Pampa Koani raised field study area, with: (1) the artificially canalized section of the Río Catari; (2) the intake of the river by-pass system, or river "shunt"; (3) the causeway on the west side may also have served as a dike, as well as an elevated roadbed; and (4) Lakaya rehabilitated raised fields. (Instituto Geográfico Militar, Bolivia sheet 20517, 10 August 1955; also based on Kolata 1991: Figure 4).

in some areas. Enormous zones of potato and *quinoa* cultivation on plains and hill slopes along the southern rim of Lake Titicaca were severely damaged by this heavy frost. Many traditional, dry-farmed fields within a few hundred meters of the experimental raised field plots experienced crop losses as high as 70 to 90 percent. One of our control plots cultivated in the traditional manner without benefit of raised field technology lost every single maturing potato plant. In contrast, damage in the experimental raised fields of Lakaya were limited to superficial frost "burning" of leaves on potato plants and

Figure 6.9   Experimental raised fields in full bloom at Lakaya in 1988. (Photograph by Alan Kolata)

an overall crop loss averaging around 10 percent. Barley, broad beans, *quinoa*, cañiwa, onions, and lettuce planted in the Lakaya raised fields showed similar, moderate crop losses in comparison to the dry-farmed fields (Figure 6.9). We attribute this tremendous differential in plant survivability to the heat storage properties of the saturated raised fields and their surrounding canals. In effect, these experiments demonstrate that prehispanic systems of raised field cultivation in the *altiplano* possess much higher thermal efficiency than traditional forms of dry farming practiced in the area since the early Spanish Colonial period. Given the high risk of crop loss through frost damage, higher thermal efficiency of the raised fields, when combined with the built-in forms of natural fertilization available to the raised field cultivator, translates into substantially higher yield performance in comparison with dry farming.

In addition to demonstrating the superior thermal properties of raised fields, our experiments in rehabilitating Tiwanaku raised fields gave us dramatic confirmation of yield differentials between traditional, dry farming and raised field cultivation. Table 6.1 illustrates the yield of potatoes planted in 12 individual control parcels in the experimentally reconstructed raised fields, along with supplemental information on the surface dimensions of the control parcels, number of planted furrows and individual plants per parcel, the achieved weight and number of tubers per potato plant, and the incidence of frost damage.

Table 6.1 Potato yield of rehabilitated raised fields in the Pampa Koani

Parcel Number	Dimensions (in meters) Length/Width	Surface area (in m²)	Number of Furrows	Number of Plants	Weight (per parcel, in kg)	Total Weight (per ha, in kg estimated)	% Exhibiting Frost Lesions*
1	3.57/2.90	10.35	4	39	40.80	39,420	10
2	4.00/3.00	12.00	4	49	45.80	38,166	20
3	3.00/3.54	10.62	4	39	39.00	36,723	10
4	2.80/3.17	8.88	4	33	38.30	43,130	0
5	2.70/7.70	20.79	4	84	82.25	39,562	10
6	3.20/3.20	10.24	4	31	43.20	42,187	25
7	2.90/2.90	8.41	4	36	44.70	53,151	10
8	2.80/3.50	9.80	4	43	38.18	38,959	20
9	2.80/2.90	8.12	4	33	29.15	35,899	0
10	3.00/5.00	15.00	9	70	70.50	47,000	10
11	3.00/5.00	15.00	9	75	63.50	42,333	10
12	3.65/3.20	18.25	5	45	57.50	49,229	0
Total		132.41		577	592.88	505,752	
Average		11.03		48	40.40	42,146**	10.41

* Percent of plants exhibiting frost lesions refers to the specific event of February 28–29, 1988, referred to in the text.
** To obtain average yield in kilograms per hectare in the raised field system as a whole, rather than the platform surfaces alone, this figure must be halved to reflect the approximate proportion of non-cultivated canal surfaces. Effective yield per hectare becomes ca. 21 metric tons/hectare.

The yields from the experimental raised fields compare favorably with those obtained from control plots that we cultivated for purposes of direct comparison using two traditional variants of *altiplano* agriculture. The two traditional forms of agricultural plots that we established were shallow furrow, rainfall-dependent plots, cultivated without the benefit of irrigation or the use of chemical fertilizers or pesticides, and shallow furrow, dry cultivated plots with added chemical fertilizers and pesticides applied both to the soil and to foliage throughout the growing season.

The first form of traditional cultivation has been the dominant mode of peasant agricultural production in the Bolivian *altiplano* for nearly five centuries, even though it is patently inefficient and destructive to soil development and fertility. As indicated by the yields in Table 6.2, this form of non-fertilized dry farming achieved an average of 2.4 metric tons per hectare of potato on five cultivated parcels. During the 1987–88 growing season, 100 percent of the maturing plants on these parcels exhibited lesions from frost, with the bulk of the damage occurring during the hard freeze of February 1988. Depending on the individual parcels of cultivated land, approximately 10 to 30 percent of these plants were only superficially damaged by frost, but the remaining 70 to 90 percent were destroyed and yielded no edible tubers.

Predictably, the addition of costly commercial fertilizers and pesticides on traditional fields increased production substantially to an average of 14.50 metric tons per hectare on eight cultivated parcels (Table 6.3). Despite the expected enhanced performance of traditional agricultural fields treated with commercial fertilizers, it is clear that the experimental raised fields significantly outperformed both the non-fertilized *and* the fertilizer- and pesticide-treated fields constructed in the traditional fashion: a remarkable and perhaps even startling outcome. On 12 cultivated parcels of experimental raised fields, potato yields reached an average of 21 metric tons per hectare, or nearly twice the yield of traditional fields treated with chemical fertilizers and over seven times the yield of unimproved traditional cultivation. The percentage of the crop planted in raised fields that was affected by frost was on average only about 10 percent, a radically different, and much smaller proportion of frost damage than experienced in the two types of traditional cultivation.

Similar experiments in raised field rehabilitation were conducted in the *altiplano* of Peru on the northern side of Lake Titicaca by a small team of archaeologists and agronomists during the mid-1980s. Their results are instructive, and generally consistent with those obtained by my own research group (Table 6.4). The Peruvian team did not

Table 6.2   Potato Yield of Traditional Agriculture Lacking Commercial Fertilizers

Parcel Number	Dimensions (in meters) Length/Width	Surface area (in m^2)	Number of Furrows	Number of Plants	Weight (per Parcel (in kg)	Total Weight per ha (in kg, estimated)	% Exhibiting Frost Lesions*
1	5.00/3.60	18.00	5	60	4.00	2,222	100
2	5.00/3.50	17.50	5	63	4.50	2,571	100
3	5.00/3.65	18.25	5	61	4.60	2,520	100
4	5.00/3.70	18.50	5	61	5.00	2,703	100
5	5.00/3.56	17.80	5	62	3.80	2,135	100
Total		90.05		307	21.9	12,151	
Average		18.01		61.4	4.38	2,430	100

* Percent of plants exhibiting frost lesions refers to the specific event of February 28–29, 1988, referred to in the text.

Table 6.3 Potato Yield of Improved Agriculture with Commercial Fertilizers (N,P,K)

Parcel Number	Dimensions (in meters) Length/Width	Surface area (in m²)	Number of Furrows	Number of Plants	Weight per Parcel (in kg)	Total Weight per ha (in kg, estimated)	% Exhibiting Frost Lesions*
1	5.00/3.68	18.40	5	45	26.0	14,130	100
2	5.00/3.40	17.00	5	40	26.5	15,588	100
3	5.00/3.60	18.00	5	40	23.0	12,777	100
4	5.00/3.80	19.00	5	40	26.0	13,685	100
5	5.00/3.20	16.00	5	41	14.0	8,750	100
6	5.00/3.30	16.50	5	46	22.5	13,636	100
7	5.00/3.30	16.50	5	51	30.5	19,062	100
8	5.00/3.50	17.50	5	44	32.1	18,342	100
Total		138.40		347	200.6	115,970	
Average		17.30		43.3	25.1	14,496	100

* Percent of plants exhibiting frost lesions refers to the specific event of February 28–29, 1988, referred to in the text.

Table 6.4   Potato Yields on Rehabilitated Raised Fields in
Huatta, Peru

Field Name	Surface Area (m²)	Yields in kg/ha 1981–1982	1983–1984	1984–1985
Machachi	110	6,760		
Candile	73	10,119		
Chojñocoto I	702		13,652	8,573
Chojñocoto II	2025			5,186
Chojñocoto III	1449			11,036
Viscachani Pampa	1405/1625		12,536	12,309
Pancha Pampa	815			10,990
Average Yield Per Hectare Per Year:		8,440	13,094	10,441
Combined Average Yield Per Hectare:		10,658 kg/ha		

Adapted from Erickson, 1988:244, Table 8.

plant control plots of traditionally cultivated fields for direct comparison, but rather relied on regional averages for the department of
Puno derived from statistics compiled by the Peruvian Ministry of
Agriculture. These averages of regional potato production on traditionally cultivated plots range from 1.5 to 6 metric tons per hectare,
which compares well with our own result of 2.4 metric tons per
hectare. On raised fields that were not treated with fertilizers over a
three-year-production cycle, the Puno group generated an average of
10.65 metric tons per hectare.

As can be seen at a glance in Table 6.4, production figures varied
considerably over time and space. Some areas did particularly well in
a given year, and even within individual blocks of reclaimed raised
fields there was considerable variability in yield depending on placement of seed in the center or along the edge of a cultivated plot,
an experience replicated in our own work on the Bolivian side of
the lake. The average yields of potato on raised fields achieved by the
Puno group are lower than those obtained on the Bolivian side in the
Pampa Koani region, although the pattern of dramatically enhanced
production on raised fields in comparison to traditional fields is identical. The higher yields that we obtained on the Bolivian side may relate to slight climatic differences between the northern and southern
sides of Lake Titicaca. The area around Puno is in higher altitude and
consequently somewhat more prone to frost damage than the area of
the Pampa Koani. Moreover, the planting and cultivating protocols
practiced by the Puno group appear to have differed from our own.
The Aymara villagers rehabilitating fields in the Pampa Koani routinely incorporated substantial quantities of organic fertilizer (green

manure, or animal waste) into the fields during tilling and sowing activities.

Despite the differences in average raised field potato production between the Puno and the Pampa Koani experiments, the general trend of significantly enhanced yields on reclaimed raised fields appears established beyond a reasonable doubt. At a minimum, cultivation on reclaimed raised fields results in production from two to three times that obtained by traditional methods. Moreover, as Erickson (1988:245) points out, raised fields are remarkably efficient in terms of the ratio of seed to producing plant: "in comparison to traditional fields, only half the seed is necessary for planting a hectare of raised fields since half the area is uncultivated canal. These high production rates are even more impressive when considering that a hectare of raised fields has only half the number of plants of a traditional potato field." If the experiments of both research groups are correct, raised fields represent a prime example of continuous, efficient, and sustainable cultivation: a system of intensive hydraulic agriculture that required no extended periods of fallow.

If the heat and nutrient conservation effects in raised fields described here are further verified, then our perception of the subsistence base of the Tiwanaku civilization will be radically altered. We must consider the possibility that the physical and thermal properties of Tiwanaku raised field agriculture in the Lake Titicaca basin routinely permitted a regime of double cropping of potato, ulluco, cañiwa, *quinoa*, and other indigenous staples of the *altiplano*. In fact, over the past several agricultural seasons, we successfully harvested two crops in the experimental fields of Lakaya: one of potato followed by a crop of barley while maintaining an average yield of approximately 20 metric tons per hectare of the potato crop. Continuous cultivation on fixed, permanent fields, short or no fallow periods, and two episodes of sowing and harvesting within the same agricultural year are inconceivable in the contemporary agrarian landscape of the high plateau. Yet these may have been routine features of Tiwanaku agricultural practice. If the farmers of Tiwanaku engaged in double cropping, the estimates of production on raised fields that I describe here may be too conservative. The experimental and empirical evidence as it currently stands leads me to conclude that such a regime of agricultural intensification was a principal strategy of Tiwanaku agricultural production. This conclusion, in turn, brings us to a reconsideration of the possibilities and limits of surplus agricultural production in the heartland of the Tiwanaku state. Reconstructing these limits offers critical insights into the questions of demographic potential and the structure of local food supply in the core of Tiwanaku's sustaining hinterland.

Carrying Capacity, Population, and Food Supply

Perhaps the most intellectually perilous enterprise undertaken by archaeologists is estimating the population size and characteristics of prehistoric cities and states, and the related concept of regional carrying capacity. By carrying capacity I mean most simply the number and density of people that can be supported at a minimal subsistence level by the resources contained within a given area. Even under the best of circumstances, population projections and the calculation of carrying capacity in the context of prehistoric societies are fraught with uncertainty. Carrying capacity is a slippery, highly context-specific concept, bound as much to the social world of cultural beliefs, values, and practice as to the physical world of natural resources. An accurate determination of carrying capacity would require detailed knowledge of what a given culture accepts as an exploitable natural resource, or as a desirable foodstuff. Few human societies were ever completely isolated in a cultural sense, or encapsulated within rigid physical boundaries, and so determining carrying capacity in its fullest sense also entails mapping out the net flow of goods and services into and out of the region of interest. Given the flexibility and uncertainty of the concept, I use carrying capacity calculations here only to generate order of magnitude estimates for population size. In other words, I cannot claim to offer realistic projections of precise population size for Tiwanaku and its near hinterland. The experiments in raised field production, however, provide us with a powerful empirical tool for calculating the range of demographic possibilities in the Tiwanaku sustaining area that possesses a measure of sensitivity not usually available to the archaeologist.

The three central valleys that were the setting for Tiwanaku's heartland of cities contain approximately 190 square kilometers of fossil raised fields, or some 19,000 hectares. This estimate of raised field distribution in the sustaining hinterland of Tiwanaku reflects only those fields that have been preserved on the surface and recorded on aerial photographs and maps. In these three valleys, huge areas of wetlands intricately criss-crossed by a web work of small streams fed by perennial springs and rivers show no evidence of raised fields on the surface. Yet geological coring in such wetlands in the Pampa Koani revealed rich organic sediments characteristic of agricultural soils deposited under clay, gravel, and sand up to two meters thick. The active river systems of these wetlands carry enormous quantities of sediments eroded from surrounding uplands. During the intense *altiplano* rainy season, these rivers often breach the natural levees that contain them, redepositing their sediment loads across the adjacent floodplain. As a result of this inexorable geological process, many raised fields lie undetected, buried deeply beneath the modern surface of the pampa. Other fields have been effaced through erosion, triggered by wind and rain and by rivers that meander across the floodplain, cutting and reshaping the unconsolidated sediments of alluvium. Cultural processes have also contributed to the physical disappearance of ancient field systems. Centuries of cattle herding across the broad plains that once were the setting for intensive cultivation and the introduction of metal plows and mechanized farming have obliterated the traces of abandoned raised fields. Despite the evident loss of some ancient raised fields, the 19,000 hectares that are documented in the Tiwanaku sustaining area most likely represent a substantial proportion of the fields that existed in Tiwanaku times, and we can use this figure as a baseline for projections of demographic potential.

In order to approximate the carrying capacity and demographic potential of the Tiwanaku hinterland based on its agricultural productivity, we must make certain simplifying assumptions concerning crop type, minimal daily caloric intake per capita, and percent of fields planted. First, all of the following calculations are based on a single index crop: potato. Clearly a wide variety of high altitude adapted plants were grown on Tiwanaku raised fields, but the tubers, particularly numerous varieties of small, frost-resistant "bitter" potatoes, were the principal food crop for the people of Tiwanaku. Second, for the purpose of comparability, I use Denevan's (1982) figures of 1,460 calories for minimal daily intake per person, and an average energy yield of 1,000 calories per kilogram of potato. In accordance with these figures, which were calculated for previous carrying capacity estimates in the ecological context of the Andean highlands, a person on the high plateau requires a yearly intake of approximately 533,000 calories which can be extracted from 533 kilograms (kg) of potato. Finally, I will initially assume 100 percent successful use of the raised fields in making population density estimates. Given potential effects of annual localized crop loss from hail, frost, pests, and spoilage, lake level fluctuations that would have inundated and taken out of production local areas of raised fields, and other such variables, this expectation is not entirely realistic. The variables which reduced gross production are not easily quantified. To account for crop attrition, I will arbitrarily adjust for the cumulative effect of these loss variables by recalculating the population density estimates a second time, assuming 75 percent use of the fields. Given this set of assumptions, what sort of carrying capacity and population densities can we generate for the Tiwanaku region using the two experimentally determined raised field production figures of 10.65 metric tons per hectare (the Peruvian group) and 21 metric tons per hectare (the Bolivian group)?

If we divide the average annual yield of potato per hectare by the annual requirement of 533 kg of potato per capita, we find that one hectare of raised fields planted in potato will support approximately 20 persons for one year according to the Peruvian experiment, and 39 persons per year according to the Bolivian experiment. Applying these figures to the 19,000 hectares of preserved raised fields in the Tiwanaku sustaining area, the carrying capacity for the region ranges between 380,000 and 741,000 assuming a single annual crop and 100 percent utilization of the fields. If we assume a regime of double cropping and 100 percent utilization, the population figures range between 760,000 and 1,482,000 (Table 6.5). Recalculating these population figures by changing the assumed percentage of field utilization to 75 percent, we find population ranges of 285,000–555,750 for a single annual crop, and 570,000–1,111,500 for a double crop (Table 6.6).

If I were asked to select from these four sets of population figures the most probable range, I would choose the option that assumes 75 percent utilization of the fields and a regime of double cropping: 570,000–1,111,500. My rationale for choosing this range is straightforward. We know that the farmers of Tiwanaku never simultaneously utilized 100 percent of the 19,000 preserved hectares of raised fields, therefore we must factor in some level of attrition. The 25 percent attrition value I have chosen, although arbitrary, is an historically plausible cumulative estimate of crop loss from frost, spoilage, fields left in fallow, and the like. On the other hand, our experimental work tells us that double cropping in the high plateau was feasible with raised field technology. To my mind, it is certain that whenever possible Tiwanaku farmers would have exploited the opportunity to produce substantial surpluses through double cropping. Almost universally, small farmers choose planting strategies that reduce risk over those that hold out the possibility of high return but with a substantially increased chance of total loss. Small farmers, like most small investors in the stock market, are risk averse. Successful double cropping represents the rare and attractive case in which the potential for high return is matched by a property of substantial risk reduction. If farmers experience total loss from frost or hail in one planting cycle, they can still recoup losses by planting and havesting in the second cycle. If both cycles of planting yield bumper crops, the farmer, of course, can expect substantial, storeable agricultural surplus. In other words, there was a powerful incentive for Tiwanaku farmers to routinely employ a regime of double cropping. Moreover,

Table 6.5 *Carrying Capacity Estimates for Tiwanaku Sustaining Area Assuming 100% Use of Raised Fields*

	Maximum Potential Population Under Assumptions Stated in Text	
Region: Raised Fields in Hectares	20 persons/ha/annum (Peruvian Group Estimate)	39 persons/ha/annum (Bolivian Group Estimate)
	Single Crop Estimate	
Tiwanaku Valley: 6,000 ha	120,000	234,000
Pampa Koani: 7,000 ha	140,000	273,000
Machaca/Desaguadero: 6,000 ha	120,000	234,000
TOTAL POPULATION	380,000	741,000
	Double Crop Estimate	
Tiwanaku Valley: 6,000 ha	240,000	468,000
Pampa Koani: 7,000 ha	280,000	546,000
Machaca/Desaguadero: 6,000 ha	240,000	468,000
TOTAL POPULATION	760,000	1,482,000

Table 6.6 Carrying Capacity Estimates for Tiwanaku Sustaining Area Assuming 75% Use of Raised Fields

Region: Raised Fields in Hectares	Maximum Potential Population Under Assumptions Stated in Text	
	20 persons/ha/annum (Peruvian Group Estimate)	39 persons/ha/annum (Bolivian Group Estimate)
	Single Crop Estimate	
Tiwanaku Valley: 6,000 ha	90,000	175,500
Pampa Koani: 7,000 ha	105,000	204,750
Machaca/Desaguadero: 6,000 ha	90,000	175,500
TOTAL POPULATION	285,000	555,750
	Double Crop Estimate	
Tiwanaku Valley: 6,000 ha	180,000	351,000
Pampa Koani: 7,000 ha	210,000	409,500
Machaca/Desaguadero: 6,000 ha	180,000	351,000
TOTAL POPULATION	570,000	1,111,500

the Tiwanaku state itself was engaged in organizing substantial estates of agricultural production, particularly in the Pampa Koani district. In order to finance public projects, the elite interest groups that constituted the command hierarchy of Tiwanaku urban society also had an interest in extracting maximum, sustainable yields from their agricultural estates through double cropping.

The indigenous technology of raised field agriculture clearly had the capacity to support large and concentrated human populations. Glancing at the figures in Table 6.6, we see that in Tiwanaku times the Pampa Koani region alone had the potential of supporting from 210,000 to 409,500 people on a sustained basis, again assuming the benchmark of double cropping and 75 percent field utilization. Even if we calculate carrying capacity using a single annual crop, the range of supportable population remains impressive: 105,000 to 204,750. Today, in the absence of raised field technology, the carrying capacity of the Pampa Koani is enormously reduced and the entire region supports only about 2,000 people at a level slightly beyond bare subsistence. Similar radical differences between past and present carrying capacity and absolute population levels can be demonstrated for the other two sectors of the Tiwanaku sustaining hinterland as well, the Tiwanaku Valley and the Machaca/Desaguadero area. To those who cling to cherished notions of inexorable human progress through the application of modern Western technology, the disjuncture between a distant past substantially better off in economic terms than the present represents an unanticipated and disturbing problem. This problem, perplexing on the face of it, dissolves when we take into account the demonstrable high productivity of raised field cultivation, an indigenous technology worked out by trial and error over the millennia by native farmers and agricultural engineers on the Andean high plateau.

If we compare the high population potentials generated by these calculations with actual population estimates for the Tiwanaku sustaining area during Tiwanaku IV and V times, what conclusions may we draw with respect to carrying capacity and the structure of food supply to urbanized populations? First, it is clear that, based on the component of agricultural production alone, the carrying capacity of the Tiwanaku metropolitan zone exceeded peak estimated population throughout the period from A.D. 400–1000. That is, Tiwanaku core populations never approached an absolute level that was sufficient to put stress on the agricultural capacity to absorb and sustain demographic growth. Based on recent systematic archeological work in Tiwanaku, its secondary urban settlements, and its hinterland, I estimate that the overall peak population for the Tiwanaku metropolitan district (the three valley system of Pampa Koani-Tiwanaku-Machaca) during this period approached approximately 365,000, distributed into a concentrated, urbanized component of some 115,000 and a dispersed rural component of 250,000. If we take into account other sources of food supply available to these populations, such as the enormous quantities of high-quality meat stored on the hoof in llama herds or the rich aquatic resources of the lake-edge environment, it is even more apparent that Tiwanaku population levels never approached our calculated ceiling of population potential. Any plausible estimate of the carrying capacity in the three-valley system comes to the same conclusion. In Tiwanaku times, there was always a substantial margin of productivity that was never extracted from Tiwanaku's sustaining hinterland. It may be that localized food supply crises developed at various times in this hinterland, but such problems were not borne of inadequately realized agrarian potential. Rather, if such crises occurred, they were generated by specific social events or processes, such as chronic conflict among competing interest groups. But they were not the result of environmental or technological limitations. Stress brought on by absolute population pressure against a fixed resource base never played a significant role in precipitating social change among the people of Tiwanaku.

We know, then, that raised field technology in combination with extensive herding and fishing activities formed the pivot of Tiwanaku's endogenous economy. This powerful troika of productive systems ensured the autonomy and self-sufficiency of food supply in the Tiwanaku core area, and provided the touchstones for supporting sustained demographic and economic growth. But several important questions remain. How was the system of raised field agriculture organized and managed? What were the economic and social relationships between the rural inhabitants of Tiwanaku's hinterland and those residing in urban centers? To what extent was the elite bureaucracy of the Tiwanaku state actively engaged in managing and intensifying these systems of production?

The Social Organization of Agricultural Production

The fundamental pediment of the archaic state was surplus labor extracted from rural populations. As Garnsey (1988:271) aptly comments in the context of the Mediterranean world in classical antiquity:

> The unique urban civilisations of antiquity were supported, when all is told, by the common labour of peasants. The survival of the

peasantry hinged on the nature of their response to environmental constraints and to the demands of those wielding political and economic power. Peasants followed a production strategy designed to minimise risk, endeavouring to reduce their vulnerability by dispersing their land holdings, diversifying their crops and storing their surplus. It was also essential for them to cultivate reciprocal relationships with their social equals, kin, friends and neighbors, and superiors who could act as patrons.

Rural commoners in the agrarian states of the Andes worked out similar tactics for survival: diversification of landholdings and crops, an in-grained ethic of mutual aid and well-elaborated reciprocal bonds with political superiors that might mitigate the tributary demand. But, the economics of these primitive states required a steady flow of surplus labor channeled toward a managerial elite residing permanently in urban centers. The organizational structure of the extractive process varied in degree and in kind according to local social context and historical circumstance.

One fundamental distinction turns on the nature of this extraction: the kind of formal exchanges (tribute coerced or voluntary) that occurred between urban elite and rural commoners. For instance, in ancient Mesoamerica, tribute between commoner and elite frequently took the form of commodities (tribute in kind), whereas this exchange relationship in the Andes relied more heavily on direct labor service. In one sense, of course, the argument could be made that this distinction is not terribly significant since tribute in kind is simply a further transformation of labor into a valued commodity. However, the potentially deeper and more subtle significance of direct labor service from commoner to elite in the ancient Andean world deserves closer scrutiny. The most detailed information that we have on tributary relationships framed in terms of labor exchange comes from our sources on Inca culture at the time of the Spanish conquest. Understanding the nature of tributary relationships that were perceivable in the early sixteenth century will aid us in reconstructing the likely forms of surplus labor extraction that powered the state of Tiwanaku.

The key to Inca extraction in the provinces was tapping into the two fundamental rural resources: land and labor. According to the Colonial period sources, one of the first steps the Inca took after absorbing a new territory was to reorganize the prevailing system of land tenure to suit the economic needs of the empire. The great Spanish cleric and chronicler of the Inca, Bernabé Cobo, writing in the mid-seventeenth century provides us with a thorough account of how this reorganization of productive lands was undertaken:

When the Inca settled a town, or reduced one to obedience, he set up markers in its boundaries and divided the fields and arable land within its territory into three parts . . . One part he assigned to religion and the cult of his false gods, another he took for himself, and the third he left for the common use of the people . . . In some provinces the part assigned to religion was greater; in others that belonging to the Inca; and in some regions there were entire towns which, with their territory and all that it produced, belonged to the Sun and the other gods . . . in other provinces (and this was more usual), the king's share was the largest. . . . In the lands assigned to religion and to the crown, the Inca kept overseers and administrators who took great care in supervising their cultivation, harvesting the products and putting them in the storehouses. (Cobo cited in Rowe 1946:265–6)

Cobo was fascinated by the manner of disposition of the third division of arable land that was to be allocated to the local inhabitants in the nature of commons. He remarks:

these lands were distributed each year among the subjects by the chief, [the local ethnic lord] not in equal parts, but proportionate to the number of children and relatives that each man had; and, as the family grew or decreased, its share was enlarged or restricted. No man was granted more than just enough to support him, be he noble or citizen, even though a great deal of land was left over to lie fallow. (Cobo cited in Rowe 1946:266)

This brief passage encapsulates a number of fundamental insights into the nature of ancient Andean rural society. It makes clear that productive lands were held in common by the local communities and ethnic groups. Beyond the level of individual nuclear families, these communities and ethnic groups were organized into *ayllus,* the group of related families who held land in common and traced their descent from a common ancestor. There was no concentration of arable land or pasturage in the hands of a few wealthy private owners. Individuals as heads of households only held the usufruct, or use right, to parcels of land, and the amount of land that could be exploited for the benefit of the household was not permanently fixed. The *kurakas* of the community determined on a periodic basis the subsistence needs of each household, and readjusted the size of the designated land allotment to reflect inevitable changes in the composition of these households. This system of communal disposition of productive lands reflects the age-old Andean ethic of mutual aid. No individuals are allowed to claim basic natural resources as their personal property, but at the same time members of each household retain the right of assured access to sufficient community farm or pasture lands to support themselves and their family.

The system of communal land tenure also played a significant role in maintaining an ecological equilibrium in the sometimes fragile agricultural environment of the Andean highlands. Since individuals were not permitted to acquire land as personal property, they had no opportunity to enrich themselves in the short term by continuously cultivating the greatest amount of land possible and then selling off surplus agricultural products at a profit. This built-in constraint on the potential for entrepreneurship and monopolization of natural resources by individuals ensured that the community as a whole would always have enough productive lands to guarantee its survival. Cobo's bemused observation that this system resulted in large sectors of land left in fallow underscores this equilibrating effect of traditional Andean concepts of communal property holding and decision making.

The Inca understood and respected these native notions of community autonomy and self-determination. Although when the Inca absorbed a new province they expropriated substantial tracts of land for the purposes of the state, they made certain at the same time that sufficient land was alloted for the support of the local communities. More importantly, they shrewdly chose not to usurp the traditional prerogative of the *kurakas* to decide how this land would be allocated among their members.

Elsewhere in his commentary, Cobo hits upon the true key to the tremendous productive capacity of the Inca state. After the Inca expropriated a certain portion of arable lands in newly conquered provinces for the support of the state cults and central bureaucracy, "the labor of sowing and cultivating these lands and harvesting their products formed a large part of the tribute which the taxpayer paid to the king" (Cobo cited in Rowe 1946:265). In addition to carving out lands from the conquered provinces for themselves, the Inca also exacted an annual tax from villagers and townspeople in the form of agricultural labor. The local inhabitants were required to prepare, plant, weed, and harvest the state fields. As Cobo describes, the products of these fields were then processed and stored under the watchful eyes of Inca overseers in immense state granaries.

In a world where money was not a principal feature of economic transactions, taxation took the form of labor service for the state. Although payments in kind, such as designated quantities of tropical forest bird feathers, honey, salt, dried fish, molluscs, and other raw products, were assessed by Inca administrators in some provinces, the principal form of taxation and source of revenue for the Inca state was this agricultural labor tax. This intense emphasis on discharging obligations to the state by labor service rather than by payments of currency, standardized manufactured goods, or other forms of primitive money, sharply distinguishes the Andes from other centers of early civilization such as Mesoamerica.

The agricultural labor tax was not an invention of the Inca, but an ancient feature of the Andean social landscape. Throughout the Andes, local political leaders and ethnic lords had extracted surplus labor in community owned fields from their subjects for generations before the coming of the Inca. The Inca, operating within an idiom familiar to any pre-Columbian Andean peasant in which work rather than money was the essential means of discharging economic and social debts, simply assessed additional labor obligations on the local communities.

Although Inca provincial administrators set quotas for the labor tax in each village and province and supervised the accounting of agricultural goods that flowed into the state storehouses, it was the responsibility of the local *kurakas* to make individual work assignments to the heads of household, who then distributed the task among its members: all able-bodied men, women, and children. With the onset of the highland planting season in August and September, the two classes of fields that belonged to the state, the fields reserved for the support of the state religious cults and the central bureaucracy respectively, were worked first, followed by those fields that remained for the support of the local populations. These fields were divided into long strips, or sections called *suyu* by the Inca, and each section of the field became the responsibility of an individual household, or group of related households. Cobo ([1653] 1979:212) explicty described how this system operated from the perspective of an individual household:

> These Indians divided the work they had to do by lines, and each task
> or section of work was called a suyu, and, after the division (made by
> the *kurakas*) each man put into his section his children and wives and
> all the people of his house to help him. In this way, the man who had
> the most workers finished his part, or suyu, first, and among them he
> was considered a rich man; and the poor man was he who had no one
> to help him finish his work, so he spent a longer time working.

By incorporating the local leaders into the supervision of the agricultural labor tax, the Inca reduced their own administrative costs. More importantly, they minimized their intrusion into the daily life of the provincial villages and towns, permitting them to maintain the politically valuable illusion that these communities retained local autonomy.

Apart from the agricultural tax that was assessed at the level of the community, the Inca also demanded a second form of annual labor service from taxpayers. This second obligation, called the *mit'a*, was variable in kind and length of labor service, and was an ancient and central principle of social interaction in Andean civilization. The *mit'a* was used by the Inca to provide temporary work gangs for construction of huge public monuments, for filling the ranks of the Inca army during its frequent campaigns in the provinces, for cultivating the private estates of the Inca elite, for extracting precious metals from state mines, and for many other similar services for the state requiring heavy manual labor. The scale of some *mit'a* operations was truly astonishing. Spanish chroniclers relate that over 30,000 men at a time were mobilized for the construction of Sacsahuaman, the great fortress-shrine of the Inca perched on the mountain slopes above the imperial capital of Cuzco.

The Inca *mit'a* labor tax system possessed a number of uniquely Andean features that distinguishes it from corvée, or other forms of forced labor routinely employed by empires elsewhere in the ancient world. Much like the agricultural tax, the *mit'a* system was administered principally through local officials of the various ethnic groups subject to the Inca. When a draft of men was required for a military campaign, or to construct a palace or an irrigation canal, the Inca governor in the affected province would call upon the heads of the various villages, towns, and ethnic groups who would each be obliged to supply a designated number of taxpayers to complete the task. These local officials would then be charged with selecting and organizing the work gangs according to principles specific to each village or ethnic group.

When the Inca assessed the *mit'a* labor tax, they acknowledged the reciprocal nature of the social obligation by holding large-scale ceremonial banquets in the principal administrative centers of the province. Local political leaders and commoners were feted with great quantities of maize beer and food drawn from the imperial warehouses. At times on these occasions, the Inca administrators would distribute clothing and sandals to the *mit'a* work gangs as well. Of course, if one compared the relative economic value of the labor service contributed by commoners with that of the hospitality and occasional suit of clothes contributed by the central government, there was no equivalency. The purpose and heart of the system was not to exchange work for an equivalent value in goods, however, but to symbolically reaffirm the fundamental social principle of reciprocity.

The symbolic nature of this reciprocity is brought into sharp relief by a telling ritual convention. In theory, the Inca were obliged to request *mit'a* work crews from the local *kurakas*; they could not compell them directly by fiat. Pragmatically, this convention was little more than a fiction. At any time the Inca had sufficient coercive power to force most subject communities into compliance. By engaging in this symbolic gesture of reciprocity and ritualized state generosity, the Inca elite confirmed, in at least a fictive sense, the authority and autonomy of local leaders and their communities, achieving in the process an enormous propaganda coup. Whenever possible, they chose to govern by persuasion through the local chain of command, respecting, at least in name, the basic institutions that formed the foundations of traditional Andean societies.

This system of preserving the local mandate of the native *kurakas* has been aptly termed indirect rule. Indirect rule was a fundamental principle of Inca statecraft in the imperial provinces, and reflects the remarkable shrewdness and political pragmatism of the Inca ruling elite. Cieza de León, among other Spanish commentators intrigued by Inca principles of command, described this phenomenon in his great chronicle of Peru:

> And they had another device to keep the natives from hating them, and this was that they never divested the natural chieftans of their power. If it so happened that one of them . . . in some way deserved to be stripped of his power, it was vested in his sons or brothers, and all were ordered to obey them. (Cieza de León [1553] 1959:57)

For an empire that was rapidly, almost frenetically expanding, and only in the nascent stages of generating formal principles of colonial governance, this system of indirect rule was simple to implement, relatively efficient, and the least intrusive in altering the daily rhythms and decision-making autonomy of potentially hostile local communities. Like many archaic states that relied on a tranquil, agriculturally productive population for revenue, as long as the tribute quotas were met, the Inca chose not to meddle directly in local affairs. The key to the success of indirect rule was the ability to secure the cooperation and at least overt political loyalty of the local *kurakas*. One strategy for co-opting these local lords was worked out through marriage alliances with the Inca elite which established irrevocable bonds of kinship. The ritualized exchange of daughters as marriage partners between Inca and local elite created powerful incentives for the provincial political leaders to buy into the Inca system. The network of real and fictive kinship ties engendered by these alliances provided rich opportunities to local lords for strategic manipulation of the resulting patron-client relationship.

Of course this strategy of enticing the local *kurakas* into the patronage system by holding out the promise of wealth and enhanced social prestige was effective only as long as the *kurakas* were able to deliver the labor and productive capacity of their people. The Inca realized this critical linkage and helped the local *kurakas* resolve this potential conflict through massive displays of state generosity: "and so, making the people joyful and giving their solemn banquets and drinking feasts, great taquis, and other celebrations that they use, completely different from ours, in which the Inca show their splendor, and all the feasting is at their expense" (Cieza de León [1553] 1959:57). Like the Roman policy of "bread and circuses" intended to diffuse the potentially explosive problem of a malcontent underclass through occasional distribution of free staples and the staging of massive public entertainments, the Inca practice of periodically redistributing warehoused food, drink, and clothing to the commoners during state-sponsored festivals was designed to dissipate social tensions and to incorporate commoners into the new economic and social order of the Inca world.

At the same time that the Inca were governing newly absorbed provinces through the practice of indirect rule, their statesmen were gradually fashioning more formal, centralized channels of tribute and labor recruitment based on a decimal system of administration. In this system, labor obligations were assessed on an ascending numerical series of tributary households that began with a minimal unit of 10 households (termed *chunka*) and terminated with the maximal unit of 10,000 households (*hunu*). Between these limits, there were decimal groupings for 50, 100, 500, 1,000 and 5,000 tributary households. The Inca state periodically took a census to account for fluctuations in the size and residential patterns of the empire's population. On the basis of the census figures recorded on imperial *quipu*, an ingenious mnemonic device of multi-colored, knotted cords, they adjusted membership in these decimal groupings of tributary households to reflect changing demographic realities.

Each decimal unit was headed by an official who, at the lower levels of the household groupings at least, was drawn from the local communities. Officers of the various decimal units were ranked in a formal, pyramid-like hierarchy with respect to one another. Some officials were appointed to their offices by higher ranking decimal administrators, others, however, appear to have inherited their positions. The chain of command and reporting responsibility began with the basal *chunka* leader and proceeded upward progressively to the *hunu* officials. Above the rank of the *hunu* heads of 10,000 households, administrative responsibility was vested in the hands of individuals with direct political or blood ties to the royal households of Cuzco. These were the surrogates of the emperor himself, serving as provincial governors, or as members of the imperial council which included extremely high ranking representatives from each of the four quarters of the realm.

As the Inca began to consolidate their authority in a conquered province, they gradually attempted to streamline the complicated political mosaic of multiple claims to power and traditional prerogatives asserted by local lords through imposition of the uniform decimal system of administration. Although this system had clear benefits for the Inca central government, permitting the state to operate with a relatively homogeneous form of political organization and labor recruitment in a pluralistic social landscape characterized by extreme ethnic, linguistic, and cultural divisions, the advantage to local *kurakas* was not as readily apparent. With the emergence of what was essentially an imperial class system of favored officials, those *kurakas* who were not designated as decimal officers saw many of their social prerogatives and traditional access to local labor pools begin to dissolve. The resulting social tensions generated by imposition of the decimal system were substantial, and we hear numerous stories in the chronicles of resentful "natural lords" of the provinces promulgating massive rebellions against Inca rule at every opportunity. The coercive techniques applied by the Inca state – calculated military violence, garrisoning of provinces, uprooting and resettling of populations in alien social settings, replacement of native with central authority – were effective, but costly and short-term solutions to the problem of political integration. Coercive mechanisms such as these, when applied indiscriminantly, inevitably generate disgust and hostility in volatile subject populations.

The relationships between the Inca and local populations were complex, fraught with insecurity for both state and local political authorities and subject to rapid change. In terms of the extraction of surplus labor, the Inca attempted to juggle the "soft" strategy of indirect rule with more intrusive, heavy-handed, centralized tactics such as imposition of the decimal system of reorganizing local populations, or establishment of permanent military garrisons. The strategic decision or capacity to employ one or the other of these forms of extraction depended on the individual political context. If there was a distinct preference for managing tributary relationships through indirect rule, this, most likely, was a reflection of the difficulty of maintaining strong Inca military presence throughout the widely dispersed provinces of the empire. When the Inca did employ more forceful techniques of command and involve themselves directly in developing massive agricultural reclamation projects that reshaped the physical and social environment of selected regions, this tended to occur in particularly strategic or core areas, such as in the near-Cuzco hinterland, or in the fertile, sub-tropical Cochabamba Valley in Bolivia. Like most archaic states, the Inca sought, or perhaps more accurately were compelled by exigency to strike a balance between force and persuasion, violence and consent.

We have a reasonably detailed understanding of tributary relationships between the Inca elite and subject populations as these were crystallized in the late fifteenth century. These relationships turned on the dual fulcrum of alienation of land for state agricultural production and the provision of labor framed as a reciprocal exchange of service between lords and commoners. How, then, can we apply these insights from the world of the Inca on the eve of their conquest by Spain to reconstruct patterns of tribute and the social organization of agricultural production in the more ancient state of Tiwanaku?

First, we must recognize that this question has an implied structure of space/time variability. Simply put, it is unlikely that we will empirically discover a single configuration that describes and explains the social organization of agricultural production as this was worked out once and for all by the people of Tiwanaku. The ways that arable land, labor, agricultural produce, and people were interrelated at the local level constitute a series of shifting and evanescent patterns. We cannot expect or falsely create uniformity. There never was a simple once and for all. Rather, the social, economic and ritual acts of farming were organized in multiple ways, and these forms of organization varied and changed within the textures of local history. By their nature as products of the interaction of people now long disappeared, the precise character and meaning of these organizational forms are forever lost to us. Yet, we know that certain social institutions, such as the *mit'a* forms of labor exchange, were elements of the cultural systems conjoining land, work, and agricultural production that have demonstrable antiquity and centrality in the native Andean world (Hastings and Moseley 1975). It is from these social principles that we can hope to reconstruct the basic contours of the organization of agricultural production at various periods in the long history of the people of Tiwanaku.

After a decade of intensive archaeological research on raised fields in the Lake Titicaca basin, we now know that these specialized agricultural systems have considerable time depth. The earliest securely documented raised fields were uncovered in excavations on the northern, Peruvian side of Lake Titicaca in the district of Huatta (Erickson 1988). Here raised fields associated with small habitation sites have been directly dated between 850–600 B.C. Erickson (1988: 438) speculates that this marshy, wetlands environment may have been colonized and exploited by farmers as early as 3000 B.C. This inference, although entirely plausible, has yet to be confirmed by substantive archaeological evidence. My own excavations in raised fields on the Bolivian side of the lake in various sites throughout the Pampa Koani and other areas in the Tiwanaku metropolitan district have recovered ceramics associated with the Chiripa peoples dating to the period from 800–200 B.C. (Kolata 1986). These ceramics were not found in direct association with the raised fields themselves, and therefore cannot be used definitively to date the agricultural works. Nevertheless, given the pattern of early reclamation of land for agricultural purposes on the northern side of Lake Titicaca, it is reasonable to assume that the lake-oriented Chiripa and pre-Chiripa peoples of the southern side were engaged in similar efforts to enhance their productive base through intensive raised field agriculture. How did these pioneering agriculturalists of the high plateau organize the process of constructing and maintaining raised field agriculture?

We can conjecture that the initial experimentation with raised field agriculture involved relatively small groups of related families who developed and elaborated this technology of cultivation along the marshy shores of Lake Titicaca. The maximal unit of social organization of these early farmers was the *ayllu*, based territorially in small villages and hamlets in the range of approximately ten to a few hundred people. The effective unit of production within these *ayllus* was the individual household, minimally a married couple and dependent children, as it remains today in the rural reaches of the high plateau. In other words, the agriculturalists who pioneered the raised field system in the Titicaca basin during the first millennium B.C. organized themselves as small, kin-based corporate groups. The clusters of related families were not differentiated socially beyond the level of the *ayllu* itself. These were quintessential pre-state social formations that functioned by community consensus without political positions defined by ascribed statuses or the intervention of civil bureaucracies. The social landscape of these groups did not incorporate distinctions drawn across class lines, nor was there a complex structure of political command. This is not to say, however, that the cultural universe of these kin-based corporate groups was primitive or parochial. Judging from contemporary ethnographic accounts from the *altiplano*, such rural *ayllus* enjoyed substantial communication and social exchange over considerable distance, and conceived of their interaction in terms of elaborate, cyclically expressed ritual actions grounded in a shared ideology (Bastien 1978; Abercrombie 1986).

Erickson (1988) has argued that such small corporate groups, organized along the lines of traditional Andean principles of kinship, were capable of constructing the immense configuration of raised fields in the Titicaca basin. In essence, he speculates that this agricultural system was originated by, and remained the province of, a wetlands-adapted cluster of ethnic groups that he associates with the ethnohistorically documented Uru and Pukina speaking peoples. He concludes that Andean raised field agriculture was never under the direct control of centralized state governments:

> In the Lake Titicaca Basin, the raised fields were associated with relatively small cooperative groups, while the dominant political organization in the basin was at the level of a state. It is unlikely that this highly productive system which functioned efficiently under local management would have been tampered with by the state. (Erickson 1988:348)

If we pose the question whether the enormous raised field systems of the Titicaca basin could have been constructed by relatively small corporate groups in a piece-meal fashion over long periods of time, the clear answer, drawn from the broadest cross-cultural perspective on analogous systems of hydraulic agriculture, is yes. The massive irrigated terrace systems of Sri Lanka described by Leach (1959) are a classic ethnographic example of this kind of gradual physical accretion of hydraulic works organized and constructed according to decentralized principles of local decision making. Similarly, Lansing (1991) provides a fascinating description of the organization of irrigation on rice terraces in Bali through a system of water temples. In this system, a complex hierarchy of temples controls the schedule of water distribution by managing the performance of rituals perceived to be essential to the growth cycle of the rice plant. The temple hierarchy itself begins with small family shrines erected by each farmer at the distal points of the irrigation canals where water first flows into individual plots. Farther upstream, collectivities representing clusters of families organized into small irrigation communities (*subaks*) establish communal temples at the heads of field systems. Continuing up the hierarchy, *Ulun Swi* regional temples shared by a cluster of *subaks* were erected to manage water distribution and maintenance of the hydraulic system at the heads of terraces. Virtually every water source had a corresponding temple, and all temples were subordinated to and overseen by a supreme water temple. Temple priests were responsible for performing three tasks fundamental to successful operation of any regional irrigation system: managing the allocation of water, organizing the physical maintenance of canals and terraces, and resolving conflicts among competing farmers. The priests of the water temple also were charged with authorizing new additions to the interlinked canal and terrace network. The striking features of the Balinese water temple system are its hierarchical design and its virtually complete disengagement from a strictly political form of organization. Each farmer is responsible for the maintenance of his portion of the irrigation canals up to his family's shrine. The *subak* is responsible for the maintenance of communal irrigation lines up to the *Ulun Swi* regional temple, and so on upstream in increasingly more inclusive social units to the supreme water temple. In this sense, there is no tightly centralized authority charged with construction and maintenance of the system. The inevitable conflicts over water rights were frequently resolved at lower levels of the temple hierachy than at the symbolic apex represented by the supreme water temple and its coterie of priests. Furthermore, the procedure for allocating irrigation water among the *subaks* is the end product of intensely conservative, traditional decisions made locally. Accordingly, there is rarely any need to consult the temples for guidance since most aspects of water scheduling and sharing are routinized and anticipated as predictable events in the agricultural cycle. The Balinese water temple system represents one instance in which relatively complex networks of hydraulic structures were constructed and maintained by locally autonomous social groups which reinforced community cooperation through the working out of shared beliefs expressed publicly in the repetitive performance of agricultural rituals. In the Balinese case, religious ideology performs considerable social work, obviating the need for centralized or even political forms of organization.

A variant on the theme of locally autonomous groups managing substantial irrigation systems can be adduced from an area closer to the focus of this book: the contemporary Colca Valley of south central Peru. Here Guillet (1987) describes a situation in which the management of terrace irrigation systems shifts in response to periodic crisis (droughts, principally) and the relative scarcity of water. Under conditions of adequate or abundant rainfall, water allocation remains vested in individual farmers or local farming cooperatives. In times of great scarcity, tensions rise and the potential for debilitating conflict over water rights surges dramatically. In such circumstances, water judges appointed by the state step in to adjudicate disputes and make "rational" decisions with respect to the timing and distribution of irrigation water. Routine canal and terrace maintenance is the responsibility of individual farmers. Occasional system-wide reconstruction projects are the province of the water judges who are

representatives of the state. The role of central authorities in Colca
is pragmatically restricted to managing crises that threaten the social
order and demand immediate, system-wide response. The Colca case
is instructive as a cautionary tale for those who might wish to typo-
logize the social organization of agricultural production in crystalline
terms, drawing hard, polar distinctions between authoritarian control
and local autonomy. Depending on ecological circumstance in Colca,
one form of organization takes precedence over the other: the categories oscillate and blur. Clearly in understanding agricultural systems
in traditional societies, we must always frame our account in terms
of particular spatial, temporal, and ecological frames of reference, as
well as historical circumstance.

This dialectical interplay of local autonomy and central authority
in the management of complex irrigation systems recurs in a particularly trenchant ethnohistorical example from the Chicama Valley of
Peru during the sixteenth century. According to Patricia Netherly's
(1984:230) reconstruction of social structure in prehispanic societies
on the north coast of Peru, all complex polities there

> were characterized by what may be called a dual corporate organiza-
> tion in which bounded, named, social groups at lower levels of organ-
> ization were integrated into higher levels by means of a series of ranked
> moieties, headed by personages we may term headmen, lords, or para-
> mount lords according to their hierarchical position . . . At every level
> in this organizational structure, each unit can ideally be subdivided
> into two unequal, subordinate groups.

Each layer in this social system, characterized by principles of duality
and hierarchy, was governed not by a single sovereign but by two
political rulers, one of whom maintained a higher status than the
other. This status distinction is reflected in the Spanish terms for
these two kinds of local, indigenous lords: *cacique principal* (paramount ruler) and *segunda persona* (lieutenant). Each of these pairs of
local lords could call upon the subjects of their own group to perform labor related to agricultural production, such as canal construction and periodic cleaning. Moreover, each of these lords could also
mobilize labor for tribute payments to paramount rulers of higher
status in this nested hierarchy. Netherly (1984:233) concludes that
this organizational structure was "infinitely subdivisible and could
accomodate an extremely large population without reorganization,"
accordingly, "[T]here was no need for a large body of supervising
bureaucrats to manage such labor." As in the case of the Balinese
water temples, this system maintained local autonomy and partitioned responsibility for labor among its constituent groups. Each

cluster of farmers maintained the irrigation canals that fed their own land holdings. They also contributed labor for the upkeep of essential common elements of the system, such as principal water intakes and the maximum elevation canals that provided water to the network of smaller feeder lines radiating out among the agricultural fields. Conflicts over labor obligations and water rights were resolved by the *kurakas* at the next highest political level in the hierarchy of governance. In Netherly's view, much like the contemporary situation described by Guillet in the Colca Valley, the only managerial role assumed by central state authorities was in responding to catastrophes (such as periodic torrential rainfall generated by El Niño events) that threatened to destroy the irrigation system as a whole.

It is abundantly clear that relatively small, autonomous social groups are capable of managing sophisticated systems of hydraulic agriculture without the intervention of state authority. We can conclude that local control of agricultural production embedded in an organizational structure similar (if perhaps somewhat simpler) to that proposed by Netherly for north coastal Peru represents the most plausible scenario for the context of the pioneering raised field agriculturalists of the Titicaca basin during the period from about 800 B.C. to A.D. 300. In the period after A.D. 300, however, when the mature Tiwanaku state had coalesced and begun a strategy of extraterritorial expansion, our research in the hinterland of Tiwanaku indicates that the paramount lords of the state promoted different and more centralized principles of organizing agricultural production.

Settlement patterns in the Pampa Koani region of the Tiwanaku hinterland indicate unambiguously that agricultural production in that zone at least was directed explicitly toward the generation of surplus, and not with an eye toward local consumption (Kolata 1986). We have located fewer than 80 small habitation mounds dispersed among the field systems of the central Pampa Koani region. Based on this sample size, I estimate that throughout the entire 75 square kilometer Koani zone, there were no more than 1,000 house mounds dating to the Tiwanaku III through Tiwanaku V phases. These structures cannot account for more than a few thousand inhabitants. Moreover, the bulk of these mounds do not appear to have been occupied permanently. The best functional interpretation of these structures is that they were seasonally occupied shelters for *kamani*, or guardians of agricultural fields who are charged with discouraging depredation of maturing crops by humans and animals.

An important, centrally located cluster of massive platform mounds clearly served administrative and ritual functions for the region (Figure 6.10). The mounds in this cluster did not develop by gradual

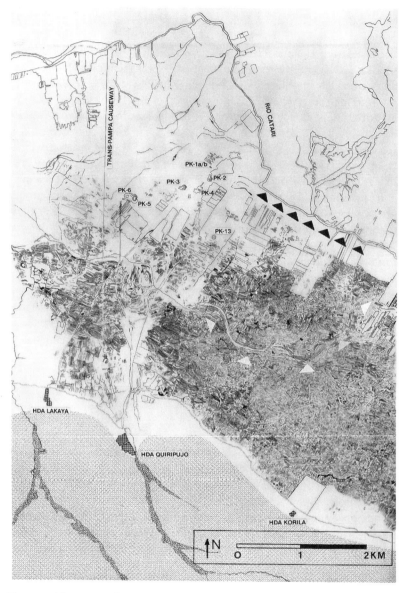

Figure 6.10   Map of Tiwanaku administrative and ritual platform mound
clusters on the Pampa Koani.

accretion of domestic residences built one atop the other, but rather through purposeful cutting and filling operations. Each of these platform mounds exhibit a measure of careful architectural treatment. Floors found intact were constructed of dense, packed clay that was, at times, coated with a layer of bone-white plaster. Adobe bricks recovered from the debris frequently possessed a thin exterior coat of stucco to which vibrant cobalt blue, blue-green, yellow, and orange pigments adhered. The largest structure in this cluster of platform mounds (PK-5) was furnished with a formal entrance, one element of which was recovered in our explorations: a plain, roughly cut rectangular stone pillar. This pillar was the fragmentary remains of a lintel that defined a gateway giving access to the summit of the mound. The summit of PK-5, itself, was spatially organized around a sunken rectangular court with an elevated platform attached to the northern end. Unlike the other platform mounds, PK-5 was not a single isolated structure. It, along with PK-6, forms part of an architectural ensemble I refer to as the dual platform-mound complex. This complex is distinguished by the disproportionate size of the two monuments, and by the unusual degree of formal design elements that characterize their construction and use. In the hierarchy of human settlements in the Koani agricultural zone, these two structures were of paramount ritual and administrative importance, subordinate only to the regional population centers of Lukurmata and Pajchiri.

Apparent status, or class stratification during Tiwanaku IV–V times is substantiated by a sharp dichotomy in residential patterns, in architectural treatment of functionally distinct structures, and in material culture. The smaller habitation mounds tested to date show little evidence of internal structure, and consist primarily of low platforms of packed earth, rather than the more elaborate adobe walls and plastered floors of the large platform mounds. The two classes of mound structures share similar kinds of faunal remains indicative of a wide-spread consumption of fish, and, to a lesser extent, llama meat. Substantial quantities of fish bones and scales were recovered from every mound tested, while relatively smaller numbers of disarticulated and frequently charred llama bones were extracted from hearths, most often within the large platform mounds.

In other regards, the material culture of the small house mounds associated with field segments versus that of the large platform mounds is palpably distinct. The house mounds contained only course, reddish-brown or black utilitarian ceramics consisting predominantly of simple bowls, basins, and jars. The kinds of simple vessels one might anticipate for facilitating ordinary household food preparation and serving needs. The large platform mounds, on the other hand, yielded substantial quantities of both domestic wares and the superb, polychrome ceramics emblematic of the Tiwanaku IV style. The exquisite, highly burnished, and carefully painted pottery from the Pampa Koani platform mounds is indistinguishable from superior vessels excavated at Tiwanaku itself, and displays all of the characteristic vessel forms of the finest quality Tiwanaku wares: *keros*, modeled, puma-headed *incensarios*, bowls, and jars. This structured distribution of utilitarian versus high-quality ceramic wares presents a strong argument for drawing both status and functional distinctions concerning the kinds of activities that were carried out on these two classes of mounds. Such distinctions are further enhanced by the distribution of metal artifacts: whole rectangular copper plaques, copper pins, and fragments of silver were recovered exclusively from the platform mounds. Most often these metal objects were found in association with seated, flexed human burials accompanied by other luxury items such as turquoise or sodalite beads and highly polished ceramics. Slag found on the surface of two platform mounds (PK-2 and PK-3) suggest that these structures were the focus of some kind of small-scale metal working industry.

The patterns that emerge from the distinctive nature, distribution and elaboration of sites and their associated artifacts suggest the following interpretation of settlement function and hierarchy on the Pampa Koani. The small house mounds physically associated or structurally merged with raised field segments were the residences of rural families engaged in primary agricultural production. A more ephemeral or rather seasonal function for some of the smaller house mounds, such as the base of huts used by *kamani* for guarding crops, is probable. The large platform mounds, on the other hand, housed a corps of administrators and their household retainers charged with organizing the seasonal cycle of agricultural activities, and accounting for the produce that flowed from the state fields of Pampa Koani during harvest time. The monumental dual platform-mound complex represents the ritual and administrative apex of settlement hierarchy on the Pampa Koani, distinguished in status from both the small habitation mounds and the other, less architecturally elaborated platform mounds (Figure 6.11). The entire settlement configuration of the Pampa Koani during Tiwanaku IV–V times revolved around the requirements of intensive agricultural production, and reflects the truly vital purpose of human activity on that plain: the construction and maintenance of a stable agricultural landscape.

The distribution and function of these settlements in the Pampa Koani region implies that the labor to construct and maintain the extensive field systems must have been drawn from a wide, non-local

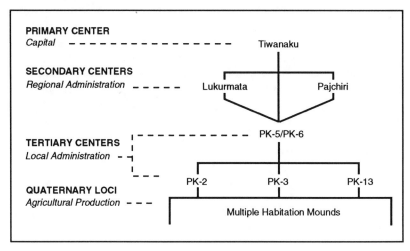

Figure 6.11   Graphic representation of Tiwanaku's hierarchical settlement network in the Pampa Koani region during Tiwanaku IV–V times.

region in a pattern attuned to the agricultural cycle of the seasons. This labor was most likely extracted by the centralized authorities of the Tiwanaku state in the form of corveé through a mechanism similar to the Inca *mit'a* tax system. The presence of massive public construction projects on the Koani plain that were designed to promote the large-scale reclamation and productivity of arable land points ineluctably to a managerial hand beyond that of locally autonomous village or *ayllu* groupings.

Figure 6.8 (see p. 191) illustrates two kinds of public construction projects on the Koani plain that served functions related to the operation of the raised fields, not as bounded, independent bundles of field plots, but as an interdependent regional system of production. The first of these public constructions is a network of elevated causeways and dikes. The principal route of the largest elevated roadbed, the trans-pampa causeway, together with its major branch, connected the marshy, low-lying zone of raised fields in the western end of Pampa Koani with roads running along mountain terraces forming the northern and southern boundaries of the pampa respectively. These contour roads running along the base of the mountain slopes lead directly to the important regional Tiwanaku urban settlements of Lukurmata and Pajchiri, as well as to the smaller towns of Yayes and Lakaya. The trans-pampa causeway itself was walled and possibly paved with cut stone in its southern extremity as it approached Lakaya.

Several smaller elevated roadbeds radiate out laterally from the trans-pampa causeway to connect field segments with the larger platform mounds in the central ritual and administrative cluster. The formal causeways on the Pampa Koani were designed to facilitate travel and transport of agricultural goods from the production zone to consuming and processing centers of population. Transport of bulk produce along the causeway and road network was facilitated by organized pack-trains of llamas.

The north-south trending trans-pampa causeway may have served another function besides that of transport. The elevated bed of this causeway runs astride the maximum elevation contour in the western end of the Pampa Koani. To the west of the causeway, the land slopes upward gradually from the shores of Lake Titicaca to this maximum elevation (3,824 masl). East of the causeway, the land slopes gently downward such that eleven kilometers inland from the shore, absolute elevation is only 3,820 masl. During the catastrophic flood caused by unusually sustained, torrential downpours that affected the Andean *altiplano* between September 1985 and April 1986, this ancient causeway acted as an effective dike, impounding the rising waters of Lake Titicaca for a time. Once the lake had risen over 2.75 meters, however, the entire stretch of the *pampa* to the east of the causeway was rapidly inundated with brackish waters to a depth of nearly 1 meter, destroying houses, pastures, and potato fields. When the flood waters finally receded by late 1988, glistening, damaging salt deposits that still depress local crop yields were left behind in thick, patchy crusts. Tiwanaku engineers may well have been aware of this natural elevation feature and sited the trans-pampa causeway along it to enhance the capacity of this feature to impound water. The causeway/dike may have been a disaster control device that prevented destruction of the raised fields in the eastern reaches of the Koani plain during years of normal rainfall.

The second regional construction project illustrated in Figure 6.8 represents a definite hydraulic control device. At some point in the history of land reclamation on the Koani plain, a long segment of the Río Catari, the principal river bisecting the pampa, was artificially canalized. The canalization of the river was achieved by diverting the natural course of the flow at a point approximately 12 kilometers inland from the lake shore into a new bed furnished with massive levees of earth, clay, and, in certain sections, cut stone. This diversion and "domestication" of the natural river achieved two important goals for the efficient operation of a regional agricultural system. First, it opened up huge stretches of land to raised field reclamation in the southern portions of Pampa Koani, and second, it permitted some

6.12   The remains of a massive earthen levee along the Río Catari. This levee is part of a canal by-pass system designed to stabilize and redirect substantial quantities of seasonal river flow, especially during periods of excessive flooding. (From Kolata 1991: Figure 5).

measure of human control over potentially disastrous river inundations of the reclaimed landscape. However, the hydraulic engineers of Tiwanaku were apparently unsatisfied with a simple diversion and canalization of the Río Catari. Excessive rainy season flow can result rapidly in bed erosion, river excursions, and potentially disastrous flooding of adjacent land. In order to augment its capacity to handle periodic flooding, Tiwanaku hydraulic engineers constructed a canal bypass system paralleling the banks of the canalized sections of the Río Catari to shunt excess flow away from critical reclaimed lands toward Lake Titicaca. The southern bank of the canal bypass (the side facing the bulk of the raised fields in the Pampa Koani region) was reinforced by a massive levee (Figure 6.12). This river shunt effectively extracted substantial quantities of seasonal flow and redirected that flow away from areas critical to agriculture.

The artificial canalization of the Río Catari is not unique in the annals of Tiwanaku hydraulic engineering. Stream canalization and river shunts were a distinct and audacious strategy of water control common to the rural and urban landscapes of Tiwanaku society. A virtually identical shunt system was identified as a crucial feature of

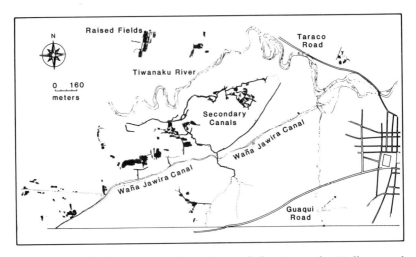

6.13 *Map of the investigated portions of the Tiwanaku Valley canal, illustrating intake near the current bed of the Río Tiwanaku and articulations with secondary irrigation canals (indicated by solid lines) and raised fields. (From Kolata 1991: Figure 7).*

the recently recognized canal that bisects the middle and lower Tiwanaku Valley (Figure 6.13). In this case, the artificial canal serves as a shunt for excess flow in the Río Tiwanaku in addition to irrigating downstream raised field complexes. As in the Río Catari system, this canal has substantial, reinforced earthen levees to stabilize extracted river flow. The Tiwanaku Valley canal illustrates a sophisticated principle of Tiwanaku regional hydraulic engineering: designed multifunctionality. The canal, together with its shunt system, was capable of implementing either a water distribution or a water extraction strategy. In the dry season, or in times of drought, the canal was capable of carrying river water from its intake on the Río Tiwanaku to secondary canals downstream for distribution to adjacent raised field complexes. During the rainy season, or during a flooding episode, the intakes of the secondary distribution canals were blocked with sluice gates and excess river flow was extracted and redirected away from the downstream agricultural landscape. In the case of the Tiwanaku Valley system, the principal canal rejoins the river at a point some 4 kilometers downstream from its intake. The enormous canal of the middle and lower Tiwanaku Valley speaks volumes regarding the organizational and design skills of the Tiwanaku elite to reshape their natural environment.

Figure 6.14   Cobblestone exterior retaining wall from an aqueduct at Lukurmata.

Designed multifunctionality of hydraulic structures integrated into a regional regime of water control was clearly a key principle in the organization of Tiwanaku agricultural production, and not an aberrant or unique occurrence. Recent investigations at the Tiwanaku regional capitals of Lukurmata and Pajchiri resulted in discovery and detailed analysis of aqueducts that possess this special attribute. Six aqueducts were discovered at these two sites, and one of these was radiocarbon dated to A.D. 950 +/– 100, or the Tiwanaku V phase (Ortloff and Kolata 1989). There are several more univestigated aqueducts channeling water into and away from raised field systems dated to the Tiwanaku IV and V phases throughout the Pampa Koani zone. The entire drainage systems of which these aqueducts were key components entailed construction, or modification, of two components: (1) an upper channel formed by an artificially modified, natural *quebrada*, or dry stream bed, and (2) a lower channel that consists of a constructed, elevated aqueduct that conducted water over an open field for eventual discharge into Lake Titicaca (Figure 6.14). The external retaining walls of the aqueducts are cobble-lined throughout their entire length, providing an outermost stable skin infilled with earth, gravel, and stone. The uppermost modified channels of these aqueducts reach into high montane basins where they were charged by precipitation runoff and by permanent springs and subterranean seeps. One of the aqueducts at Pajchiri, which crosses a sector of raised fields constructed on a series of massive terraces, was furnished with well-elaborated, cut-stone drop structures and secondary feeder canals (Figure 6.15). Such drop structures may have been incorporated into some aqueducts to mitigate the effects of periodic droughts that afflict the Andean *altiplano*. Fresh water from the montane basins frequently flows continuously (if at a reduced rate) even during the most pernicious drought, and these precious sources of perennial water were clearly jealously guarded and improved by the people of Tiwanaku through elaboration of efficient distribution networks.

In the volatile environment of the Andean high plateau, agricultural disaster lurks in many disguises, and one of these, as potentially catastrophic as drought, is torrential rainfall and flooding (the 1985–6 occurrence being the most recent). Inundation can have an exceptionally long-term impact by generating high groundwater conditions and supersaturation of soils that are deleterious to crop growth. Most of the aqueducts that we have excavated did not possess drop structures and were not articulated with secondary feeder canals. These hydraulic structures supported continuously functioning drainage canals that were designed to remove excess water from areas of field reclamation, and thereby reduce the incidence of dangerously high groundwater conditions. By diverting excess water from the raised fields, such structures may have helped stabilize the water table at a point below that of the critical zone of crop root development. In other words, the aqueducts of Pajchiri and Lukurmata, like the river shunt systems, were technologically sophisticated hydraulic structures responsive to the severe inundation-drought cycles that are characteristic of the *altiplano*.

These river canalizations, *quebrada* modifications, aqueducts, dikes, and causeways functionally integrated the agricultural landscape of the Pampa Koani zone into a regional system of production. Agricultural production on the Pampa Koani, to some degree, may have served the needs of local consumption. But the enormous capital investment in reclamation of arable land and in alteration and control of the hydrological regime directly implies the action of a regional political authority. Although the initial, pioneering construction of raised field plots was most likely the product of an autonomous, uncentralized social order, the subsequent reshaping of the Koani plain into a regional system of agricultural production under the hegemony of Tiwanaku elite in the period from A.D. 400 to 900 entailed the periodic mobilization and coordination of a substantial non-resident labor force. The logistic requirements of repeatedly

Figure 6.15 One of the aqueducts at Pajchiri, constructed of cut-stone blocks, which formed part of a complex drainage system designed to conduct water over open fields for eventual discharge into Lake Titicaca.

organizing the deployment of a concentrated, non-local labor force demanded a political order with powerful regional authority to alienate land and co-opt labor, and at least a rudimentary bureaucratic system to track the extraction of labor service from subject communities and the subsequent flow of produce from state operated fields.

My interpretation of the organizational framework of production in the Koani zone implies that Tiwanaku established proprietary agricultural estates in which ownership and usufruct rights were vested directly in state institutions, or perhaps more precisely in the hands of the elite classes. These corporate estates or production zones were bound directly to the capital of Tiwanaku through a network of secondary urban centers with administrative functions. Dispersed, rural hamlets and individual households occur in the Tiwanaku area outside the zone of optimal lake-side agricultural soils. These settlements were probably engaged in small-scale subsistence dry farming and herding of llama and alpaca, and, along with the commoner populations of the larger cities, provided corvée labor for the state fields.

By about A.D. 500, we can best understand the Tiwanaku hinterland as a constructed landscape of state production. The labor invested in shaping that landscape was drawn from taxation of both local and non-local groups headed by political leaders who acted as intermediaries and surrogates for the Tiwanaku political elite. But the autonomy of these local *kurakas* must have been constrained by the needs and prerogatives of the more highly ranked non-local elite who resided in the network of urban centers in the greater Tiwanaku metropolitan zone.

If we recall Inca state strategies of agricultural production and tribute extraction vis-à-vis local communities, we see a context-specific mix of indirect rule that did not impinge on local autonomy counterposed with authoritarian expropriation of land and labor that abrogated the political will and self-determination of local communities, particularly in strategic production zones. Investment in landscape capital (terrace and irrigation systems, aqueducts, and dikes) that served the purpose of expanding or stabilizing regional agricultural production goes hand in glove with this latter strategy of direct state intervention. The paramount elite of Tiwanaku operated with similar fluid, context-specific strategies of economic development. The group or perhaps class interests of this elite demanded the creation of strategic, directly controlled production zones that ensured long-term stability in access to surplus crops and commodities. This economic surplus, of course, was the foundation of their political power. It furnished them with the means to sustain personal and group prestige through dramatic public expressions of generosity and abundance during the cyclical calendar of agricultural festivals and ritual events. The opulent lifestyle permitted to them by this surplus product was a kind of essential social theater that publicly ratified their personal and positional status within Tiwanaku society.

At the same time that social and ideological necessity demanded that Tiwanaku elite carve out corporate estates to ensure a direct supply of surplus agricultural production, political reality dictated that their relationships with most local communities and ethnic groups under their, at times, uncertain dominion follow the path of least resistance. In most instances, coercion of local populations and mass alienation of land and labor was not a viable political option for the Tiwanaku elite. The political and logistical costs entailed in dominating a huge, diverse physical territory were too great to sustain, and local resistance to the complete encroachment of an authoritarian regime was too much of a present threat to the social order to justify a posture of unalloyed hostility. Instead, the Tiwanaku elite, much like their Inca counterparts some 700 years later, struck a balance between force and persuasion. They established with ruthless efficiency key proprietary estates of production that assured them of a stable fund of product that could be invested in sustaining the social roles demanded of them. At the same time, outside of these core areas of directly controlled production, where necessary, discretion was the better part of valor, and they moved by indirection and subtle attention to the local political context. In the latter circumstance, tributary relationships between the cosmopolitan elite of Tiwanaku and their distant rural counterparts were most likely framed in terms of patron-client exchanges. Such clientage relationships, in which the state confirmed the traditional authority of local *kurakas* in dealing with their own communities, were strategic elements of Inca statecraft, reflecting the remarkable shrewdness and political pragmatism of native Andean elite.

Herders and Fishers

If intensive agricultural production was in part vested in the hands of the ruling elite, what can be said of the two other economic touchstones of Tiwanaku society: fishing and herding? To what extent did these two activities fall under the purview of central authorities in Tiwanaku's urban centers? Or were these distinct lifeways and economic pursuits the realm of individual, familial, or ethnic entrepreneurs? How did the products of these two modes of non-agricultural production find their way to the metropolitan centers of the people of Tiwanaku?

The relationship between humans and camelids in the Andean high plateau was ancient and pervasive, a peculiarly intense form of symbiosis. The economic uses of the llama and alpaca speak only superficially to the complementary social and ritual roles that these animals played in the minds of the people of Tiwanaku. The llama was a source of food and tools, clothing and transport. It was an avatar of the supernatural, an animate creature both sacred and profane. Llama sacrifices marked critical episodes of the human life cycle, and punctuated and defined temporal transitions in Tiwanaku's sidereal-lunar agricultural calendar. Llama husbandry, rituals of llama sacrifice, and agricultural fertility were intimately associated with this calendrical system, reflecting social, symbolic and ecological relationships between pastoralism and agriculture in the high plateau. The social and physical ecologies of agriculture and pastoralism, although in and of themselves potentially antagonistic, were made to mesh by formulation of the ritual calendar: the rhythms of rite, crop, and herd were brought into productive synchrony.

But who were the herders in Tiwanaku society? Who owned, or perhaps more aptly phrased, possessed and managed the herds? It is likely that in the gradual process of human domestication of the llama and alpaca in the Titicaca basin, beginning perhaps as early as the seventh millennium B.C., the principal herding groups were semi-sedentary bands that practiced a mixed economy of tuber agriculture and pastoralism. Animals were possessed and managed by family groups. Adolescent children were frequently charged with guarding herds in the high *puna* pastures. Grazing rights to specific pastures and access to breeding stock was maintained within the autonomous nuclear family, or in the lineage cluster that formed the *ayllu*. The population size of these early family and *ayllu* herds were probably maintained at a sufficiently moderate level to enable periodic regeneration of the natural fodder in available pastures. Browman (1981:408–9) suggests that these early herding societies were oriented toward "carnivorous pastoralism," breeding animals primarily for their meat and the marrow content of their bones. Over time, he envisions a transition toward more industrial use of the animals as sources of wool and long-distance transportation of bulky commodities among consumers. Interestingly, Browman (1981:409) derives certain social and moral implications for native high plateau societies embedded in this proposed transition:

> In hunting societies, and to a lesser extent in carnivorous pastoralism, the highest value is on sharing the kill. Men are motivated to produce by an ideal of generosity, and status is achieved through the prestige

associated with generosity. In carnivorous pastoralism, the emphasis is basically on ownership of the dead animals. By contrast, when wool and transport become paramount, the emphasis is on the live animals. Status and wealth are now based on the number of transport animals an individual owns, the amount of wool produced, and the number of animals that can be loaned or given. An earlier ideal of generosity is replaced, one might argue, by an ideal of parsimony. To gain social and political status, an individual must control a large number of animals.

Browman's suggested transition also implies distinct strategies of herd management. Under a regime of carnivorous pastoralism, emphasis was placed on "maximizing sustained yields and thus implicitly limiting herd size"; in contrast, pastoralism focused on wool production and transport demands maximizing herd size and "implicitly limiting caloric yields, since direct consumption of the animals in effect entails the destruction of wealth" (Browman 1981:409). Browman speculates that this shift in the use and management of camelid herds occurred sometime before the first millennium B.C., and that therefore the people of Tiwanaku bred and maintained llama and alpaca herds explicitly for use as wool producers and pack animals. This is entirely consistent with his view that Tiwanaku economy relied principally on long-distance movement of commodities mobilized through llama caravan trade.

Although there is a certain internal logic to such a postulated transformation in cultural use of camelid herds, archaeological data from our recent excavations at Tiwanaku and its affiliated settlements does not support the proposition. In every area of domestic residences excavated to date, we have encountered enormous quantities of disarticulated, burned, cracked, and cut llama bones. Frequently, these bones, split longitudinally for extraction of marrow and for tool production, are found in abandoned hearths, or discarded in huge, ashy refuse pits. Many bones show clear evidence of butchering by stone knives and cleavers. Butchered and cooked llama bones are found associated with residences pertaining to the entire spectrum of Tiwanaku social hierarchy: from the elaborate palatial complexes in the city's center to the adobe huts of the poorer quarters on the site peripheries. Tiwanaku society was extravagant, even profligate in its exploitation of llamas and alpacas. This empirical evidence that llama meat and marrow was consumed avidly and in substantial quantities by all social classes in Tiwanaku society indicates that "carnivorous pastoralism" was not simply a more ancient evolutionary phase in the relationship between humans and camelids. Llamas remained squarely on the menu in Tiwanaku times.

The tremendous supply of llamas available for butchering and consumption in Tiwanaku's urban centers forces us to draw several provocative conclusions with respect to the role and likely organization of herding in Tiwanaku society. The people of Tiwanaku clearly placed a cultural value on maximizing herd size to accommodate the constant demand for meat from concentrated urban populations, to maintain sufficient numbers of animals for the caravan trade, and perhaps more importantly, to provide adequate supplies of raw wool for the textile industry. Satisfaction of this triple demand required not so much the parsimonious ethic of herding envisioned by Browman, but rather well-articulated and enforceable rules and social codes that governed human management of the reproduction and disposition of camelid herds. The huge economic demand for llama and alpaca products and services could not be met reliably by autonomous herding *ayllus* alone. The state of Tiwanaku had an enormous stake in assuring the reproductive success of llamas and alpacas: the elite could not afford to assume a *laissez faire* posture concerning herd management.

But what precisely were these rules, social codes, and techniques of herd management? I cannot offer a definitive answer. But by employing analogy from ethnohistoric descriptions of the treatment of llama herds in the Inca state, we can at least suggest some intriguing possibilities. Bernabé Cobo's ([1653] 1979:215–6) extended account of herd management under the Inca offers some key insights:

> The Inca had the same division made of all the domesticated livestock [llama and alpaca], assigning one part to religion, another to himself, and another to the community; and not only did he divide and separate each one of these parts, but he did the same with the grazing land and pastures in which the livestock was pastured, so that the herds were in different pastures and could not be mixed. The Inca divided these pastures and had them marked in each province. The pastures of religion and the Inca were called *moyas* . . . and it was unlawful to put the livestock of religion in the *moyas* of the Inca, nor could the opposite be done, for each herd or flock had its own specified district. The borders between provinces were also divided; the pasture lands of different provinces were not common even for the livestock of the same owner. For example, there were pastures in the province of Chucuito where the Inca's livestock were raised in that province; and the animals that the Inca himself had in the bordering province of Pacajes could not cross over there to graze. In keeping these animals, great care was taken to assign herdsmen and foremen to count the increase in the flocks and animals that died; and in contributing the people necessary for this purpose, the towns paid a considerable amount

of their tribute. The part of the livestock that belonged to the common people was much smaller than either of the other two parts, as can be noticed by the names that were given to each one. The herds belonging to religion and to the Inca were named *capac llama*, and the herds owned by either the community or privately were named *huacchac llama*, which means "rich herds" and "poor herds." Moreover the king took animals from the part belonging to the community; these were given to caciques and persons who served him as a favor to them; the king also ordered that the residents be alloted the number of animals that they needed. None of the animals that the king gave as a favor to develop and start herds could be divided or transferred, any more than the lands; thus, the heirs of the first owner possessed his herds in common. This domesticated livestock of llamas was one of the greatest riches that the Indians had. In order to conserve it so that it would always be on the increase, the Inca had ordered two very important things. First, any animal that got *caracha* (a certain illness like mange or scab which these animals often catch, and many die of it) was to be immediately buried alive and very deep, and no one was to try to cure the sick animal or kill it for food, and this was done in order to prevent the disease from spreading, for it is extremely contagious; second, the females were not to be killed for sacrifices or for any other reason. Owing to these measures, the vast number of these animals in their kingdom was incredible.

This passage elegantly conveys the Inca elite's obsession with the reproductive success and health of their llama herds. It also explicitly describes some of the mechanisms and sociology of herd management. Much like the principles of land tenure and production on agricultural fields, the Inca divided the llama and alpaca herds into three broad categories of possession, control, and use: state, religion, and local community herds. These three principal categories of herds were rigidly segregated spatially as an accounting technique to keep track of the animals and their annual fluctuations in population, and, most likely, as a reaction to localized scarcity of good pastureland as well. Cobo recounts that much of the tribute obligations of subject towns was discharged by providing herdsmen for the state's elite and religious cults. In fine indigenous Andean fashion, the Inca reciprocated the tributary labor provided by subject towns by periodically redistributing llamas to local *kurakas* and their communities.

We cannot be certain that the same well-elaborated set of managerial techniques and behavioral codes concerning camelids described by Cobo for the Inca were employed by the elite of Tiwanaku. Nevertheless, given the enormous numbers of animals that were consumed and used for ritual and industrial purposes by the people of Tiwanaku, it is certain that the state of Tiwanaku possessed specific pasture

Figure 6.16 Herd of llamas grazing near the shore of Lake Titicaca. (Photograph by Nicole Couture).

lands for maintaining herds. I believe that the modern Bolivian province of Pacajes was one of the principal local zones of dedicated pasture lands maintained by the people of Tiwanaku (Figure 6.16). Even today, this area contains the highest concentration of llamas in the near-shore regions fringing Lake Titicaca. Vast, seemingly desolate landscapes of dissected plains extend far to the southwest from Pacajes skirting the modern frontier between Bolivia and Chile. This high, seasonally dry plateau is a natural habitat for the camelids, and was clearly one of the principal source areas for breeding and replenishment of camelid stock. We can infer that the care of Tiwanaku state herds was the responsibility of subject populations living in proximity to these dedicated pastures. It is likely that the state of Tiwanaku, like the Inca, assessed a labor tax on herding communities that constituted a substantial proportion of their tribute obligations. The huge demand for llamas in Tiwanaku urban centers required concentrated herds that, in turn, necessitated labor intensive forms of organization characterized by occupational specialization. In other words, provisioning Tiwanaku and its metropolitan district with llamas was the province of specialized herding communities bound in a symbiotic economic and ideological relationship with the elite of Tiwanaku. We can extend this analysis with a somewhat less certain speculation:

these specialized herding communities were ethnically and linguistically proto-Aymara.

It is likely, then, that the exploitation of llamas and alpacas by the people of Tiwanaku was context specific, occurring in both centralized and decentralized forms. The structural form of the organization of camelid production depended, to a great extent, on association with either the rural or cosmopolitan realities of Tiwanaku society. That is, the huge supply of camelid products and services necessary to accommodate the demands of Tiwanaku's cities required well-orchestrated techniques of herd management. In the context of Tiwanaku urban society, llama, alpaca, and their requisite pasture lands were key natural resources upon which the ruling elite exerted substantial, centralized control, much as the Inca were to do several centuries later. Yet, away from the dense nucleus of lake edge cities, in the remote rural reaches of the empire, the relationship between human and camelid populations, although no less intense, was structured more loosely. In the rural contexts of Tiwanaku society, where the bulk of the population resided, this relationship flowed not from the inflated, artificial demands generated by urban demand, but from the natural rhythms established by the seasonal cycle of the agro-pastoral lifestyle. Each hamlet and small village dispersed across the face of the great southern high plateaus maintained their own llama and alpaca herds. The population size of the herds tethered to these small communities was regulated by the local availability of good pasture lands. Here the extent to which herd size was manipulated was more the product of local, internal community needs and choices.

If there were multiple organizational forms in the sociology and economy of herding that describe a complex response to the demands of rural versus urban milieux, can we identify similar context-specific forms of organization in the specialized fishing economy? The short answer is most likely no. Aquatic foraging and fishing was an ancient and extremely productive mode of food production in the Lake Titicaca basin. Perhaps the earliest experimenters with raised field agriculture were initially oriented heavily toward exploiting the rich biomass of the lake. Although there may have been instances in which these lake dwellers engaged in fish farming in the canals between raised fields, most fishing activities on the lake entailed harvesting of a wild resource, the population characteristics of which were not substantially affected by human activities or purposive management. Today most fishing on the great lake is the product of individual or family initiatives, and, in most circumstances, it is a part-time occupation of the household to supplement income and diversify the family diet.

Before the European conquest of the Andes, however, Lake Titicaca supported substantial populations of specialized, aquatic foragers and fishers. Ethnohistoric accounts from the sixteenth and seventeenth centuries concerning the lake district indicate that substantial populations of the Uru ethnic and linguistic group traditionally, if not exclusively, earned their daily subsistence by intensive aquatic foraging. I have inferred from archaeological evidence that Uru, or Uru-affiliated groups lived in similar fashion during the Tiwanaku hegemony.

As Wachtel (1986) points out, during the early Colonial period the Uru were not exclusively dedicated to aquatic foraging. They frequently served as agricultural hands on the lands of the Aymara and, in return, planted some of their own plots of potato and *quinoa*. Certain "rich" Uru owned their own agricultural lands and camelid herds. But the mixed economy of foraging, agriculture, and some herding engaged in by Colonial-era Uru may very well have been a late adaptation to a changing social and historical reality that was characterized by massive demographic collapse of the indigenous populations. With the destruction of the old social networks of complementarity between populations oriented to and specialized in the terrestrial and aquatic realms, the remnant Uru during this time were forced into a more generalized pattern of subsistence. To survive they expanded into other ecological settings and adopted other modes of production. In many respects the Uru of the Colonial period were already substantially transformed, undergoing a process of Aymarization, engaged in inexorable movement toward loss of ethnic identity.

We get a sense from these ethnohistoric documents, from historical linguistics, and from the little archaeology of the Uru done to date, that the ancient economic orientation of the Uru was toward the lake and its tributaries. In the prehispanic past, the Uru were distributed along an 800 kilometer aquatic axis of the high plateau from Lake Azángaro in the north to Lake Titicaca, down the Desaguadero River to the great saline lakes of Poopó and Coipasa in the south (see Figure 3.3, p. 44). The Uru populations fished and gathered the wild resources of this lacustrine and riverine world as a full-time occupation. They exchanged fresh and dried fish, edible algae, water fowl and eggs, totora reed, and other lake products for the agro-pastoral goods such as llama wool, potatoes, and *quinoa*, of their more terrestrially oriented neighbors.

Working with census data from the general inspection ordered by the Spanish Viceroy Francisco de Toledo between 1573–1575, Nathan Wachtel (1986:285) projected that approximately 80,000 Uru lived along this aquatic axis in the late sixteenth century, representing approximately 24 percent of the indigenous population. Today this population is drastically reduced. Remnant families of Uru still live around Lake Titicaca and along the Desaguadero River, although their numbers continue to dwindle and their language is rapidly moving toward extinction. In the contemporary Bolivian nation state, the Uru are a minority embedded in the larger, more powerful native world of their Aymara neighbors. In many respects, the Uru are doubly dispossessed, regarded as primitive curiosities by the urbanized populations of Bolivia, and lacking the nationally influential native political organization of their far more numerous Aymara counterparts. They persist in a reality that becomes increasing marginal to the modern world, a twilight existence tinged with a curious penumbra of the past.

The Uru's name for themselves is Kot'suñs, or "people of the lake" clearly reflective of their special identification with the aquatic environment. This linguistic marker essentially sets the Uru apart self-consciously from those they conceptually refer to as the "dry people" (Wachtel 1986:284). They consider themselves to inhabit a separate reality: the aqueous realm, physically and symbolically distinct from the telluric, earth dependent setting of the agrarian lifestyle. Again we find embedded in the mind of the indigenous Andean peoples a reflexive mapping of the social universe onto, or perhaps more precisely into the deep contours, or contrast points of the physical universe: in this case, the sharp, sensually apparent opposition between the terrestrial and the aquatic, the dry and the wet.

Colonial period documents also tell us something else important about the social landscape inhabited by the Uru. In the famous 1567 Garci Diez *visita* to the province of Chucuito, the two principal lords of the ancient Lupaqa Kingdom, Qari and Qusi, describe their traditional world as pluriethnic, and one in which the Aymara were the "better people ... those more notable," in contradistinction to the Uru who "are the poor folk, who do not cultivate and live only by fishing and roaming about the lake" (cited in Wachtel 1986:285). Here we catch glimpses of an ancient system of class and political stratification in which the Aymara are portrayed as noble overlords to the poorer, less prestigious Uru. We can reconstruct the contours of a caste-like social order drawn along lines of ethnic-linguistic-occupational stratification. In this stratified system, the Uru occupied the lowest tier, associated symbolically with the treacherous watery world they inhabited: nomadic, barbaric, unconstrained by the norms and social conventions of native civilization. If the Uru were in some respects outside of culture and thereby relegated to low status and political dependency on their Aymara overlords, they nevertheless successfully, perhaps even aggressively maintained their social identity.

Importantly for this analysis of Tiwanaku's political economy, the Uru technology of production was non-complex and available to all members of the group. Simple watercraft, nets, hooks, snares, and atlatls, or dart throwers, were all that was necessary to fish and forage successfully on the lakes and rivers of the high plateau. Unlike herding and agriculture which depended on specific management techniques, scheduling of activities, and localized distribution of good pasture lands or potentially arable soils, the fishers and aquatic foragers responded to the natural population cycles of the wild resources they harvested. They could not domesticate or maximize the population size of the animals on which they depended as could herders, nor could they artificially intensify food production as could agriculturalists. Unlike the agro-pastoral complex, the Uru foraging economy was not linked to fixed, landscape capital. In the jargon of economists, Uru subsistence was characterized by easy entry, relatively low risk, but small potential return. The implication of these structural characteristics is that the production activities of the Uru were never centrally controlled. They remained the province of specialized entrepreneurs who could capture the economically useful resources of the aquatic environment and trade them for the terrestrial products they lacked. Unlike the huge numbers of camelids bred for consumption and use in Tiwanaku's cities, the products of the lake were introduced into the urban milieu through a decentralized network of exchange. The urban dwellers of Tiwanaku had as much of a taste for the delicate meat of fish and water fowl as for the red meat and *ch'arqi* of llama, but the means and organization of supply were distinct.

Paradoxically, the Uru were the most aggressively insular of ethnic groups, and yet simultaneously the people of the high plateau who depended most for their livelihood on established relationships of exchange with their terrestrial neighbors. In this sense, the Uru intersected with the broader agropastoral economy of Tiwanaku, but never became an integral, managed part of that economy: they were in it, but not of it.

Political Economy and the Social Nature of Tiwanaku

The foregoing analysis of Tiwanaku's political economy generates some provocative, perhaps even unorthodox, interpretations regarding the nature of the social world inhabited by the people of Tiwanaku. The world of Tiwanaku was clearly multi-ethnic and plurilinguistic. We can identify at least three distinct social groups that appear to have intense, primary associations with particular ecological settings, socioeconomic structures, and ideologies. The Pukina, now extinct, were distributed along the lake shores and in the sub-tropical valleys of the Andes' eastern slopes and may have been the principal wetland originators of raised field technology. They were linked intimately with an agrarian lifestyle. The Uru, slipping gradually toward extinction as a distinct ethnic group, were fishers and foragers along the high plateau's aquatic axis. The Aymara, ethnohistorically the classic agro-pastoralists of the high, dry western punas of the *altiplano* were traditionally associated with large-scale herding of llama and alpaca complemented by rainfall-dependent tuber agriculture. I would suggest that the organizational genius of Tiwanaku resided precisely in the effective synchronization and synthesis of these three linguistically distinct ethnic groups into a single, dynamic political economy. The perceptual boundaries of ethnic purity did not inhibit a process of economic and political mutualism, although we can assume with a certain measure of confidence that there remained embedded among these three groups significant distinctions in status and access to natural resources, and, as a consequence, inherent contradictions and sources of tension. The economy of Tiwanaku entailed development of a technological and managerial mesh among three distinct systems of production: fishing, farming, and herding. But, perhaps more importantly, it required forging with delicacy and diplomacy enduring cross-ethnic ties that could bring historically autonomous societies into creative conjunction.

Tiwanaku, then, was not a single identifiable culture or ethnic group. Nor was it an ethnic melange, or pastiche. The ethnic constituencies of Tiwanaku retained their individual public identities as distinct cultures. This was no idealized, American-style melting pot. Tiwanaku was a created, intensely hierarchical, culture of the state. If there were dominant actors in this Tiwanaku state culture, they were, most likely, of Aymara or Pukina descent. One of these two languages was Tiwanaku's elite lingua franca, or court language. The Uru, although recognized players in the game, were conceptually outsiders, foreigners, in a sense, in their own country. The Aymara and Pukina between them controlled the dominant agro-pastoral axis of the Tiwanaku political economy. We can conjecture, although not demonstrate archaeologically, that the Aymara and Pukina formed political alliances based on strategic dynastic marriages, and perhaps more generalized bride exchange. The ruling lineages of Tiwanaku may very well have been a created nobility born of cross-ethnic marriages.

The touchstone of the multicultural economic and political conjunction that I describe here was the dynamic power relationships among the various ethnic *kurakas* and paramounts who were the natural lords of these disparate ethnic groups. The merging of the command hierarchy into a unified structure created an organizational framework that unleashed enormous energy in the form of human labor. One enduring legacy of this labor remains visible today around the shores of Lake Titicaca in the immense, artificially transformed landscape of agricultural fields and hydraulic works that once formed the economic foundations for Tiwanaku civilization.

7

The Empire Expands

At some point after A.D. 400, Tiwanaku's growing economic and political power transformed it from a locally dominant force into an aggressive, predatory state with a penchant for territorial expansion. Within two centuries, Tiwanaku's power was extended throughout the Lake Titicaca basin, as well as into the *yungas* regions at lower altitude, particularly into agriculturally fertile enclaves such as the Cochabamba Valley to the east of the Bolivian high plateau and the Moquegua Valley to the west (Figure 7.1). But, apart from a few exceptions, the expansion of Tiwanaku was not the product of a militaristic grand strategy worked out self-consciously by the lords of Tiwanaku and implemented through force-of-arms. Tiwanaku's empire was not of the same order of magnitude as that of the Inca, or the classical empires of the Old World, nor was its expansion primarily the work of warrior-kings with huge, standing armies ready at an instant to conquer, intimidate, and oppress local populations. Military stratagems and conscious efforts to conquer territory played a relatively small role in the movement of Tiwanaku into foreign territories. Rather, we must think of the state as a dynamic mosaic of populations linked at times imperfectly by a mosaic of strategic policies and political relationships devised by Tiwanaku's elite interest groups in an almost *ad hoc* fashion. These political stratagems responded to local cultural diversity and specific historical contingencies.

Tiwanaku's elite manipulated a variety of economic and political techniques to link themselves with local populations. Among those favored by Tiwanaku's ruling class were direct conquest and administration of strategic regions, large-scale regional colonization or selective enclaving of populations in foreign territories, administered trade, propagation of state cults, and the establishment of clientage relationships between themselves and local elite. These techniques

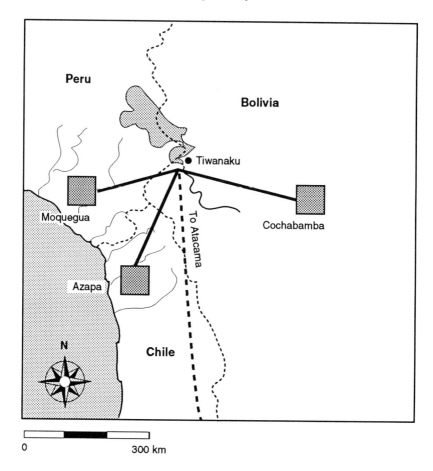

Figure 7.1 Map of the southern Andean highlands, illustrating the expansion of Tiwanaku into agriculturally rich enclaves, including the Cochabamba Valley to the east, and the Moquegua and Azapa Valleys to the west.

could be either coercive or consensual, depending upon the specific geographic and political context. As a result, Tiwanaku's imperial administration took a variety of forms: it could be direct or indirect, centralized or decentralized, and it could take strong or weak forms. The ability to incorporate other societies and other ethnic groups into a greater, productive whole required that Tiwanaku shrewdly balance force and persuasion, coercion and consent.

Given the bewildering diversity in social and physical landscapes which confronted Tiwanaku during its drive to empire, it is not surprising that Tiwanaku's elite never established a uniform strategy of administration throughout its realm. The humid, sub-tropical *yungas* to the east of Tiwanaku's high plateau heartland were radically different from the arid *yungas* lying to the west. The *altiplano* around Lake Titicaca was vastly more fertile and suited to intensive agriculture than the higher, drier reaches of the southern Bolivian high plateau, where llama and alpaca pastoralism dominated. Each of these areas differed substantially in natural resources, and the size and degree of organization of the resident human populations. In the rich, but tortuous terrain of the eastern *yungas*, Tiwanaku faced agricultural societies subsisting on slash-and-burn agriculture on steep mountain slopes, a form of shifting cultivation still practiced today. Along desolate stretches of the Desaguadero River flowing southward toward Lake Poopó, Tiwanaku's mobile caravan traders encountered and bartered with small clusters of Urus who fished and foraged for food along the river banks and on the lake itself. In the dry, western *yungas* of the Peruvian and Chilean coasts, local populations were well-established in large, densely settled villages. These coastal peoples were well-accustomed to trading with highlanders and had done so for centuries. In the Titicaca basin itself, Tiwanaku shared long-standing cultural ties with neighboring groups, and was simply the most brilliant exemplar of an urban civilization that had deep roots extending back to Pukara, Chiripa, and Wankarani. Here Tiwanaku was not so much a society different in kind from the others, but different in scale and cultural influence. South of the Titicaca basin, cities never developed and any sense of urban civilization among local populations was gained from contact with visitors and resident colonists from the lake district. Yet, because of Tiwanaku's vigorous political expansion from the fifth through eleventh centuries, many people who never saw the great, glittering cities along the shores of Lake Titicaca still participated, however remotely, in Tiwanaku's urban civilization.

It is evident that the Tiwanaku elite was not loath to apply force against local populations and competing polities whenever necessary. Policies of forceful, direct appropriation of productive lands were implemented in areas that were of prime importance to the economic and political well-being of the state, such as in the Lake Titicaca basin. Without secure sources of improved agricultural land for surplus crop production and high-quality pasturage for their herds, the power of Tiwanaku's elite classes to expand into foreign territories would have been tenuous at best. It is equally evident that Tiwanaku did not rely solely on coercion to pursue its expansionist economic ends. Tiwanaku state religion and imperial ideology performed much the same work as military conquest, but at significantly lower cost. In many instances, particularly in areas over which Tiwanaku held demographic and organizational superiority, the prestige of Tiwanaku religion and elite beliefs was sufficient to command respect and political subordination. Of course, along with the adoption of Tiwanaku's state cults, local people, or at least local elite received the distinct economic advantage of being incorporated into a wider social network controlled by their *altiplano* patrons. To understand Tiwanaku as an imperial society, we must grasp the multiple ways in which its elite interest groups responded to the challenge of extending their power and influence into a world replete with an almost riotous diversity of terrain and of people.

Ideology and Imperialism in the Titicaca Basin

Intensive agriculture was the fundamental source of Tiwanaku's wealth. The great agricultural estates of the Tiwanaku hinterland churned out surplus production on a grand scale. This surplus was transformed into political power by Tiwanaku's elite through its capacity to recruit and maintain local loyalties. The elite controlled an enormous fund of rich agricultural land and camelid herds with which it could manipulate the strings of power through its ability to redistribute wealth to dependent populations. As the Tiwanaku elite's power intensified, their interest in reclaiming agricultural land expanded beyond the narrow confines of their capital's sustaining hinterland. After about A.D. 400, we see a distinct pattern of strategically located, state-built administrative centers being established by Tiwanaku all along the agriculturally optimal lands of the Lake Titicaca coast (see Figure 5.4, p. 103). Impressive cult and administrative centers, similar to those in the Tiwanaku hinterland, were founded on the northern side of Lake Titicaca, strongly implying that the Tiwanaku state unified the Titicaca basin under its rule no later than A.D. 500. This "Pax Tiwanaku" permitted expansion of agricultural production, and offered access to new pasture lands.

Imperial expansion into the northern Titicaca basin fortified Tiwanaku's fundamental sources of wealth, economic vitality, and political power. Unfortunately, there are very few detailed archaeological reports bearing on these religious and political centers. Apart from noting their existence, we can say little specifically about their nature, size, and relationship to the surrounding countryside. However, we can reasonably conjecture that these sites functioned much like the secondary urban settlements of the Tiwanaku hinterland. Like Lukurmata, Pajchiri, and Khonko Wankané, they were important to

Tiwanaku both as centers of cult activity and as nodes of political and economic administration. The imposed centers in the northern Titicaca basin inevitably contain temple architecture that mimics that of Tiwanaku itself, but on a significantly smaller scale. Cult activities were presumably presided over by Tiwanaku elite in concert with their local counterparts. The performance of cultic rituals in these centers merged almost imperceptibly with the nitty-gritty business of managing agricultural production. Agricultural work in the Andes was always performed in the context of public rituals, and the rituals themselves were the means of organizing and synchronizing labor on a grand scale. Rite and crop intermingled to the point that the act of performing a prescribed ritual in the agricultural cycle of the seasons was simultaneously an act of administration, one that called forth and organized commoners to prepare fields, clean irrigation canals, plant, or harvest. In this sense, Tiwanaku state religion and politics were one and the same.

We do have reasonably detailed information on Tiwanaku's expansion into one area of the Lake Titicaca basin outside of its immediate hinterland: the Juli-Pomata region on the southwest side of the lake (see Figure 2.1). Here Stanish (1991) reports that a systematic survey of nearly 500 square kilometers discovered 39 Tiwanaku sites dating to the Tiwanaku IV and V phases. These sites range from small house mounds associated with raised field complexes to large ceremonial centers with cut-stone architecture constructed on artificial terraces. One of these ceremonial centers, the site of Tuma Tumani, consists of a dual mound configuration like that of the PK-5/PK-6 complex on the Pampa Koani in Tiwanaku's near hinterland. Many of the Tiwanaku settlements discovered in this recent survey consist of domestic residences set on terraced hillsides. The terraces themselves are artificial, stone-faced constructions similar to those found at the Tiwanaku regional capitals of Lukurmata and Pajchiri. Although the numbers of sites are smaller, the pattern and purpose of settlement in this region virtually replicates that of the Tiwanaku hinterland.

This survey demonstrates unequivocally that the southwest Titicaca basin was heavily populated in Tiwanaku times, and that the Tiwanaku state established strong political control over this strategic area. The central purpose of Tiwanaku expansion into this region was development and exploitation of the lake-side agricultural landscape. Enormous tracts of raised fields are directly associated with these Tiwanaku sites. The organization of this agricultural landscape was similar to that of the Tiwanaku hinterland. Tiwanaku ceramics recovered from these sites include both imported finewares that came directly from the Tiwanaku core terrritory and local imitations of Tiwanaku elite ceramics. As Stanish (1991) notes, the presence of locally produced ceramics that imitate Tiwanaku stylistic conventions implies a complex exchange relationship between the expanding state and local populations. Fine ceramics imported directly from Tiwanaku occur disproportionately in sites in the Juli-Pomata region that contain sunken courts and cut-stone architecture: the architectural emblems of Tiwanaku authority and dominion. This correlation hints at the presence of foreign administrators installed directly by the lords of Tiwanaku who were charged with the obligation of organizing the region into productive agricultural estates. The imitation ware may represent the efforts of local *kurakas* to integrate themselves into the administrative system imposed by the Tiwanaku elite. Tiwanaku presence in the Juli-Pomata region extended from arable lands along the lake edge suitable for intensive raised field agriculture up into the high *puna* grasslands over 4,000 masl. The Tiwanaku elite established a pervasive, thoroughgoing control of the southwest Titicaca basin that enabled it to dominate the most productive natural resources of the region: rich agricultural fields and prime pasture lands.

With the expansion of Tiwanaku outside of its immediate core territory, we see clear evidence that an essential element of Tiwanaku imperial policy was the exportation of state cults. In particular, after A.D. 400, the figure of the Gateway God appears on sculptures, ceramics, textiles, and other media in Tiwanaku-related sites throughout the high plateau, as well as in the lower altitude *yungas* zones of Peru, Bolivia, and Chile. Recall that this figure represented a celestial high god ancestral to the Aymara weather deity, Thunupa. The Gateway God, as a personification of elemental natural forces such as wind, rain, and hail, was embedded in a complex religious ideology that related royal authority, ritual calendars, and agricultural production. The cult of the Gateway God, linked so essentially to the state's agricultural calendar, was imposed, or at least layered over, multiple local cults and shrines.

That the entire Lake Titicaca basin population did not voluntarily embrace Tiwanaku state religion with messianic fervor is made apparent in the archaeological record. We now know that a major stone stela from the site of Arapa near Puno on the northern shores of the lake was broken at its base in antiquity, transported over 150 kilometers by raft, and incorporated into one of the palace complexes at Tiwanaku (Chávez 1975). This stela was associated stylistically with the early, north Titicaca basin urbanized culture of Pukara (Figure 7.2). The implication of this violent political and ideological act is clear: in the process of subjugating the northern Titicaca basin, a

Figure 7.2   The "Thunderbolt Stela," part of a larger stela originally from the Pukara site of Arapa near Puno on the northern shore of Lake Titicaca. This stela fragment was transported 150 kilometers to Tiwanaku, where it was incorporated into a local palace complex. The "Thunderbolt Stela" is now housed in the site museum at Tiwanaku.

ruler of Tiwanaku ritually debased and appropriated a sacred emblem of the concentrated spiritual power, or *huaca* of the Pukara nation, and, in so doing, demonstrated both the religious and secular superiority of the Tiwanaku state. This ideological act of *huaca* capture is not rare in the annals of Tiwanaku. The puma-masked, crouching figure holding a trophy head found during recent excavations at the Akapana pyramid betrays influences from the classic Pukara style, and may represent another instance of *huaca* capture in the old Pukara homeland. As we have seen, the Semi-subterranean Temple at Tiwanaku is filled with an eclectic group of stone stelae and sculptures carved in distinct styles, representing the *huacas* of various times, places, and ethnic groups. These sculptures were carefully placed in a subordinate position to the great, centrally located Bennett monolith which itself visually encoded the essential tenets of Tiwanaku state ideology, cosmology, and royal prerogative. The symbolic statement made by the lords of Tiwanaku when they captured the *huacas* of other nations and reincorporated them into their own capital's palaces and temples was intense and unambiguous. They were publically affirming the centrality of their own society in the universal world order, justifying their conquest of and supremacy over other lands and other peoples.

But Tiwanaku's rulers did not attempt to eradicate the local cults and their sacred *huacas*. Rather they absorbed them, and made them subordinate to the state cults. In this manner, they anticipated the actions of the Inca state many centuries later who used the same shrewd policy of absorption of local cults and beliefs into the imperial religion. By incorporating local cults into the state religion, both Tiwanaku and later the Inca mitigated the intense hostility of conquered populations to state interference in their most personal beliefs and religious practices. In fact, the prestige and efficacy of the local cults and shrines may have been enhanced in the eyes of the local populations by their new association with the obviously successful imperial cults. The power of religion and cult to conquer hearts and minds should not be underestimated.

The lords of Tiwanaku avidly pursued military conquest and annexation of foreign territory in the Lake Titicaca basin. In a sense, if Tiwanaku was to expand, it was imperative that its rulers gain dominion over the lands encircling the lake. The lake basin was an area of great productivity and of great potential opposition to Tiwanaku rule. This was a lesson that the Inca were to learn some 1,000 years later. After establishing control over the Cuzco valley, the Inca's first foray of foreign conquest was aimed against the Aymara kingdoms around Lake Titicaca. The Inca knew full well that if they were to be the new emperors of their world, they would have to control the Titicaca basin. Subsequently, the Inca fought constant rear-guard actions against the native lords of these kingdoms who bitterly contested Inca rule in their homeland through outright rebellion and subtle subterfuge. Just so, there were many potential competitors to Tiwanaku within the Lake Titicaca region who had comparable access to the rich resources of the lake and its surrounding lands. Tiwanaku's effort to incorporate these Titicaca basin competitors into its expanding state was a pragmatic and necessary strategy. In other areas of their empire, the lords of Tiwanaku pursued different strategies of expansion that relied less directly on military confrontation and complete domination of local populations.

The Yungas Zones: Colonial Agricultural Provinces

Tiwanaku imperial expansion intimately linked to the appropriation of agricultural land did not stop at the edges of the high plateau. Tiwanaku directly colonized and subsequently controlled key lands in lower altitude regions such as the Cochabamba Valley in Bolivia, the Azapa Valley of northern Chile, and the Moquegua Valley of southern Peru, among others (Figure 7.1). Perhaps the most interesting element of the interaction between highland *altiplano* and lowland valley populations during the Tiwanaku regnum was the motivations that each side may have had for fostering and perpetuating a colonial relationship.

From the perspective of the Tiwanaku state, establishing agricultural colonies in regions at lower elevation would have permitted access to crops otherwise unavailable in the high, cold *altiplano*. But what is most significant is the nature of the two principal crops that were grown at lower elevation: maize and coca. If my estimates of the productivity of intensive grain and tuber agriculture in the high plateau are correct, then *altiplano* populations under Tiwanaku had achieved economic self-sufficiency. That is, the high plateau under Tiwanaku control would not have required a massive influx of bulk food crops from lower elevations to sustain its urbanized populations. Producing food crops was not the principal intent of Tiwanaku colonization schemes in the *yungas* zones. Maize and coca were highly valued as ceremonial and prestige crops in the Andes. They were state crops *par excellence* under the Inca, produced in many areas under the centralized, monopoly control of the government through the labor of forcibly resettled colonists. The motive force underlying Tiwanaku agricultural colonization in the *yungas* zones was expansion of the cultivation of prestige crops, particularly maize. These prestige crops provided the raw material for the production of ritually important commodities, such as maize beer, that were consumed prodigiously during state-sponsored festivals. Such festivals demanded of the elite elaborate ritual hospitality and the ceremonial display of abundance. Maize and coca as primary products were channeled into the redistributive networks manipulated by the Tiwanaku elite classes. They provided a storable, high value, state-controlled medium of exchange that could be used by the elite to "purchase" labor from commoners. The agricultural provinces of the Tiwanaku state in the *yungas* zones were essential, not as sources of basic food crops, but as a source of prestige and ritual commodities that fueled the age-old Andean system of reciprocity between lords and their subjects.

From the perspective of local populations, in return for a portion of their product and labor, the Tiwanaku state provided both a measure of political security and the technological and administrative expertise in developing massive reclamation projects that had been gained through centuries of creating similar hydraulic works around the edge of Lake Titicaca. Perhaps even more importantly, through shared participation in a unified economic and religious system, the Tiwanaku state also offered native populations incorporation into a more inclusive social universe that mitigated the risks of survival in the harsh, natural environment of the Andean world. For the non-urbanized populations of the *yungas* zones, Tiwanaku's urban values and rich culture themselves must have held a powerful attraction. Coercion may not have been necessary to incorporate the *yungas* into Tiwanaku's realm. The subtle implications of Tiwanaku cultural superiority and the promise of sharing the wealth of a powerful new society on the rise may have been sufficient to bring the *yungas* populations into line.

Until recently, the history of Tiwanaku expansion into the *yungas* zones was almost exclusively the province of speculation and reconstructions based on the thin ice of insufficient data. There have been innumerable discoveries of Tiwanaku tombs in the arid coastal regions of Chile and Peru, and the contents of these burials have found their way into many private and public collections in Europe, the United States, and Latin America. Thousands of objects related to the time of Tiwanaku expansion have been extracted, but few of these have been studied systematically. Worse still, we have virtually no intensive excavations of habitation sites with which to reconstruct the character and intensity of Tiwanaku colonization schemes. Agricultural reclamation projects inspired by Tiwanaku expansion into the *yungas* have mainly gone unexplored. Canals and fields that once flourished lie hidden beneath tons of sediment or under drifting sand dunes awaiting discovery.

Yet the tempo of explorations focused on the phenomenon of Tiwanaku expansion outside the high plateau has increased dramatically in the past decade. Ongoing archaeological projects in southern Peru, northern Chile, and eastern Bolivia promise to provide new, primary information concerning Tiwanaku's role in the geopolitics of the ancient Andean world (Rice et al. 1989; Watanabe et al. 1990). For instance, recent research in the Moquegua Valley of southernmost Peru has begun to clarify the nature and extent of Tiwanaku state expansion from the *altiplano* to the western Andean slopes and Pacific coast (Goldstein 1989; Moseley et al. 1991). The largest expanse of arable land in the river valley, comprised of fertile flatlands formed around the confluence of three major tributaries, is found in the mid-valley region around the modern city of Moquegua (Figure 7.3). Given the Tiwanaku elite's obsession with reclaiming agricultural land, it is not surprising that this zone was the focus of dense and long-term Tiwanaku occupation.

Tiwanaku sites in Moquegua are concentrated in the lower agricultural zones of the mid-valley region where farming was supported by irrigation canals drawn from rivers and streams. Tiwanaku settlements range from multi-room farmsteads or hamlets associated directly with agricultural fields and irrigation canals to dense communities of several hundred structures grouped around formal plazas. There are

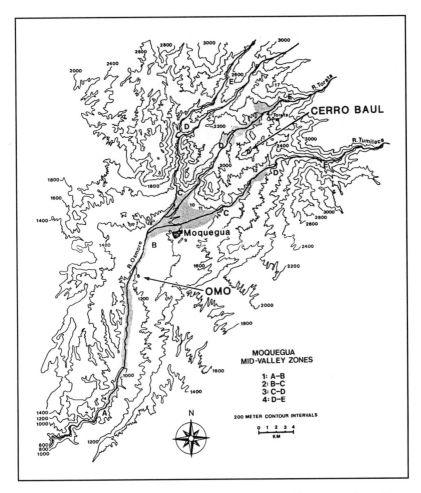

Figure 7.3 Topographic map of the Moquegua Valley in southern Peru, illustrating the key archaeological sites of Omo and Cerro Baul, as well as the valley's four principal agricultural zones. The largest zone of flat arable land is Zone 2 (B–C). (Based on Moseley et al. 1991 and Goldstein 1989).

special purpose sites such as the extensive settlement of Omo, where massive adobe architecture and formal, stepped-terrace layout imply an administrative and ceremonial function similar to that of the secondary cities of Lukurmata and Pajchiri in the *altiplano* (Figure 7.4). Other specialized sites include two mid-valley hills with large adjoining settlements that were heavily fortified with formidable masonry perimeter walls, and the exceptionally large cemetery of Chen Chen that apparently served as the central burial ground for the mid-valley

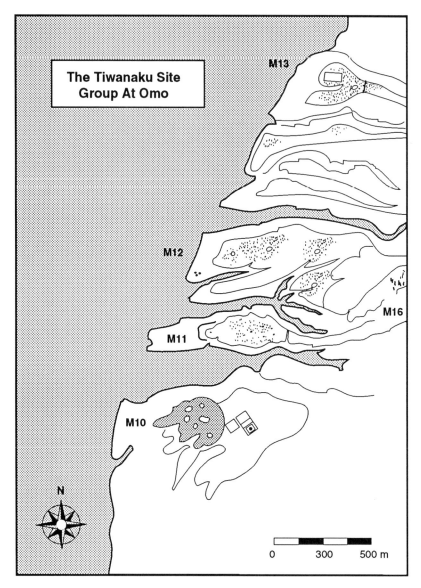

Figure 7.4 Map of the Tiwanaku site group at Omo, located along the Osmore River in the Moquegua Valley. (Based on Goldstein 1989).

population during the Tiwanaku V period (c. A.D. 750–1000). Three major Tiwanaku settlements are situated at the base of Cerro Baul immediately adjacent to irrigated bottom lands of the Torata and Tumilaca rivers (Figure 7.3). Agricultural terraces at higher elevations were only used extensively after the decline of the Tiwanaku state in the region around A.D. 1000. Additional Tiwanaku cemeteries cluster along the coast and in the lower reaches of the Osmore River. Chen Chen and the other mid-valley sites have abundant decorated ceramics stylistically associated with Phase V of the Tiwanaku sequence. Tiwanaku IV (c. A.D. 400–750) material occurs less commonly than that of the later phase, but is present in quantity at the large site of Omo. This pattern suggests that Tiwanaku influence in the Moquegua Valley began as early as A.D. 400 and was initially focused in key enclaves such as Omo. Through time, Tiwanaku cultural influence intensified and became more inclusive, penetrating into the households and villages of local populations.

This pattern seems a familiar one to students of empire. Frequently the first step in incorporation of a new province is establishment of a military garrison. Over time, if the imperial enterprise is successful, the garrison aspects of the enclave gradually disappear as relationships with local populations stabilize and move beyond the stage of initial confrontation. Constant, day-to-day interaction between growing numbers of state colonists and local populations creates a sense of social and economic interdependence. Mutualism replaces repression. Many features of the intrusive state are readily adopted by local populations, and the flow of cultural influences becomes reciprocal. The benefits to the local populations of linking into a more inclusive social universe outweigh the natural resentments and hostility born of forced incorporation into an alien state. To sustain an imperial province over the long run, this movement from garrison to colony is essential. Niccolo Machiavelli ([1532] 1952:37–8), author of *The Prince*, that great Renaissance manual of statecraft, perfectly captures this prescription for creating empire in a few, well-chosen phrases:

> plant colonies in one or two of those places which form as it were the keys of the land, for it is necessary either to do this or to maintain a large force of armed men . . . but by maintaining a garrison instead of colonists, one will spend much more, and consume all of the revenues of the state in guarding it, so the acquisition will result in a loss . . . In every way, therefore, a garrison is as useless as colonies are useful.

The lords of Tiwanaku apparently followed this prescription to the letter in the Moquegua Valley, establishing a "beachhead" early on at Omo, and gradually infiltrating the daily life of the area through

increasingly intense colonial relationships with the locals. If he had
been on the scene, Machiavelli would surely have admired the mach-
inations of the state of Tiwanaku. They were sensitive to the need to
establish alliances with the local populations, and to inculcate a sense
of loyalty and identification with the prestige and power of the state.
They founded substantial colonies in the Moquegua region, promoting in the process a pluralistic, multi-ethnic state with which many
could identify and prosper.

The impressive settlement of Omo provides us with our clearest
and most detailed insights into the nature and process of Tiwanaku
colonization in the Moquegua Valley. The site spans a series of dramatic escarpments overlooking the floodplain of the Osmore River
(Figure 7.4). The setting of Omo is quintessentially Tiwanaku: the
blufftop location is above, but immediately adjacent to the valley's
richest expanse of readily arable land. This land could be irrigated
with either river water or with groundwater percolating from natural
springs that emerge below the Omo escarpments. Omo itself occupies
nearly 40 hectares across three separate bluffs, giving it the distinction of being the largest archaeological site in the valley, and the
largest known Tiwanaku settlement outside of the *altiplano*. However, not all of these 40 hectares were occupied simultaneously.
Through time, the community structure of Omo evolved in response
to changes in the intensity of Tiwanaku's engagement in the Moquegua
region.

The earliest Tiwanaku occupation at Omo was a substantial colony
established around A.D. 500–600 during the Tiwanaku IV phase. This
colony betrays its Tiwanaku affiliation through its distinctive architectural plan, and through the kinds and patterning of objects recovered
in recent excavations of domestic residences (Goldstein 1989). Although not exceedingly formal, the overall plan of the Tiwanaku IV
phase settlement evinces certain principles of community planning.
Houses and artisans' workshops in the community are arrayed around
and oriented to three distinct plazas that were clearly designed as
spaces for public congregations (Figures 7.5 and 7.6). Materials for
house construction were simple, locally available, and of a perishable
quality. Nothing more elaborate than cane walls, wooden posts, and
thatching was required in the arid, temperate environment of southern
coastal Peru. All of the houses were built with a similar technique.
A series of closely spaced wooden posts or canes were erected to
form the structure's walls. Houses were generally rectangular in form
and densely packed. Woven textiles or mats were hung over this cane
framework. Within the house, a series of posts were sunk into the
floor to provide the frame for a thatched roof. Generally, one or two

Figure 7.5   Aerial photograph of the extensive M10 settlement at Omo. M10, which can be seen in the left side of the photograph as the large tripartite rectangular enclosure and its adjacent residential architecture, provides the clearest and most detailed evidence of a substantial Tiwanaku colony in the Moquegua Valley. (Photograph courtesy of the Servicio Aerofotográfico Nacional, Peru, 1837–19).

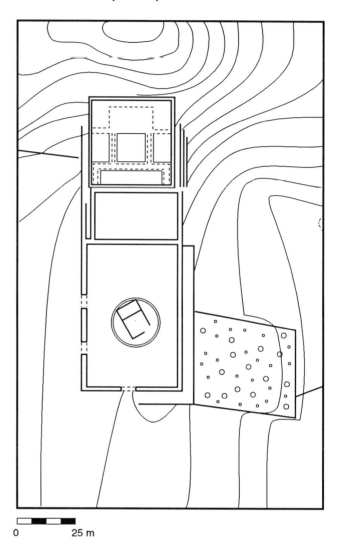

Figure 7.6   Plan of the Tiwanaku ceremonial complex at the Omo site of M10, composed of three plaza groups. (From Goldstein 1989: Figure 62).

informal hearths were dug into the floor of each house for cooking purposes and to heat the structures on the rare occasions when night-time temperatures dropped below a comfortable range. Across the community, all of the households seem to have engaged in some kind of craft production. Spindle whorls, needles, and spun and dyed camelid wool all point to a widespread, household textile industry.

In the western plaza group, one household seems to have specialized in cutting, drilling, and polishing ornamental shells from the Pacific Ocean for export. The remarkable preservation of organic material on the arid coast permitted recovery of a cornucopia of both food and industrial crops within the kitchens and living areas of the community's houses. Among these crops were maize, beans, squash, chile pepper, pumpkin, gourd, and coca. The daily life of the Omo colony clearly revolved around farming, complemented by a cottage industry of textile production, and a few more exotic crafts meant for export, such as the ornamental marine shell.

Although there are no obvious distinctions in the degree of elaboration of architecture among the three plaza groups, artifacts recovered in excavations point to significant social differentiation within the community. The southernmost plaza was isolated from the other two house and plaza clusters by a deep *quebrada* that forms its northern border. Intensive investigations in this plaza group recovered elaborate ceramics from the surface, such as incense burners boldly modeled in animal shapes and vessels produced as portraits of Tiwanaku elite, many of which are depicted chewing coca (Figure 7.7). The density, high quality, and elite character of this material suggested that this area held a distinct status and fulfilled a different function than the other two plaza groups. This conclusion was subsequently confirmed by excavation (Goldstein 1989). One of the structures in this plaza group was found to contain several enormous ceramic vessels with a minimum capacity of 90 liters, as well as many broken pieces of thick-walled pottery in the debris. This type of large, thick-walled, globular vessel with a constricted neck (Figure 7.8) has been used for generations in the Andean world as a fermentation chamber for alcoholic beverages, including both maize and grain-based beers. Producing the maize beer entailed a rather elaborate process that consumed considerable time and energy. Today the process involves quantities of corn meal mixed with warm water and heated in large fermentation pots. Apart from the fermentation and beer storage pots, one of the two rooms in this modest structure contained a disproportionate number of exceptionally fine, portrait head vessels that were clearly used for consuming the alcohol (Figures 7.9a and 7.9b). Scattered throughout the structure were pieces of red ochre and an ochre-stained pestle used for grinding this mineral. If the ceramic portrait heads give us an accurate representation of human facial ornamentation, the ochre may have been used for ritual face-painting during a drinking ceremony.

The picture that emerges from the debris of this structure is one familiar to any student of the ancient Andean world. This plaza group

Figure 7.7   An example of a ceramic vessel produced as a portrait head of a Tiwanaku elite chewing coca. (Museo Nacional de Arqueología, La Paz, Bolivia. Photograph by Alan Kolata).

and the structures within them were home to the community's elite. As we have seen, one of the principal obligations of the community leaders or *kurakas* was to host banquets and drinking bouts. There are some compelling Spanish accounts of *kurakas* from the early Colonial period that emphasize, albeit unintentionally, this consummately political act of sponsored drinking ceremonies. For instance, in 1567 Juan de Matienzo described the *kurakas* as "an idle, elite class" who he implied were given much to drinking, wenching, and generally laying about, providing no useful service to the state (Matienzo [1567] 1967:21). But, at the same time, in document after document from this period, we see the native peoples themselves, presumably the

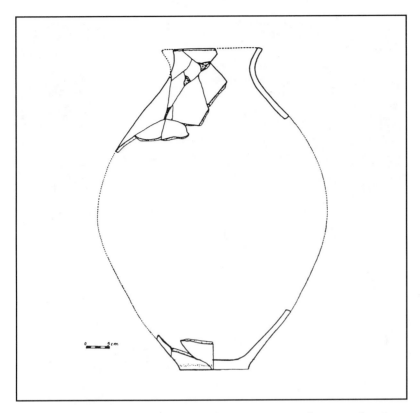

Figure 7.8   Reconstruction of a large fermentation vessel recovered at Omo that was probably used to brew alcoholic beverages, such as maize beer. (From Goldstein 1989: Figure 5.6).

class exploited by these layabouts, entreating the Spanish courts to confirm the *kurakas* in their position, because, they argue, without them everything would fall into chaos, and no one would know when and where to plant. This is our first clue that these "exploiters" actually performed a service for the masses. Matienzo's extended description of the *kurakas* gives us deeper insight into the service provided by the elite: "their function is to be idle and drink, and to count and divide up, they are very capable at this . . . more so than any Spaniard . . . and they keep accounts with multicoloured stones (quipus), so ably that it is a pleasure to watch them" (Matienzo [1567] 1967:21). This brief account points up the basic administrative and political role of *kurakas*. What the *kurakas* were dividing up and counting is essentially land, or, more precisely, the social map of

Figures 7.9a and 7.9b   Two examples of fine ceramic portrait vessels from Tiwanaku that were used for consuming alcohol. (Fig. 7.9a: Museo Nacional de Arqueología, La Paz, Bolivia. Photograph by Alan Kolata). The vessel illustrated in Figure 7.9b was recovered in excavations on the Akapana pyramid during the 1989 field season.

who had access to land for agricultural production. Production, especially agricultural production, was organized as a cycle of religious festivals. One could say of these societies that what was produced in the agricultural cycle of the seasons was social and religious solidarity as much as corn or potatoes, and it was the critical role of the *kurakas* to oversee the conjoined agricultural and ceremonial cycle. This entailed considerable cost to the *kuraka* in that ritual acts of public generosity were a part of the job description for organizing a religious festival. According to Felipe Guaman Poma de Ayala, the great native American author of the late sixteenth century, a good *kuraka* was generous and hospitable. Juan de Matienzo's complaint that the *kurakas* were idle and drank to excess was a glorious misinterpretation of what the *kurakas* were actually doing when they sponsored drinking bouts. They were not simply drinking to get drunk, aspiring to be the Jay Gatsby's of the Andean world. They were performing their essential ritual, political, and administrative functions, organizing religious festivals during which participants simultaneously consumed a prodigious quantity of drink and produced a substantial amount of work. This pattern of *kuraka*-sponsored religious festivals was an ancient one in the Andean world, one in which the elite of Omo were clearly engaged.

The Omo community during the Tiwanaku IV phase was an agricultural colony of *altiplano* origins. Many of the ceramic vessels discovered in the excavations of houses from this period were direct imports from the high plateau (Goldstein 1989). Frequently these vessels have distinct marks, often a y-shaped emblem, engraved into their bases. Identically engraved emblems have been found on Tiwanaku ceramic vessels from Arica on the north coast of Chile, from San Pedro in the high Atacama desert, and from Cochabamba, in the temperate *yungas* regions of eastern Bolivia. This pattern strongly implies that the Tiwanaku state was mass producing fine ceramic vessels, and other sumptuary objects such as particularly fine articles of clothing, for export to its colonies. The state monitored the production and distribution of these vessels through use of these distinctive, engraved emblems. These objects were identified with the power and religious ideology of the Tiwanaku state and their distribution was controlled directly by the state. The selective distribution of these wealth, or perhaps better phrased, status objects were an essential tool of statecraft for Tiwanaku. They were exported from the prestigious *altiplano* centers to the colonies where they circulated among the households of both Tiwanaku colonists and the local *kurakas* as public markers of their engagement with the state authorities. These objects must have been particularly coveted by the local

Figure 7.10   Fragment of a fine Tiwanaku tapestry, probably from the north coast of Chile. (Photograph courtesy of the American Museum of Natural History, New York).

elites who could elevate their own social status by their possession, display, and manipulation in rituals.

Through time, Tiwanaku state involvement in the Moquegua Valley intensified, a process reflected on the ground in an expansion of labor-intensive irrigation systems in the mid-valley and the appearance of monumental religious and administrative architecture at Omo. This intensification of Tiwanaku presence most likely occurred all along the coastal valleys of southern Peru and northern Chile during the Tiwanaku V period from A.D. 750 to 1000. Population in these valleys peaked during this time as a direct response to Tiwanaku investment in major hydraulic works and the expansion of trade relations between the *altiplano* and the coast. Local prosperity was being driven by the economic engine of the Tiwanaku state economy. Caravans laden with raw materials, local produce, and manufactured goods wound their way laboriously upward into the high sierras to reach Tiwanaku's cities on the lake. On the return trip, they brought with them the emblems of Tiwanaku society, fine ceramics, and iconographically rich textiles. Tiwanaku clothing may have been the most important *altiplano* export to its provinces. Brilliantly colored and technically superb tapestry bags, belts, tunics, and distinctive four-pointed hats are found by the hundreds in the tombs of local elite on the Peruvian and Chilean coasts (Figures 7.10 and 7.11). These items

Figure 7.11 An example of the distinctive four-pointed Tiwanaku hats, which are usually recovered from tombs of local elites on the Peruvian and Chilean coast. (Brooklyn Museum of Art, New York. Photograph by Alan Kolata).

of clothing were not simply fashionable attire for those who could afford them. They were laden with meaning and embued with an aura of power. Local elite and *altiplano* colonists who wore these elaborate costumes were publically affirming their intimate relationship with the lords of Tiwanaku. They were advertising their cultural and social superiority, and confirming their elevated status in the social hierarchy. More importantly from the perspective of the local commoners, they were identifying themselves as agents of Tiwanaku state authority. Access to *altiplano* goods and influence could be had through these agents of the state. Clothing here really did make the man.

Growing Tiwanaku influence in the Moquegua Valley during the Tiwanaku V phase took a particularly clear form. The agricultural colony at Omo was transformed in both size and character during this time. The most distinct expression of this transformation was the

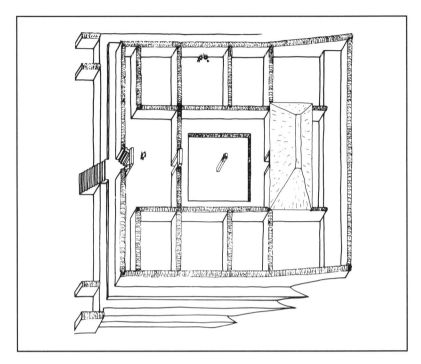

Figure 7.12   Reconstruction of the administrative and ceremonial complex from the M10 site at Omo. (From Moseley 1992: Figure 107).

construction of a monumental ceremonial and administrative complex on a second bluff-top setting at the site. The complex was designed as a set of three adobe-walled courts, each constructed on a different level. Surrounding and oriented to this ceremonial complex was a dense area of habitations significantly larger than the earlier agricultural colony at Omo (Figure 7.12). A visitor to the complex would have first entered the lowest court which is the largest of the three and capable of accommodating a considerable concentration of people. Moving toward the southeast, the visitor would next ascend to the middle court which was enclosed on three sides by low adobe walls, and on the fourth, uphill side by a massive stone and adobe wall three meters tall. Excavations in this middle court uncovered a particularly beautiful fragment of a Tiwanaku tapestry depicting the image of a figure in profile grasping a puma-headed staff. The tapestry is of the finest quality, woven in a complex pattern using eight colors: red, white, black, turquoise, green, maroon, orange, and gold. This splendid textile attests to the elite character of this complex. The floor of the middle court was surfaced with a dense, red clay similar to the architectural elaboration of floors in elite structures at Tiwanaku itself. Ascending to the upper court, the visitor would finally penetrate into the most intricate, private space within the complex. This space consists of a series of rooms arrayed around an inner, sunken atrium. The central sunken atrium was insulated from public view by these encircling rooms and access to it was controlled and most likely restricted to the elite. The atrium served as the *sanctum sanctorum* of the entire ceremonial complex. The walls of the upper court were constructed of adobe layed on a foundation of stone. Walls and floors were well plastered and were most likely painted in vibrant colors as well.

An offering placed on the floor of the upper court emphasizes the special, ritually charged character of the structure. In the southern corner of the structure, the excavator encountered the remains of a llama fetus and a starfish. Such dedicatory offerings during the construction, or renovation of a structure are commonly found in archaeological sites throughout the Andes. Even today in the modern city of La Paz, Indians and non-Indians alike will bury a llama fetus under the foundations of a new building. But the starfish in this offering is rather unusual. The juxtaposition of these two very different kinds of animals as dedicatory offerings in the upper court may have been a powerful symbolic statement. The llama, of course, is a domesticated, terrestrial animal of highland origin, while the starfish is a wild, marine animal from the coastal zones. By placing this offering in the ceremonial core of the site, the architects of this complex may have been signaling, among other things, that the state of Tiwanaku had political and symbolic dominion over both highland and coast. A similar conjoining of highland and coastal objects in dedicatory offerings occurs on the Templo Mayor, the principal pyramid in the Aztec capital of Tenochtitlan in the Valley of Mexico (Broda et al. 1987; Matos Moctezuma 1987). There too the offering was interpreted symbolically as an expression of Aztec control over wide-ranging, ecologically diverse landscapes.

Although smaller in scale, the elite complex at Omo replicates the basic canons of Tiwanaku ceremonial architecture. The essence of Tiwanaku ceremonial architecture was the terraced platform mound constructed around an interior sunken court. The triple-stepped platform mound appears in Tiwanaku both as a three-dimensional architectural form and as a salient element in Tiwanaku sculptural iconography. The Omo complex's three walled courts, which dominate the site visually and step up in ascending levels, reflect the same design principle of measured progression and ascent. The inner sunken

atrium of the upper court at Omo is a clear architectural reference
to the sunken courts emblematic of Tiwanaku ceremonial architecture
throughout the Lake Titicaca basin. Even more explicity, Omo's upper
court may have been modeled directly after the Semi-subterranean
Temple at Tiwanaku itself. Two anthropomorphic sculptures were
recovered from the complex. One of these is a highly weathered, but
recognizable head fragment of a Classic Tiwanaku style stela, similar
in form to the Ponce or Bennett monoliths. The other sculpture is
entirely different, closely resembling the tenon head sculptures in
Tiwanaku's Semi-subterranean Temple: it represents a grotesque
human face, oval in shape with a protruding nose, gaping round
eyes, and a broad smile. The stone sculptures are made of local materials and were clearly not imported from the highlands, as were the
more portable, elite ceramics. The designers of the Omo ceremonial
complex were well familiar with the architectural and sculptural
tradition of Tiwanaku, and drew their inspiration directly from
Tiwanaku's central monuments. They were most likely colonists who
had come directly from the high plateau itself to settle in Omo as
part of Tiwanaku's state expansion into the western *yungas*. The Omo
ceremonial complex can be understood best as an imposed center of
Tiwanaku political and religious domination.

    Ethnohistoric and archaeological research has demonstrated that
ethnic groups of *altiplano* affiliation have periodically colonized or
otherwise occupied key resource-bearing lands in the Moquegua and
other river valleys to the south. Evidence from work completed over
the past few years strongly supports the interpretation that ethnic
altiplano occupation in the Moquegua region was an ancient and
profoundly influential geopolitical pattern (Goldstein 1989; Mujica
1978). Both settlement surveys and tomb excavations have revealed
substantial quantities of early *altiplano* ceramic materials including
classic Pukara pottery from the northern Titicaca basin, and the fiber-
tempered wares characteristic of the Chiripa sites of the southern
Titicaca basin. If we combine this evidence with the history of
Tiwanaku occupation sketched above, it is very difficult to escape the
conclusion that, at various times, the Moquegua Valley was the object
of resource hungry *altiplano* ethnic groups wishing to expand their
economic base. During the Tiwanaku regime, we can speak of
Moquegua as an integrated economic province of an *altiplano* state.

    In this respect, the political importance of the Omo ceremonial
complex cannot be overemphasized. Like the mound and sunken
court complexes of Tiwanaku sites in the Lake Titicaca basin, Omo's
ceremonial architecture was the public focus of agricultural rituals
that related elites to commoners, and colonists to locals. Agricultural

ritual was an essential component of the technology of farming, and it was intensive agriculture that was the *raison d'être* of Tiwanaku colonization schemes in the Moquegua Valley. Although the Omo complex replicates the ceremonial and administrative architecture of similar Tiwanaku centers in the Lake Titicaca basin, the agriculturally oriented mid-valley of the Moquegua region was most likely not organized by the state of Tiwanaku in the same hierarchical fashion as the high plateau sustaining area. Rather, I envision a more symbiotic relationship between state and provincial governments that encouraged a stronger measure of local autonomy in the organization of production. In contrast to the situation in the high plateau where labor for reclaiming and maintaining productive agricultural lands was non-local, that is, specifically brought in by state government for that purpose, all evidence indicates that in the Moquegua Valley the land was worked by the local resident populations in part for their own benefit, and secondarily for the benefit of the reigning political power from the *altiplano*.

In this scenario, state intervention was more indirect and local autonomy may not have been completely abrogated as in the case of the Pampa Koani and the other crucial sustaining areas surrounding Tiwanaku itself. Nevertheless, despite its significant organizational differences from the core agricultural zones around Lake Titicaca, the Moquegua region and its counterparts in other Peruvian and Chilean coastal valleys were in a real sense politically, economically, and culturally embedded in an influential and enduring social matrix of *altiplano*, particularly Tiwanaku, origin. Tiwanaku influence at Omo and other Tiwanaku V sites in the Moquegua Valley penetrates to the smallest households. At this time, the local populations had access to a wide variety of *altiplano* exports, particularly textiles and the distinctive, standardized ceramics characteristic of this period. If the inventory of goods they used and to which they aspired is an accurate index, the local people were behaving like true provincial citizens of an imperial state. They clearly identified culturally with Tiwanaku, and avidly sought to acquire and consume products from the high plateau.

If the arid, coastal valleys of southern Peru and northern Chile were economic provinces of an expanding Tiwanaku state, what of the sub-tropical valleys of the *yungas* zones to the east of the high plateau? Intensive archaeology here is only in its inception, and we still have little information regarding the history of Tiwanaku occupation in these zones. We do know that the remarkably fertile region around the Cochabamba Valley was the focus of intense Tiwanaku colonization and sustained close relationships with the populations of the high plateau. Thousands of Tiwanaku period tombs have been uncovered inadvertently in the modern city of Cochabamba during construction projects and in the course of agricultural activities in surrounding rural regions. More than one soccer field lies atop the razed and forgotten remains of terraced mounds that once provided the foundations for Tiwanaku houses and temples. Museum collections are replete with fine, polychrome ceramics from these sacked tombs and ruined structures. These beautiful ceramic vessels demonstrate that Tiwanaku stylistic influence in the region was long-standing and pervasive. Some of these vessels were clearly imported from the high plateau to Cochabamba as objects of special beauty, prestige, and ritual significance. Others were produced locally according to models provided by the imported vessels. We can even speak of local Cochabamba variants of the quintessential Tiwanaku ceramic styles. Cochabamba produced vessels appear in domestic residences in Tiwanaku itself, indicating that the flow of cultural and artistic influences was not imposed or unidirectional, emanating solely from the capital to the provinces. Rather, we can envision the relationship between Tiwanaku and Cochabamba as a dense network of social and economic relations that constantly intermingled people, ideas, and commodities.

On the evidence of ceramics alone, Cochabamba was clearly participating avidly in the Tiwanaku sphere of cultural influence. Unfortunately, beyond the realm of ceramics, many of which themselves were encountered fortuitously and lack a precise provenance, we have little primary evidence to reconstruct the history of Tiwanaku in Cochabamba. Clusters of preserved terraced mounds still punctuate the landscape, but no systematic investigation of Tiwanaku habitations and ceremonial architecture has yet been undertaken. We still do not have a grasp of how Tiwanaku might have contributed to realizing the agricultural potentials of the valley through large-scale reclamation programs. No Tiwanaku period irrigation canals, terraces, or other agricultural systems have been thoroughly described for the region.

Yet, it is apparent that the verdant landscapes and deep, rich soils of Cochabamba were particularly prized in prehispanic times for their agricultural fertility. Today, Cochabamba remains a key agro-industrial center in Bolivia, producing huge quantities of maize, potato, *quinoa*, wheat, barley, alfalfa, and a wide range of vegetables for the urban market. Coca, of course, continues to be one of the principal crops of the region. This sacred plant, transformed into the hugely profitable, primary material of the narcotics trade, thrives in the humid, heavily forested, mountainous terrain of Cochabamba's lower-lying Chapare district. We know that the Inca state took an intense interest in the valley. Huayna Capac, the last, independent emperor of the Inca, expelled the native populations of the Cochabamba Valley in order to install 14,000 new colonists from a variety of ethnic groups who were placed under the direct control of two Inca governors (Wachtel 1982). These multi-ethnic colonists were brought to Cochabamba explicitly to produce maize for the state. The vast quantities of maize that flowed into the Inca's imperial storehouses in Cochabamba were eventually shipped to Cuzco for ultimate consumption by the Inca army.

Huayna Capac completely reorganized the system of land tenure in Cochabamba to accommodate this grand scheme of repopulation and intensive state maize production. He divided the entire valley into 77 long strips, or *suyu*, and then assigned individual ethnic groups to work the land of *suyus* or fractional parts of *suyus*, depending on the topographic context of the designated strip and the population size of each colonizing ethnic group. Only 7 of these strips of land, interspersed among the other 70 *suyus*, were alloted to the 14,000 colonists for their own subsistence. The remaining portion, over 90 percent of the arable land in the valley, was given over to intensive production of maize for the state. The work assignments and other internal affairs of each ethnic group were governed by its own political leaders. These leaders were then responsible to the two Inca governors who headed up the political hierarchy. In return for their service to the Inca, the various ethnic *kurakas* were rewarded with small plots of land within the valley, with some Inca prestige goods such as cotton mantles, and occasionally with women for secondary wives.

Although we do not yet have primary archaeological evidence, it appears likely that Tiwanaku's interest in Cochabamba, like that of the Incas, turned on its immense potential for sustained agricultural production. Maize, coca, chile pepper, tropical fruits were all avidly sought by consumers on the high plateau unable to produce these warm lands crops themselves in quantity. We can conjecture, although not yet demonstrate unequivocally, that Tiwanaku organized its agricultural exploitation of the Cochabamba region in a manner similar to that of the Moquegua Valley. Although Tiwanaku colonists from the high plateau were undoubtedly resident in the Cochabamba Valley, we have no reason to suspect that Tiwanaku implemented a Huayna Capac-style reorganization of the local populations in the valley. Forced resettlement of entire villages and towns was a costly strategy, and one that was unnecessary and counterproductive for Tiwanaku. Rather, as in the Moquegua Valley, Tiwanaku social and economic influence and cultural style was pervasive, familiar, and readily absorbed by the local populations. Political relationships between local *kurakas* and the Tiwanaku state were most likely cast in a manner that was mutually beneficial. Rather than an icily autocratic domination of local populations through the threat of military coercion, the Tiwanaku elite relied upon economic mutualism and long-standing cultural relationships to gain access to the fertile lands of Cochabamba.

Caravans, Clients, and the Far Periphery

In the far reaches of Tiwanaku cultural influence, the nature of the interaction between the *altiplano* state and local populations was more attenuated than in the core regions of the Lake Titicaca basin and adjacent *yungas* lands. This attenuation of direct state action is reflected in material culture. In areas such as the San Pedro de Atacama oasis in northern Chile, the central Chilean valleys, and the Quebrada de Humahuaca in northwestern Argentina (Figure 7.13), Tiwanaku-related artifacts are concentrated disproportionately in elite tombs, and consist principally of portable art associated with Tiwanaku state cult and belief systems. The materials recovered from these specialized contexts include fine textiles, ritual drinking cups wrought of precious metals, featherwork associated with elaborate costumes, and a broad spectrum of elements associated with the ritual consumption of hallucinogens, including mescaline bearing cactus, vines from the tropical forest, and a variety of other plants with psychoactive properties. The contents of these Tiwanaku-related tombs strongly imply that the social linkage between locals and representatives of the distant *altiplano* state revolved intensely around cults and shared religious experience.

In each of these different areas on the far periphery of the Tiwanaku realm, the precise artifact assemblages and combination of iconographic elements derived from Tiwanaku state art vary, suggesting a selective adoption and local reinterpretation of ideological concepts (Browman 1978). Unlike the standardized, imposed, and pervasive character of Tiwanaku imperial art, architecture, and agricultural construction in the core areas of the state, current evidence from the far peripheries suggest a more fluid, opportunistic, and transactional relationship between the state and local populations. Each such region seems to have selected those elements of the state belief system that were appropriate to its own cultural setting, generating in the process a multitude of synchretic ritual and religious concepts that were complementary with the ideological system of the *altiplano* state.

The societies on the far peripheries of the state were connected to Tiwanaku's elite and their beliefs through an extensive network of long-distance trade. In the desertic, virtually trackless wastes of the

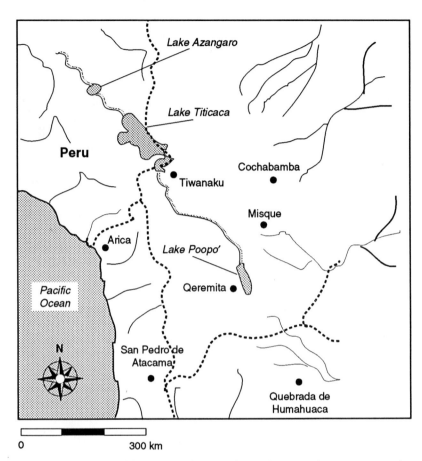

Figure 7.13 Map of key areas of Tiwanaku exchange and interaction in the south-central Andes.

southern Bolivian *altiplano*, long-distance exchange was accomplished through the medium of organized llama caravans, a pattern that persists to this day, although contemporary caravans are vastly reduced in scale, frequency, and economic importance. Sixteenth-century documents from the Lake Titicaca region reveal that the Aymara kingdoms of that time controlled immense herds of llamas and alpacas (Diez de San Miguel [1567] 1964). Some wealthy nobles controlled up to 50,000 animals. These native lords organized llama caravans with hundreds of pack-bearing animals to transport a wide array of food products, salt, textiles, pottery, aromatic and fuel woods, medicinal plants, special clays and natural minerals, metals, and much more throughout the south-central Andes. We can conjecture with confidence that Tiwanaku's caravans were of equivalent scale, diversity, and geographic reach.

But how were these caravans organized, and what might the relationship have been between Tiwanaku and its trading partners in distant lands? It is likely that there were different kinds of caravan trade. Perhaps the largest number of caravans were operated strictly on an inter-local basis. These would have been relatively small in terms of the number of animals involved and the quantity of commodities transported in any given caravan. Communication among the isolated villages dispersed across the hostile landscapes of the southern Andes depended on these local caravans. Such caravans linked long-term trading partners in a constant stream of barter and social visits. Trading partners themselves were frequently related by kin ties. The purpose of these caravans was to visit relatives, share gossip, and attend ceremonies as much as it was to exchange goods. Villagers must have greatly anticipated the arrival of the *caravaneros* with their large herds of llamas bearing goods and news as a welcome respite from the daily grind of making a living. We can imagine a lively, dense network of caravans radiating out from one village to another, connecting trading partners, reaffirming the essential bonds of kinship, and, not incidentally, circulating desired raw materials and manufactured goods.

Inter-local caravans have been a part of the social landscape of the south-central Andes for at least 3,000 years, binding dispersed towns, villages, and hamlets in regional webs of exchange. Other caravan traders, however, specialized in long-distance exchange between ethnically distinct groups. This form of caravan trade operated with different assumptions concerning the social identity of the trading partners. Relationships of this sort were conceived not so much as an exchange between intimate kinsmen, but as more of an impersonal transaction, with economic goals as the predominant motive force. These long-distance caravan traders were accommodated in the distant communities, and provided with a central location to display and exchange their wares with local consumers. This sort of affair had more of the feel of a medieval European trading fair, attracting people from the surrounding countryside to the town to examine exotic merchandise brought from afar, to converse with the foreign caravan traders and more often than not, to drink, feast, and sacrifice to the lineage ancestors.

Although these specialized *caravaneros* plied their wares for many centuries before the expansion of Tiwanaku, this kind of long-distance trade intensified under Tiwanaku's hegemony. Concentrated natural resources were monopolized by Tiwanaku's elite and funneled into these lucrative caravan networks. For instance, the site of Qeremita, a spectacular volcanic outcrop on the shores of Lake Poopó some 300 kilometers southeast of Tiwanaku, was intensively exploited for its marvelously dense basalt (Figure 7.13). This durable stone was the primary material for Tiwanaku's heavy-duty tools and weapons. High-quality agricultural hoes, knives, scapers, anvils, hammers, and other basic tools fashioned from this special basalt blanket Tiwanaku settlements throughout the *altiplano*. Shafts driven deep into the Qeremita outcrop attest to mining activity that may date back to the original inhabitants of the high plateau. Thousands of turtle shell-shaped basalt cores, the by-product of tool production, litter the slopes of the outcrop, indicating that the site was the locale of both large-scale extraction and manufacturing. Distinct paths lead down from the mines of Qeremita to small Tiwanaku settlements on the shores of Lake Poopó. These sites served as caravansaries and staging areas for shipping the finished product to avid consumers, as well as basic lodging for the mine workers and tool makers. Enormous pack trains of llamas must have converged periodically on the shores of Lake Poopó to transport this bulky, heavy mineral northward to Tiwanaku's urban settlements. The scale of Tiwanaku mining, manufacturing, and export at Qeremita is truly breathtaking and the closest one comes to organized industrial production in the ancient Andean world.

In addition to concentrated sources of critical raw materials, the state of Tiwanaku monopolized and forcefully administered strategic routes of the caravan trade, such as the trunk line to the San Pedro de Atacama oasis (Figure 7.13). The Atacama oasis served as an entrepôt, or trans-shipment point for other independent caravan traders who brought goods for exchange and distribution with established trading partners. Recent archaeological research in San Pedro de Atacama indicates the presence of substantial colonies of *altiplano* people from the Tiwanaku core area around Lake Titicaca. Tiwanaku colonization schemes in the Atacama area, as well as along the north Chilean coast, began at least as early as the Tiwanaku IV phase, or sometime after A.D. 400. Such colonization, or enclaving of populations emphasizes the geopolitical importance of the Atacama oasis to the lords of Tiwanaku.

One cemetery at the site of Coyo (Figure 7.14) reflects the pervasiveness of Tiwanaku presence in the Atacama oasis, and offers insight into the relationship between Tiwanaku colonists and local populations. At Coyo, foreign groups from Tiwanaku coexisted with local populations. Foreign colonists and locals were buried in a single, large cemetery, but individual tombs were distributed into two rigidly

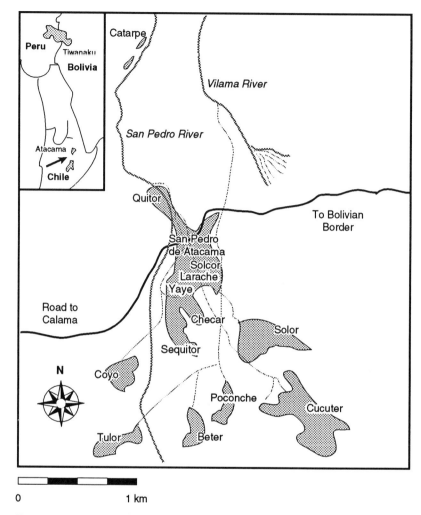

Figure 7.14 Map indicating the location of the Coyo cemetery within the San Pedro Atacama oasis. (Map courtesy of Amy Oakland Rodman).

segregated clusters, reflecting the distinct ethnic identity of the dead (Oakland 1990, 1992). Although buried together in one place, the dead retained strict affiliation with their social group of origin. Distinct styles of clothing and headdress expressed one's ethnic origin in the ancient Andean world, and, in certain rural areas, they still do so today. The difference in death shrouds, tunics, hats, bags, belts – in truth the total costume ensemble – between these two groups in the

Coyo cemetery was not subtle. Color patterning, iconography, and even basic weaving structures differ radically in the textiles worn by these two groups. Local costume was executed in fluid, curvilinear designs, while that of the intrusive, colonizing group from Tiwanaku emphasized rectilinear and recursive, geometric patterns, such as checkerboard and stripe designs (Figures 7.15a and 7.15b). The mortuary textiles associated with Tiwanaku colonists were rich in the visual codes of symmetry, duality, and the progressive replication of structural elements. As Oakland (1992:335) comments, "the geometry of checkerboard patterning with two colors above and two below is essential to the design and meaning" of these Tiwanaku tunics. It is tempting to read the symbolic "text" woven into these textiles as a metaphor for Tiwanaku society and social organization in which duality and hierarchy were the key operative principles. However one interprets the intricate design schemes, the elaborate iconography, and distinctive weaving structures of these textiles make it abundantly clear that they were intended to represent and publicly display the social, political, and religious world of Tiwanaku to the local populations.

But who exactly lived in the Atacama oasis and were buried wearing this distinctive Tiwanaku clothing? What was their relationship with the local populations? Given the richness, complexity, and beauty of these distinctive textiles, the dead entombed in the Coyo cemetery were most likely themselves Tiwanaku elite dispatched to the Atacama region as representatives of the state. The fact that these elite were buried in Atacama implies a fair measure of permanence to their position, much like the agents of England's colonial empire who, together with their families, lived out their lives in distant outposts of India, Malaysia, and Africa. But, unlike England's colonial agents, who maintained strict class and racial distinctions between themselves and their subjects, Tiwanaku's representatives in provincial outposts maintained closer personal ties with the local populations. The single cemetery at Coyo argues for a strong measure of intimacy and shared belief, even if the tombs themselves were ethnically segregated. Over the centuries of Tiwanaku influence, there may have been considerable intermarriage between these resident foreigners and the locals.

The relationship between foreign colonists, as representatives of a powerful, although distant state and locals was organized along the lines of a clientage relationship. In such an arrangement, local *kurakas* of these distant lands maintained personal relationships with the lords of Tiwanaku and their agents. In concert with their *altiplano* patrons, the local *kurakas* managed the production and long-distance exchange of desired commodities. In the case of the Atacama region, the local resouces of interest to the lords of Tiwanaku were most likely

Figure 7.15a   Tiwanaku tapestry tunic from the Coyo Oriental cemetary, San Pedro de Atacama, Chile. (Museo R. P. Gustavo Le Paige, S. J., San Pedro de Atacama, Chile. Photograph courtesy of Amy Oakland).

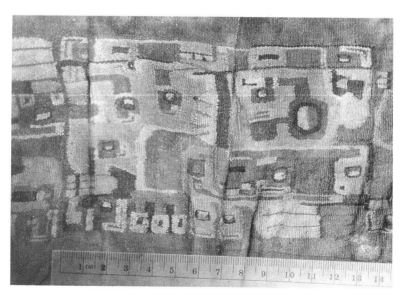

Figure 7.15b   Detail of tunic illustrating repeated motif of running bird-headed figures arranged in geometric panels. (Museo R. P. Gustavo Le Paige, S. J., San Pedro de Atacama, Chile. Photograph courtesy of Amy Oakland).

minerals. Many hafted hammer stones that have been associated with mining activities are found in the tombs of cemeteries like Coyo throughout the Atacama oasis (Oakland 1992).

In return for compliance and active participation in trading and exploiting local natural resources for the benefit of the state, Tiwanaku's lords granted emblems of status and authority, and perhaps women of high status to these local *kurakas*. We know that Inca rulers used certain women as diplomatic tools to cement relationships with local elite. Specially selected young females were gathered together to live communally in special residential compounds referred to as the *acllahuasi* (or house of the chosen women) in the larger cities of the empire (Rowe 1946). There these women performed a variety of services for the state: spinning cotton and wool for the clothing of the Inca elite, weaving particularly luxurious textiles, cooking delicacies and brewing maize beer in great quantities for public ceremonies, tending to the daily chores of maintaining the principal shrines of the state cults. Some of the *aclla* were drawn from the families of the highest nobility, and these frequently served as concubines to the emperor himself. Others were distributed by the Inca ruler and his generals as secondary wives to warriors who had distinguished themselves in battle, or to local kings and *kurakas* who had demonstrated loyalty to the Inca cause. In essence, the *aclla* were simultaneously sources of concentrated skilled labor for the state, and precious commodities for the conduct of diplomacy. Of course, females who were direct descendants of the royal household in Cuzco were the most desirable marriage partners for the highest status native lords of the provinces. These marriages constituted true dynastic alliances, and frequently resulted in heirs with aspirations to high positions in the central governmental bureaucracy, or even with pretensions to the throne itself. But the genius of Inca statecraft was to take this somewhat circumscribed notion of dynastic alliances among the princes and princesses of royal households and generalize it to virtually every rung in the social hierarchy of control. The tremendous concentration of unencumbered *aclla* in the provincial capitals of the Inca state was the key to this institutionalization of strategic marriages. By virtue of their elevated status as "chosen women" of the Inca, the *aclla* were transformed into desirable marriage partners, imbued with the prestige of the state, holding out the promise to provincial nobility of identification with the power and authority of the central government. Although we would stand on shaky ground to project the specific institution of the *aclla* back into the Tiwanaku state, like most court societies throughout the pre-industrial world, the lords of Tiwanaku surely relied on strategic marriages to consolidate their political ties with provincial nobility. The evidence from state-imposed sites like Omo in the Moquegua Valley and from the cemetery of Coyo in the San Pedro de Atacama oasis demonstrating that Tiwanaku elite were intimately associated with local populations strongly supports this supposition.

The personal relationships between *altiplano* patrons and local clients may well have been cast in the metaphor of fictive kinship among the elite. Such a series of elite, client-patron relationships accounts for the peculiar distribution, specialized context, and clustering of Tiwanaku artifacts in the peripheries of the empire. The overwhelming focus in the distant provinces on rich personal attire, on rare and precious commodities, on ritual paraphernalia linked closely with Tiwanaku state cults, and on objects of great value for public display emphasize the personalized, transactional quality of the relationship. In the far peripheries, the actions of the lords of Tiwanaku were pervasive, influential and perduring, but not fundamentally transformative. Unlike in the core regions around Lake Titicaca, more basic patterns of settlement, farming practices, and local political organization do not seem to have been altered directly by interaction with the *altiplano* state.

The role of Tiwanaku state religion similarly seems quite different in the far peripheries of the realm. Here the state cults did not act as monolithic, conceptual givens constructing and justifying cultural identity. Rather, the cults served as a fertile medium for generating personal and group prestige by establishing a shared idiom of communication between the lords of Tiwanaku and the local elite. The locals appropriated the state cults to open up channels of communication with the agents of Tiwanaku's elite. The isolated populations of southern Bolivia, the Atacama oasis, the central Chilean valleys, and northwestern Argentina had much to gain from inclusion in the social world created by the people of Tiwanaku. They benefited economically and socially from incorporation in secure, far-reaching caravan routes that placed them in contact with distant lands. But they were not passive recipients of an urban civilization propagated by Tiwanaku. Although the lords of Tiwanaku, like empire builders elsewhere in the pre-industrial world, may have portrayed themselves as a noble, civilizing force, the "barbarians" on the peripheries of their realm had their own ideas about the meaning of the relationship between themselves and the agents of Tiwanaku. This was not an autocratic relationship built on coercion. Unlike the populations of Moquegua, Cochabamba, and the Lake Titicaca basin, these people did not become absorbed culturally by Tiwanaku. They did not become citizens of a Tiwanaku state. Rather, they selectively and opportunistically adopted elements of Tiwanaku culture and society to enhance their political and economic positions, while maintaining their own unique ethnic identities. They actively engaged in the long-distance caravan trade that linked their communities with a broader social world, but they negotiated the terms of this engagement.

As states expand they incorporate a multiplicity of local populations possessing divergent demographic, political, and economic potentials. Some of the regions in the Lake Titicaca basin into which the Tiwanaku state expanded, such as the heartland of the old Pukara polity, contained human settlements with high population density, emergent nobility, class stratification, large investment in labor intensive systems of production, and well-developed mechanisms for allocating and redistributing economic surplus. This was a pre-existing social landscape of interdependent cities. In high contrast, other areas toward the peripheries of the state, such as the desolate *puna* of southern Bolivia, were characterized by small-scale, dispersed, kin-based communities that emphasized local community autonomy, and self-sufficiency. More inclusive economic relationships in these isolated communities were restricted to exchange based on principles of reciprocity among kinsmen.

The impact of Tiwanaku on these divergent communities in the south-central Andes likewise varied greatly, ranging from total political and economic absorption into the heart of the empire to desultory, indirect trade relationships on the margins. Some local communities, by choice or necessity, became citizens in the Tiwanaku state. Their home territories became true economic provinces of the empire. Others, by virtue of their distance from the capital, interacted with the state's agents through their traditional *kurakas*, but assiduously maintained their own ethnic identities. Tiwanaku urban values and ideology penetrated to these more isolated communities, but they were selectively adopted and encapsulated in the local culture, and did not come to dominate the local social landscape.

The cultural force of Tiwanaku's expansion was long-standing and so intense that it left a heavy imprint on societies throughout the south-central Andes. Generations after Tiwanaku itself had fallen into ruins and began its centuries-long slide into myth, local cultures still produced ceramics and textiles studded with motifs drawn from Tiwanaku's prestige-laden state art. Even 400 years after the fall, the Inca avidly sought to identify themselves with Tiwanaku as a mystical place of origin and as a sacred seat of dynastic power. The enduring impact and legacy of Tiwanaku's distinctive civilization was the product of its rare capacity to bind diverse social groups into long-term relationships of shared production, exchange, and belief.

8

The Decline and Fall of Tiwanaku

In the concluding chapter of his magisterial work on the history of Rome, Michael Rostovtzeff (1971:318) posed a question that has engaged and puzzled scholars for generations: "Why did such a powerful and brilliant civilization, the growth of ages and apparently destined to last for ages, gradually degenerate?" Rostovtzeff located the cause of Rome's decay and dissolution in the corruption of its once dynamic economic system. According to his analysis, deteriorating economic conditions in the third century A.D. generated empire-wide class and labor conflicts and sowed anarchy among the military which, in turn, shattered the over-arching, elitist political structure of the state. The end-product of this process was the fragmentation of the state marked by an inevitable shifting of political boundaries and a multiplication of centers of local power. Despite the acknowledged complexity and interlocking character of the social forces contributing to political fragmentation of the imperial system, one symptom and cause of Rome's degeneration particularly intrigued Rostovtzeff (1971:310):

> one feature of the economic condition is especially remarkable – the complete change in agricultural methods throughout the empire. Scientific cultivation backed up by capital and intelligence disappears utterly and is replaced everywhere by a system which merely scratches the surface of the soil and sinks lower and lower into primitive routine.

Rostovtzeff's apocalyptic vision of the empire's decline as a product of complete devolution in Rome's agricultural techniques and productive capacity, although perhaps overdrawn, illustrates a fundamental axiom of any theory of state collapse. Unless a state can assure a reasonable measure of economic well-being for its populations, it will inexorably lose competitive advantage and either disintegrate through internal disaffection, or fall prey to competing powers that will dissolve or absorb its political structure. In other words, there is an undeniable material basis to the political integrity of states, whether archaic or modern, and a large part of any explanation of state collapse resides in the vicissitudes of the production and distribution of wealth.

In the special case of the pre-industrial state, economic well-being was synonymous with agriculture. Wealth was generated primarily not by industry or by commerce, but by intensive farming of arable land. This essential truth holds even more rigorously in the context of the precolumbian Andean world where markets and merchantile activities were, on the whole, nonexistent, or severely constrained in geographic and economic scope. In lieu of unrestricted commerce and free market exchange, there was no other source in the ancient Andes for generating substantial wealth beyond the margin of subsistence than intensive agriculture. Of course, the deterioration of a state's agricultural base may just as well be a symptom as a cause of state collapse. We can readily imagine a scenario in which agricultural collapse is implicated as a contributing, rather than a proximate cause of state collapse. For instance, internal political disputes may disrupt the capacity of a state to invest systematically in its wealth-producing agricultural systems. Weakening or loss of political consensus results in declining production which further erodes the state's economic foundations. The ultimate result is a cross-linked, downward spiral in which interdependent economic and political institutions become increasingly debilitated and subject to rapid collapse.

Despite these potential complexities of causation, in a thoroughly agrarian world like the Andes, agriculture is inevitably implicated in some fashion in the process of state collapse. Here I explore the collapse of Tiwanaku's empire through the lens of its agricultural history. Based on a rich spectrum of new ecological data for the geographic region dominated by Tiwanaku, we can now perceive Tiwanaku's political decline as the product of the deterioration and ultimate abandonment of its regional-scale agricultural systems. The collapse of Tiwanaku's once-productive agro-economy was the result of a natural catastrophe of unprecedented proportions: hemispheric change in climatic conditions that shrank the always narrow environmental margin for effective agriculture in the Andean high plateau to the point at which surplus production became impossible. Under the burden of a deteriorating economic base, the overarching political structure of the empire fragmented, and the complex set of elite statuses that had evolved over the centuries of Tiwanaku domination of the south-central Andes was shattered. Tiwanaku's royal dynasty and court life dissolved.

In most pre-industrial states, the king was the ultimate guarantor of agricultural success. One of the primary cult obligations of the royal household was to perform continuing, seasonally regulated sets of agricultural rituals designed to ensure abundant harvests. Often rulers in these agrarian states were symbolically associated with the concept and achievement of agricultural fertility. Not only was the king perceived as the provider of political protection for his subjects, but, in his role as a ritual practitioner of the agricultural arts, he also, quite literally, provided daily sustenance for the common people. The nexus between political legitimacy and agricultural success could not be more intimate: uneasy lies the crown of a pre-industrial king who presides over an agricultural disaster. The rulers of the Tiwanaku world during the final century of that state's existence had the great misfortune to witness one of the most dramatic changes in climatic conditions experienced by humans in the southern hemisphere. The result for them and for Tiwanaku elite society was catastrophic. Their complex and carefully nurtured systems of hydraulic agriculture disintegrated beneath them, and with it went the pediment of their power and authority.

Climate and Collapse

After approximately 700 years of growth and colonial expansion, the Tiwanaku state disappeared as a regional political force in the south-central Andes between A.D. 1000 and 1100. Through progressively complex statecraft and economic opportunism, Tiwanaku had expanded from its core territory in the Lake Titicaca basin to establish a dispersed network of cultural and economic centers in diverse ecological settings. In the lower *yungas* zones that lie both to the east and west of the *altiplano*, Tiwanaku established large-scale colonizing populations for the purpose of directly exploiting lower-altitude, arable land. The case of the Moquegua Valley of south coastal Peru was a particularly clear example of intense, *altiplano* colonization of a *yungas* environment.

Although Tiwanaku colonies exploited *yungas* zones to produce a number of products otherwise unavailable at high altitude, the economic key to the functioning of the state was the integrated agricultural core area in the Lake Titicaca basin that operated by means of regional manipulation of land, labor, and most especially, water resources. Technical expertise stemming from centuries of empirical observation and experiment is evident in the planning, engineering, construction, and maintenance of this state agricultural system. The development of regional administrative centers, each with agricultural field systems under their control that incorporated refined hydrological engineering practices, formed a strong regional agricultural base for economic and political stability. Over the course of nearly a millennium of experimentation, the Tiwanaku state constructed an interlocking, redundant, and optimum agricultural supply base resistant to collapse and disintegration. Yet, despite an apparently secure basis for continued expansion and economic growth, the empire and its colonies collapsed and faded into history toward the end of the historical period denoted as Tiwanaku V (A.D. 800 to 1100). The collapse mechanism of the Tiwanaku state is only now emerging as the result of research into the function and vulnerabilities of the agricultural base of the Tiwanaku heartland and colonies.

Recent climatological and ecological data have provided the unanticipated key to explaining the causal mechanisms underlying the decline of Tiwanaku. In particular, data on climate variation obtained from ice cores taken at the Quelccaya glacier in southern Peru (Thompson et al. 1979, 1982, 1985, 1988) and from my own research group's sediment cores extracted from Lake Titicaca (Binford and Brenner 1989; Binford et al. 1992) has permitted correlation of Tiwanaku culture history with changing ecological conditions. Analysis of these data indicate a radical climate change in the south-central Andes during the post-A.D. 1000 era that took the form of a significant decrease in annual precipitation. The decrease in precipitation was so severe and persisted for so long that we can legitimately refer to this event as a great drought. This great drought led to a progressive abandonment of the agricultural systems of the Tiwanaku colonies followed by the collapse of the raised field systems of the heartland area.

In searching for the underlying causes of the decline of Tiwanaku, we are fortunate to have one of the most highly resolved records of regional paleoclimates derived from recent ice coring work at the Quelccaya glacier (Thompson et al. 1985, 1988). The Quelccaya ice cap is located in the Cordillera Blanca mountain range of southern Peru approximately 200 kilometers northwest of Lake Titicaca (Figure 8.1). In overview, during Tiwanaku IV and V times, the Quelccaya record indicates wetter periods from A.D. 610 to 650 and 760 to 1040 and periods of decreased precipitation from A.D. 650 to 730. In the post-Tiwanaku period from A.D. 1245 to 1310, the region experienced a severe precipitation deficit. High dust concentrations in the ice core with peaks around A.D. 600 and 920 have been associated with periods of major earth-moving, including raised field construction in the *altiplano* around Lake Titicaca (Thompson et al. 1988).

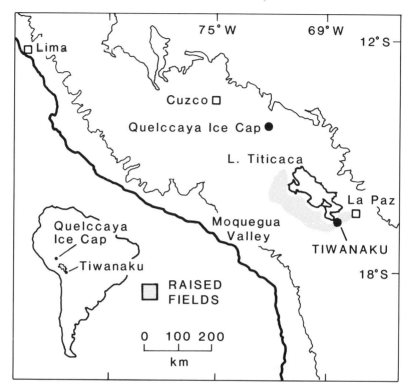

Figure 8.1   Map of the south-central Andes, indicating the location of the Quelccaya glacier between Cuzco and Lake Titicaca and the distribution of raised field agriculture.

Prevailing winds from the *altiplano* transport particles of dust and organic debris toward the Quelccaya glacier where they are deposited in snow layers. These particles serve as datable boundaries within the accumulated snow layers and as indicators of unusual events such as volcanic eruptions, or large-scale earth moving with its attendant generation of wind-born dust.

The proximity of the Quelccaya ice cap to Lake Titicaca and the main urban centers of the Tiwanaku empire is significant in that climate history derived from analysis of the ice cap data applies directly to the historical development of the state. The currently analyzed sections of the Quelccaya ice cap are a record of climate variation in the south-central Andes over the period from A.D. 400 to 1980 (Thompson et al. 1988, 1989; Thompson and Mosley-Thompson

1987). The basic data are cumulative measurements of annual snow layer deposits (Figures 8.2a–c). In simplest terms, in these graphs, large snow layer thickness is indicative of heavy annual rainfall at lower altitudes; small layer thickness implies an annual period of lower rainfall. While numerous wet periods exist in the record as illustrated in these figures, and severe drought is certainly indicated in the period from A.D. 1245 to 1310, the data only reveal clear trends through statistical analysis. Over 200-year intervals from A.D. 800 to 1400 the mean annual snow layer thickness progressively declines. While vigorous fluctuations in precipitation certainly exist over individual decades, there is a statistically significant change in mean moisture level beginning after A.D. 1000.

If the ice core thickness distributions are displayed in a different way, the decline in annual precipitation after A.D. 1000 becomes even more apparent and dramatic. Figure 8.3a illustrates a gradual change in precipitation starting around A.D. 950 followed by a precipitous change in moisture content commencing with the post-A.D. 1000 period. This reflects the significant decline in mean levels of precipitation between the pre- and post-A.D. 1000 time periods. A short upswing in moisture level at circa A.D. 1300 in this curve is represented together with a subsequent decline starting from about A.D. 1350 and extending at least up to A.D. 1400. Generally this result translates into a much drier climate on average in the post-A.D. 1000 period than in earlier times (Figure 8.3b).

Paleolimnological work by my own research team based on cores extracted from sediments from the bottom of Lake Titicaca supports the ice core evidence for climate change. According to these sediment cores, the lake level was significantly higher than usual between circa A.D. 350 to 500, implying increased precipitation. This period of elevated lake level is indicated in ancient pollen collected from one of our cores and is marked by a dramatic rise in certain aquatic plants and planktonic algae. The sediments in this section of the core have been radiocarbon dated to about A.D. 300 to 700, with the highest lake level peaking at around A.D. 500 (Figure 8.4). This increase in aquatic plants and algae co-occurs with a decrease in sedges, such as the Lake Titicaca *totora* reed. This particular distribution of ancient pollen indicates that during this time lake levels rose over the core site drowning the sedges and promoting the expansion of aquatic plants and algae. Subsequently, the sediments in the upper sections of the core show a dramatic decline in deeper water plants and algae, and a resurgence of *totora*, which is a shallow-water plant. This pollen distribution in the upper third of the core reflects a lowering of lake levels and a return to littoral conditions at the coring site (Leyden

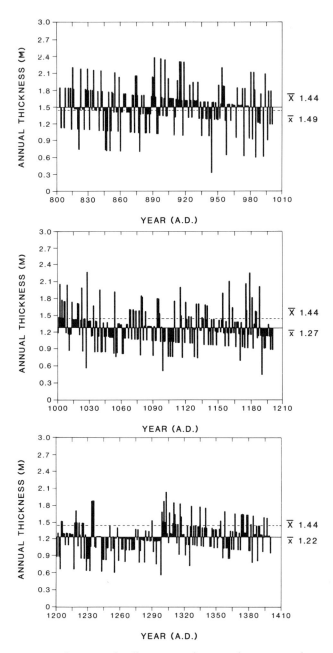

Figures 8.2a-c   Three graphs illustrating the cumulative annual snow layer deposits on the Quelccaya ice cap from A.D. *800 to 1410. (Figure based on privileged, unpublished data courtesy of L. G. Thompson).*

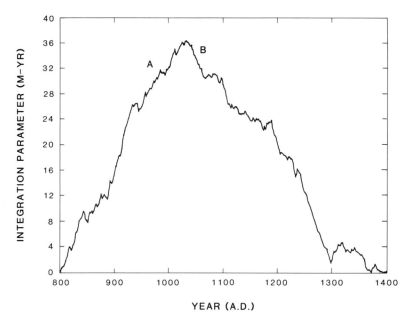

Figure 8.3a Time-dependent graph of changes in snow layer accumulation on the Quelccaya ice cap. The graph illustrates a gradual change in precipitation starting around A.D. 950 (point A) followed by a precipitous decline in rainfall after A.D. 1050 (point B). Relative drought conditions persisted in the south-central Andes until the early fifteenth century. (Figure based on privileged, unpublished data courtesy of L. G. Thompson).

1989). Age estimates on these sediments place the decline in lake level precisely in the post-A.D. 1000 period of dessication recorded in the Quelccaya ice cap. In other words, lake sediments and ice cores tell the same grim tale: the south-central Andes suffered from a catastrophic and persistent drought that began around A.D. 1000 and persisted virtually unabated for many decades.

In addition to recording changes in precipitation, a measure of the prevailing temperature at the Quelccaya glacier can be inferred from isotopic oxygen measurements (Thompson and Mosley-Thompson 1989). These measurements indicate a rise in mean temperature of about 1° C beginning around A.D. 1000 and persisting until at least A.D. 1400 coincident with the evidence for drought. A similar A.D. 1000 to 1400 temperature rise has been observed in Europe, a phenomenon designated there as the Medieval Warm Epoch (Anderson 1991; Lamb 1965, 1982). Crops normally grown in the southern parts of Europe flourished in the colder climate of the Scandinavian

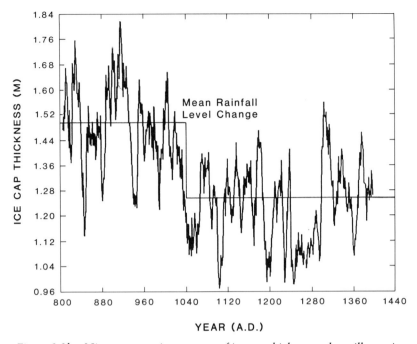

*Figure 8.3b   Nine-year moving average of ice cap thickness values, illustrating the dramatic post-*A.D.* 1000 decline in mean rainfall levels in the south-central Andes. (Figure based on privileged, unpublished data courtesy of L. G. Thompson).*

countries leading to a period of economic prosperity throughout Europe. Vineyards and associated wine production peaked during this time due to the mildness of the climate. However, the general rise in temperature was not without negative collateral effects: devastating torrential rains occurred frequently in Europe in the fourteenth century destroying the agricultural gains of earlier periods (Lamb 1965). As indicated by the Quelccaya ice cap data, this temperature rise appears to extend into the Western Hemisphere suggesting that this climate change was a global phenomenon.

The climate changes during the post-A.D. 1000 era documented in the Quelccaya ice cap and in our lake sediment cores had an agro-ecological impact on South American civilizations equally as profound as the historically documented effects on Western European societies. This new evidence that climate change in the form of chronic drought conditions in the post-A.D. 1000 period was the mechanism that triggered the collapse of Tiwanaku's agricultural base and ultimately the disintegration of the state itself is compelling. This is not to say that

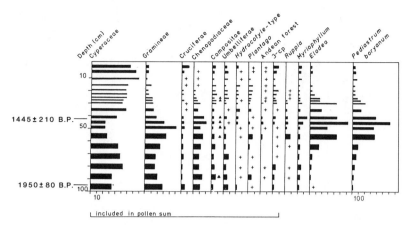

Figure 8.4 Pollen percentage diagram for a Lake Titicaca sediment core taken near the site of Lukurmata. Pluses represent percentages less than 2 percent. All profiles are drawn to the same scale except for Pediastrum boryanum *which is displayed at 1/10-scale. Redrawn from Leyden (1989:270) with addition of radiocarbon dates on sediments in basal and mid-core sections.*

this great drought is a complete explanation for the collapse of Tiwanaku's political system. The process of political collapse in the face of declining agricultural returns undoubtedly required a few generations and was accompanied by historically specific instances of social competition, conflict, and realignments that are unrecorded in the archaeological record. Nevertheless, when we look carefully at the nature and potential vulnerabilities of the agricultural systems that Tiwanaku's populations created, and then became totally dependent upon, it becomes painfully clear that chronic drought conditions were the ultimate threat and the proximate cause for the collapse of the Tiwanaku state.

Vulnerability of Tiwanaku Agricultural Systems

Tiwanaku agricultural systems in both its *altiplano* core territory and in its coastal colonial outposts reflect consummate skill in conception and construction. Nevertheless, both core and colonial Tiwanaku agricultural systems fail and are abandoned in the immediate post-A.D. 1000 period. Given the different ecological, technological, and organizational characteristics of these various agricultural technologies, we can detect a distinct sequence in the extinction of these systems based on their relative vulnerability under the severe drought conditions recorded in the Quelccaya ice cap. The vulnerability of agricultural technologies used in different geographic regions of the Tiwanaku empire directly depends on the relationship of water source and water distribution techniques to field systems, and on the effects of drought conditions on the function of a given system. Since water supply ultimately relates to climate-dependent rainfall, river runoff, or groundwater storage, the agricultural systems that depend on these distinct sources will be affected differentially by changing climatic conditions.

Altiplano *Agricultural Systems*

The immediate environs and near hinterland of Tiwanaku were characterized by extensive raised field systems and by *cochas*. *Cochas* are essentially sunken-gardens excavated into the water table (Flores-Ochoa 1983). Many of these sunken-gardens are still used today on the Andean *altiplano* as small, family gardens and as water holes for cattle. There is strong evidence that *cochas* were part of the sophisticated repertoire of Tiwanaku farmers, although cultivation of these sunken-gardens was clearly secondary to raised field farming. These two kinds of agricultural systems were both fed by deep groundwater and by perennial springs, sources of water that render them resistant to drought. Of all the agricultural systems employed in the Tiwanaku empire, these two were least vulnerable to collapse from drought conditions. Two types of canal-fed raised field systems are also found in the Tiwanaku hinterland. One such irrigation network was discovered in the Pajchiri area to the northwest of the Pampa Koani. This aqueduct-based network was driven by local, high-elevation springwater. A second and more extensive system of canal-fed raised fields is found in the valley of Tiwanaku and in the Catari river sub-basin (see Chapter 6). These raised fields were supplied by canals that drew water from local rivers and streams. If these canal-fed raised fields had operated with surface runoff as their *sole* source of water, they would have been highly vulnerable to drought conditions. However, these systems were simultaneously supplied by groundwater, and they therefore retain lower vulnerability, similar to that of the deep groundwater-fed raised fields and *cochas*.

Moquegua *Valley Agricultural Systems*

In many respects, the Moquegua Valley can be considered a paradigmatic case of Tiwanaku agricultural colonization outside of the *altiplano*. Aridity and broken, difficult terrain severely constrain agriculture in the 140-kilometers-long drainage area of the Moquegua Valley. Although this drainage system rises above 5,000 meters, less that 20 percent of the area lies within the zone of seasonal rainfall. Cultivation requires artificial, canal-based irrigation. The use of scarce runoff is itself subject to topographic constraints that divide Moquegua agriculture into four ascending zones (see Figure 7.3, p. 253). The second zone, which lies at the heart of the mid-valley, contains the largest expanse of arable land, comprised of fertile flat-lands formed around the confluence of the three major valley tributaries. As we have seen, this zone was the focus of heavy and long-term Tiwanaku occupation.

Several native agricultural techniques designed to exploit available water resources were developed in the Moquegua Valley. These techniques include rain-fed agricultural terraces, canal irrigated field systems in the floodplain of the Moquegua River and local wetlands agriculture supplied by seepage from spring and groundwater at coastal sites near Ilo (Clement and Moseley 1989). Tiwanaku sites are concentrated in the lower agricultural zones where farming was supported by canal systems that reclaimed relatively flat land. Irrigated floodplain agriculture is associated with both Tiwanaku IV and V phase colonies (c. A.D. 400–1000) in the Moquegua Valley. The agricultural systems in the Moquegua Valley were all highly vulnerable to drought since their sources of water are most directly linked to precipitation levels. Rainfall, river water, and shallow groundwater springs supplied the irrigation needs of Moquegua's agricultural landscape. All of these sources of water are affected rapidly by decreasing rainfall.

In contrast, Tiwanaku's groundwater-based raised fields in the high plateau were much less vulnerable to drought conditions than the agricultural systems in the *yungas* areas. Because of the nature of the groundwater reservoir, evaporation through the surface is limited. Seepage rates into the canals of raised field complexes is similarly a slow process further limiting the effects of evaporation. Since the collection zones supplying groundwater to the raised fields in the Tiwanaku hinterlands are immense and the flow of groundwater to the fields is extremely slow, with typical velocities on the order of centimeters per month, depletion of this resource is minimal under normal seasonal or periodic drought conditions. In periods of prolonged drought, however, the groundwater level will eventually decline as resupply diminishes. In these circumstances, raised field systems will ultimately fail. *Cochas* are even more resistant to drought than raised fields. They can be continuously excavated to follow a decreasing water table. Although least vulnerable to drought of all the agricultural systems employed by Tiwanaku, by their nature, *cochas* offer limited planting surface area and give a relatively low rate of agricultural return relative to labor invested. The farmers of Tiwanaku could not replace the production of extensive raised field networks with these labor intensive sunken gardens: the scale and magnitude of the raised field systems were simply too great.

The Sequence of Agricultural Extinction

Under chronic drought conditions, each of the agricultural systems within the Tiwanaku heartland and in its agricultural colonies located in the lower-lying *yungas* region ultimately failed. But they failed sequentially and not simultaneously. The systems that possess delayed delivery characteristics (*cochas* and raised fields) sustained production longer than those systems directly tied to the precipitation regime (river irrigation, rainfall dependent terraces, localized springs tied to shallow groundwater sources). In the presence of extended drought conditions, there was a distinct sequence of extinction of agricultural systems based on their relative vulnerability. Given this sequential extinction effect, one immediate agro-ecological consequence of the climate change documented in the Quelccaya ice cap was shifts in the agricultural supply zones available to the Tiwanaku state. These supply zone shifts generated grave social problems for a political system experiencing increasing economic stress.

As precipitation levels began to decrease gradually after A.D. 950, irrigated, canal-based agriculture characteristic of the Tiwanaku V colonies in the Moquegua Valley were early casualties of reduced rainfall and reduced river flow rates. The Tiwanaku V colonies in the middle Moquegua Valley relied almost exclusively on canal-fed irrigation systems to support their populations. Even more vulnerable to minor rainfall and runoff decreases were the small communities along the Peruvian and Chilean coasts dependent upon shallow groundwater seepage as a source of irrigation water (Clement and Moseley 1989). Since only a small fraction of the river flow supplies the groundwater reservoir, coastal communities depending upon springs and seepage for water supply to field systems were the first to experience minor changes in the water supply. These small spring-based agricultural communities may have gone into decline as early as A.D. 850 to 950 with the initial shifts to a drier climate (Bermann et al. 1989).

Despite the deterioration of the Tiwanaku V Moquegua colonies' agricultural base, the heartland agricultural system dependent upon raised fields was still relatively viable due to the time lag in groundwater change even under incipient drought conditions. Further, the potential crop supply base from heartland systems far exceeded the demand, leading to excess agricultural capacity. Even if these raised fields operated at partial capacity due to gradually changing groundwater conditions, sufficient agricultural supply to sustain the local population was still possible. But the agricultural system as a whole lost substantial capacity for surplus production.

Ultimately, chronic drought conditions began to lower the water table height in the raised field complexes in the Tiwanaku heartland, changing the delicate moisture balance derived from continuous replenishing of water in the critical canals between elevated planting beds. Declining availability of fresh water supply caused subtle changes in the heat transfer characteristics of the raised field systems. The formation of dry soil surface layers changed the heat conduction and moisture transport characteristics of the raised fields and increased chances of crop loss from frost damage, exacerbating the agricultural problems caused by the drought itself. As the groundwater level dropped, however, the most devastating effect was the drought-related withdrawal of water supply from the root systems of plants cultivated on the raised field platforms. Given a receding water table, there was no economically feasible method to reconfigure the water supply and reproduce production results similar to those achieved under fully functioning raised field systems.

The Evidence of Changing Settlement Patterns

In this scenario of climate-induced collapse, the heartland area was the last survivor, but only in the presence of an observable loss in agricultural capacity from year to year. Given predictable and non-reversible decline in the principal agricultural supply base, regionalization and opportunistic exploitation of declining water resources replaced previous centralized state control of an integrated agricultural landscape. Since available water resources were dispersed and limited, the size of the group deriving sustenance from each water source was commensurate with the source itself. Post–Tiwanaku settlement patterns in the valley of Tiwanaku dramatically reflect this process of population dispersion.

In the Tiwanaku IV and early Tiwanaku V phases, the lower and middle valley of Tiwanaku was organized into an integrated, agricultural production zone characterized by a distinct settlement hierarchy similar to that of the Pampa Koani region. During this time, a series of sites was established along hillside terraces on both the north and south sides of the valley immediately above the Tiwanaku river's floodplain. These Tiwanaku settlements are spaced regularly, each approximately 2 kilometers apart, all along the adjacent hillside terraces from the city of Tiwanaku itself to the shore of Lake Titicaca some 17 kilometers away (Albarracín-Jordan and Mathews 1990). These settlements vary in size from one to ten hectares, and show evidence of dense occupation. Several have elaborate, stone-faced terraces on which houses and craft workshops were constructed. Some of the larger sites were substantial villages associated directly with the administration of agricultural production on raised fields in the adjacent river plain (Albarracín-Jordan and Mathews 1990). Substantial numbers of agricultural hoes recovered from these sites indicate unambiguously that the residents of these villages were engaged primarily in agricultural production for the state. During the florescence of Tiwanaku society, the valley was clearly a dedicated agricultural landscape of the elite.

In sharp contrast, the immediate post–Tiwanaku settlement pattern in the region exhibits a complete disintegration of this organized exploitation of the valley for the purposes of intensive agricultural production. Although there are still substantial numbers of sites in Tiwanaku's hinterland after A.D. 1000, they are widely dispersed across the landscape and few exceed one hectare in size. Most dramatic of all in terms of settlement pattern transformations, the cities of Tiwanaku and Lukurmata themselves are virtually abandoned at this time. Radiocarbon dates on Tiwanaku V phase households in these cities cluster between A.D. 750 and 950, and *no* radiocarbon dates on domestic occupations are associated with these urban centers past A.D. 1000. There was, in short, a dramatic redistribution of population in the Tiwanaku hinterland characterized by complete deurbanization. If as Saalman (1968:11) suggests "there is only one criterion of failure for cities: depopulation," then after A.D. 1000 Tiwanaku and its secondary urban centers were clear failures. As a corollary to this proposition, when cities and urban culture fail, so do the state political systems in which they are embedded.

There is some evidence for localized raised field cultivation in the post–A.D. 1000 environment (Albarracín-Jordan and Mathews 1990; Graffam 1990). However, despite subsequent periods of relatively higher precipitation that would have again made this form of cultivation technologically feasible, the earlier regional system of large-scale agricultural production was never reactivated. This serves to illustrate that societies possess thresholds of irreversibility. Once fragmented, precarious structures of organizational complexity characteristic of imperial societies never permit a return to the original state.

Similar settlement pattern surveys on the southwestern margins of Lake Titicaca provide a portrait of agricultural collapse and settlement transformation in that region consistent with this scenario in the Tiwanaku hinterland. There recent archaeological research found evidence of intrusive human occupation and tombs in previously productive raised field complexes in the immediate post–A.D. 1000 period. With the collapse of Tiwanaku raised field agriculture in the region, there seems to have been a shift to increasing emphasis on llama and alpaca pastoralism to replace lost food resources (Stanish 1991). Such a shift would entail dramatic changes in the structure of the prevailing social order, toward a more dispersed, mobile and potentially aggressive society.

Relocation and regionalization of populations around increasingly scarce water resources also occurred outside of the *altiplano* in the Tiwanaku colonial outposts of the Moquegua Valley. This process of climate-induced, settlement reorganization is directly reflected in the emergence of post–Tiwanaku groups in the upper Moquegua Valley sierra zones. Agriculture in the Moquegua region shifts away from the irrigated cultivation of the mid-valley floodplain characteristic of the Tiwanaku V colonies toward higher elevation agricultural terraces tied to a restricted water supply derived from snow melt and available precipitation (Bermann et al. 1989; Rice et al. 1989). Water supply was now critical to survival and defensive structures appear in profusion in the sierra zone apparently guarding and controlling access to the supply canals (Kolata 1983; Rice et al. 1989). But the water supply from this source was limited, given declining precipitation and lack of replenishment of the sierra snow pack in the post–Tiwanaku environment.

The Tiwanaku empire experienced collapse of its agricultural base after A.D. 1000 due to a dramatic decline in annual precipitation beginning around A.D. 950. Recovery in terms of return to the precipitation levels of the pre–A.D. 1000 period began only centuries later. Since the Tiwanaku empire was based on a surplus-producing agricultural system that was sustained over a period of at least seven centuries, the intense drought conditions of the post–A.D. 1000 period can be understood as an extraordinary and catastrophic episode of climate change beyond any experienced during the formation and design of the raised field system. Over the course of these centuries, Tiwanaku society became dependent upon a system of agricultural production that was well adapted to the rigorous environmental conditions of the *altiplano*: a system that could adjust to normal cycles of drought and inundation characteristic of that environment. The state organized labor on a grand scale to construct raised field systems in their final Tiwanaku Phase IV and V configurations. The intricate drainage and water shunting systems to control groundwater level and intercept runoff are eloquent testimonies to indigenous understanding of the hydrological environment and its manipulation. Nevertheless, despite centuries of sophisticated manipulation of the hydrological regime for the benefit of agricultural production, Tiwanaku agro-engineers were incapable of responding to a drought of unprecedented duration and severity. In the prolonged decades of drought conditions that ensued in the post–A.D. 1000 era, there was insufficent production and storage capacity to support the urbanized populations that had grown up in the lake district during previous periods of agricultural expansion and prosperity. The end-product of a climate-induced deterioration of the agricultural base was predictable. Tiwanaku cities were abandoned and the surplus-extracting apparatus of state administration disintegrated. The royal dynasty, tied so intimately to the success of its state-run agricultural estates, lost both its fundamental source of power and its social relevance.

The Aftermath of Collapse

The psychological impact of this chronic drought on the people of Tiwanaku must have been devastating. For untold generations, their sophisticated hydraulic agriculture had generated unprecedented wealth and power. Their empire controlled the great Lake Titicaca basin and made them undisputed lords of the high plateau. In time, their political reach extended into the exotic, resource-rich lands of the *yungas* to the east and west of their *altiplano* homeland. The people of Tiwanaku were accustomed to dominating the essential elements of their environment. These were a people obsessed with diverting great rivers and completely reshaping intractable mountain landscapes for the purpose of intensifying their agricultural power. They were virtuosos in the art and science of farming. Their consummate skill in controlling stone and water, land and people converted their society into one of the truly brilliant achievements of native Andean civilization. Yet, the urbanized world they created for themselves was vulnerable precisely at the point they least expected.

The demands of concentrated human populations on the food supplies of the empire were enormous. Tiwanaku's urban culture flourished as long as a constant stream of agricultural produce flowed from the country to the cities. Over the centuries, Tiwanaku's urban food supply had come to rely upon an intensely productive, yet highly specialized form of cultivation. Raised field agriculture could stand many different kinds of environmental stress through clever use of aqueducts and canals, dikes and river shunts. But, in the face of such a persistent, deep drought, no agricultural system could survive for long under the rigorous environmental conditions of the *altiplano*. In a sense, after a successful run of at least 800 years, Tiwanaku, like the dinosaur driven to extinction by the environmental consequences of asteroid impacts on the earth, became the victim of cosmic bad luck. The people of Tiwanaku themselves did not perish *en masse*, but their special form of social organization, their economic power impelled by imperial conquests and intensive production on rich agricultural lands, their cities studded with the monumental displays of former glory, all of these went the way of the dinosaur.

What replaced Tiwanaku society was markedly less powerful, and considerably less splendid, if monumental architecture and art, a refined court life, and a distinct cultural aesthetic are a few of our indices. The evidence of the archaeological record speaks unambiguously. After the decline of Tiwanaku, cities and urban civilization disappeared in the Lake Titicaca basin for nearly 400 years. Central organization and management of intensive agriculture, craft production, long-distance trade, and other sources of wealth broke down. Across the south-central Andes, human populations dispersed across the landscape, and settled into smaller, defensible settlements. The demise of the Tiwanaku empire brought with it widespread political instability. The "Pax Tiwanaku" imposed by the empire could no longer repress ingrained, inter-ethnic hostilities, and the former provinces of the empire dissolved into small polities bitterly contesting land, water, and other natural resources. The political disturbances and economic chaos that followed in the wake of Tiwanaku's collapse are brutally reflected in the characteristic pattern of settlement of this period: the fortified village. Núñez and Dillehay (1978) speak of a "cordon" of fortifications ranging along the upper valleys of the north Chilean and south Peruvian coast that appears at this time. Vast stretches of formerly productive land in the highlands and along the coast were abandoned as populations retreated into protected redoubts, subsisting principally on the production of small-scale agricultural terraces in arable pockets.

This state of political instability marked by a proliferation of competing micro-polities persisted until the late fourteenth century. It was only in the decades immediately prior to the irruption of the Inca onto the high plateau around A.D. 1450 that well-organized kingdoms associated with Aymara speakers began to reassert their hegemony over large expanses of productive territory. In the fifteenth and sixteenth century, coincident with the re-establishment of more normal precipitation levels, the Lake Titicaca basin was again under the sway of powerful political coalitions. Bouysse Cassagne (1986:211) identifies at least twelve Aymara señorios or kingdoms in the highland territories of the old Tiwanaku empire, including the Pacajes in the area of Tiwanaku itself. Two of these kingdoms, the Lupaqa and the Qolla, centered on the western shores of Lake Titicaca, appear to have been organized nearly at the state level, restoring some of the political power that had once been wielded by Tiwanaku alone. The Lupaqa and Qolla sustained a series of heavily populated towns and dominated relatively large territories, including distant colonies on the coast of Peru and in the *yungas* region on the eastern slopes of the Andes. By the mid-fifteenth century, these two native kingdoms were in a bitter battle for political supremacy of the lake district. If their further development had not been truncated by the Inca's conquest of their territory, the outcome of the contest between the Qolla and the Lupaqa might have been the emergence of a new Tiwanaku-style empire.

Instead, the imperial armies of the Inca moved swiftly to gain the submission and rich tribute potential of the native Titicaca basin kingdoms. Appealing to a mythical association with the ancient Tiwanaku dynasty, the Inca attempted to construct an identity with the past, to appropriate the mystique of Tiwanaku's distinct civilization as their own. The Inca conquered farther and faster than Tiwanaku ever had. But, unlike Tiwanaku, their impact on the local population was short lived. The coercive techniques liberally applied by the Inca, calculated military violence, garrisoning of provinces, uprooting and resettling of populations in alien social settings, were effective, but energetically costly and short-term solutions to the problem of political integration. Coercive mechanisms such as these, when applied indiscriminately, inevitably generate instability and hostility in subject populations. It is the shared beliefs and practices of a coherent ideology, and not a preponderance of naked force, that bind pluralistic states into durable political and economic formations. The nearly 1,000 year reign of the lords of Tiwanaku in the south-central Andes may be attributed as much to their conceptual understanding and manipulation of the interpenetrating institutions of ideology and economy, as to their technological prowess in force-of-arms.

In 1532 another wave of conquerors stormed the Andean world and transformed it forever. After the Spanish vanquished the ill-fated empire of the Incas, they began at once to implant European modes of economic and political behavior. Their attempts to restructure the native Andean world in terms they could understand, and better manipulate, were immeasureably aided by the scourge of virulent diseases to which the natives had little resistance. In province after province of "Alto Peru" (the Spanish term for the great Andean *altiplano*), colonial tribute lists record the terrible toll on natives exacted by foreign diseases, and by other introduced evils, such as forced labor in the deadly mines of Potosí in southern Bolivia. In some provinces of Alto Peru as much as 90 percent of the indigenous population disappeared within 50 years of the Spanish conquest. Some fled the foreign invaders, disappearing into the trackless deserts of the high plateau, or into the lush forests east of the Andes. Many were murdered in the aftermath of the conquest or died rapidly from smallpox or measles. Others suffered an even more agonizing fate: they were consigned to the mines to labor for their Spanish overlords until death. For the miners, death came slower, but it came surely and in bitter ways: starvation, exhaustion, poisoning from the mercury used to extract the precious silver, despair. And the waves of killing pandemics kept coming. A contemporary account from northern Peru in 1585 vividly and awfully captures the terror and the terrible social cost of these epidemics:

> They died by scores and hundreds. Villages were depopulated. Corpses were scattered over the fields or piled up in houses or huts . . . The fields were uncultivated; the herds were untended; and the workshops and mines were without laborers . . . The price of food rose to such an extent that many persons found it beyond their reach. They escaped the foul disease, but only to be wasted by famine. (Moses 1914:385)

It was not long before the sophisticated agricultural techniques worked out by the natives of the high plateau over the millennia were lost to the world. The population that survived the conquest was not large enough to justify investment in terraces and dams, dikes and aqueducts. The Spanish overlords were more interested in precious metals, cattle, and a few crops that fueled their mining industry: vineyards for wine, olives for oil, and a few cereal grains to sustain their workers. The once innumerable banks of fertile agricultural terraces fell gradually into disuse, the once vast herds of llamas and alpaca dwindled to nothing, and the once bustling network of caravans and colonies atrophied, bringing isolation to the native populations where there had once been alliance. The native Andean peoples have persisted in this state of marginality to this day.

But, ironically, the mystique of their brilliant past lingers in the imagination of all the citizens of the modern Andean republics. The people who conceived and lived in Tiwanaku's world disappeared 1,000 years ago. But their cultural legacy persists in strangely stubborn ways in the minds of the Bolivian people. Like the Inca before them, contemporary Bolivans, both Indian and non-Indian alike, seek to appropriate and absorb as their own what they perceive as the greatness of an ancestral civilization.

In 1989, a major politician aspiring to the presidency of the Republic of Bolivia declared his candidacy on national television outside the ruins of Tiwanaku. In 1990, the newly elected president, Jaime Paz Zamorra, declared Tiwanaku a "diplomatic capital" of Bolivia, and hosted a meeting of the presidents of the Andean republics within the great temple precinct of the Kalasasaya, the ancient seat of Tiwanaku's kings. In 1992, a group of Aymara symbolically reclaimed their heritage by planting the *wipala*, a multi-colored flag emblematic of a unified Aymara nation, squarely and visibly on the summit of the Akapana pyramid. Their leaders declared unequivocally that the site belonged to the Aymara people, and not to the Bolivian nation. The hulking, eroded pyramids of Tiwanaku retain an essence of native Andean spirituality. Local shamans still offer sacrifices to the *huacas* of the Akapana and Puma Punku and invoke their names in the long, ancient litany of the mountain deities. Although reduced utterly to ruins, Tiwanaku's monuments maintain their ineffable power to evoke feelings of ethnic pride and wonder. In some sense, this intense, symbolic contest over the shattered remnants of a world long gone is a fitting and enduring testament to the cultural achievements of the people of Tiwanaku.

Bibliography

Abercrombie, T. 1986. *The Politics of Sacrifice: An Aymara Cosmology in Action.* Unpublished Ph.D. dissertation, Department of Anthropology, University of Chicago, Chicago.

Albarracín-Jordan, J., and J. Mathews. 1990. *Asentamientos Prehispánicos del Valle de Tiwanaku,* vol. 1. La Paz, Bolivia: Producciones Cima.

Albó, X. (con equipo de CIPCA). 1972. Dinámica en la estructura intercomunitaria de Jesús de Machaca. *America Indígena* 32, 773–816.

Anderson, I. 1991. Global warming rings true. *New Scientist* 21, 23.

Arriaga, José de [1621]. 1968. *Extirpación de la Idolotría del Perú,* vol. 209. Madrid: Biblioteca de Autores Españoles.

Bandelier, A. 1911. The ruins at Tiahuanaco. *Proceedings of the American Antiquarian Society* 21, part 1.

Bastien, J. 1978. *Mountain of the Condor: Metaphor and Ritual in an Andean Ayllu.* St. Paul, Minn.: West.

Bellamy, H., and P. Allen. 1948. *The Calendar of Tiahuanaco.* London: Faber and Faber.

Bennett, W. 1934. Excavations at Tiahuanaco. *Anthropological Papers of the American Museum of Natural History* 34, 359–494.

Bennett, W. 1936. Excavations in Bolivia. *Anthropological Papers of the American Museum of Natural History* 35, 329–507.

Berdan, F. 1982. *The Aztecs of Central Mexico: An Imperial Society.* New York: Holt, Rinehart and Winston.

Bermann, M., P. Goldstein, C. Stanish, and L. Watanabe. 1989. The collapse of the Tiwanaku state: a view from the Osmore drainage. In D. Rice, C. Stanish, and P. Scarr, (eds.), *Ecology, Settlement and History in the Osmore Drainage, Peru,* Oxford: British Archaeological Reports International Series 545(ii), 269–85.

Bertonio, Ludovico [1612]. 1984. *Vocabulario de la Lengua Aymara.* La Paz, Bolivia: Edicion Ceres.

Betanzos, Juan de [1551]. 1987. *Suma y Narración de los Incas,* Maria del Carmen Martin Rubio (ed.). Madrid: Ediciones Atlas.

Binford, M., and M. Brenner. 1989. Resultados de estudios de limnología en los ecosistemas de Tiwanaku. In A. Kolata (ed.), *Arqueología de Lukurmata,* vol. 2. La Paz, Bolivia: Producciones Puma Punku, 213–36.

Binford, M. W., M. Brenner, and D. R. Engstrom. 1991. Patrones de sedimentación temporal en la zona litoral del Huiñaimarca. In C. Dejoux and A. Iltis (eds.), *El Lago Titicaca: Síntesis del conocimiento limnológico actual*. La Paz, Bolivia: ORSTOM and Hisbol, 47–58.

Bird, R., D. Browman, and M. Durbin. 1983–4. Quechua and maize: mirrors of central Andean culture history. *Journal of the Steward Anthropological Society* 15, 185–240.

Bouysse-Cassagne, T. 1986. Urco and uma: Aymara concepts of space. In J. Murra, N. Wachtel and J. Revel (eds.), *Anthropological History of Andean Polities*. Cambridge: Cambridge University Press, 201–27.

Broda, J., D. Carrasco, and E. Matos Moctezuma. 1987. *The Great Temple of Tenochtitlan: Center and Periphery in the Aztec World*. Berkeley: University of California Press.

Browman, D. 1978. Toward the development of the Tiahuanaco (Tiwanaku) state. In David Browman (ed.), *Advances in Andean Archaeology*. The Hague, The Netherlands: Mouton, 327–49.

Browman, D. 1981. New light on Andean Tiwanaku. *American Scientist* 69, 408–19.

Browman, D. 1984. Tiwanaku: development of interzonal trade and economic expansion in the altiplano. In D. Browman, R. Burger, and M. Rivera (eds.), *Social and Economic Organization in the Prehispanic Andes*. Oxford: British Archaeological Reports International Series 194, 117–42.

Brush, S. 1977. *Mountain, Field and Family: The Economy and Ecology of an Andean Valley*. Philadelphia: University of Pennsylvania Press.

Calancha, Antonio de la [1638]. 1939. *Crónica moralizada de la Ordén de San Agustín del Perú*. La Paz, Bolivia: Imprenta Artistica.

Castelnau, Francis de [1850–1]. 1939. El pueblo de Tihuanacu. In G. Otero (ed.), *Tihuanacu: antología de los principales escritos de los cronistas coloniales, americanistas e historiadores bolivianos*, Biblioteca Boliviana 2. La Paz, Bolivia: Imprenta Artistica, 53–66.

Chalon, P. [1882,1884]. 1939. Monumentos religiosos y militares de Tihuanacu. In G. Otero (ed.), *Tihuanacu: antología de los principales escritos de los cronistas coloniales, americanistas e historiadores bolivianos*, Biblioteca Boliviana 2. La Paz, Bolivia: Imprenta Artistica, 78–87.

Chávez, S. 1975. The Arapa and Thunderbolt stela: a case of stylistic identity with implications for Pucara influence in the area of Tiahuanaco. *Ñawpa Pacha* 13, 3–25.

Chávez, S. 1988. Archaeological reconnaissance in the province of Chumbivilcas, south highland Peru. *Expedition* 30 (3), 27–38.

Chávez, S., and K. Mohr-Chávez. 1975. A carved stela from Taraco, Puno, Peru and the definition of an early style of stone sculpture from the altiplano of Peru and Bolivia. *Ñawpa Pacha* 13, 45–83.

Cieza de León, Pedro de [1553]. 1947. *Primera parte de la Crónica del Peru*. vol. 26. Madrid: Biblioteca de Autores Españoles.

Cieza de León, Pedro de [1553]. 1959. *The Incas of Pedro de Cieza de Leon*, H. de Onis (trans.), V. von Hagen (ed.). Norman: University of Oklahoma Press.

Clement, C., and M. Moseley. 1989. Agricultural dynamics in the Andes. In D. Rice, C. Stanish, and P. Scarr, (eds.), *Ecology, Settlement and History in the Osmore Drainage, Peru*. Oxford: British Archaeological Reports, International Series 545(ii), 435–55.

Cobo, Bernabé [1653]. 1890–5. *História del Nuevo Mundo*, Marcos Jiménez de la Espada (ed.), 4 vols. Seville: Biblioteca de Bibliófilos Anadaluces.

Cobo, Bernabé [1653]. 1939. Del templo y edificios de Tihuanacu. In G. Otero (ed.), *Tihuanacu: antología de los principales escritos de los cronistas coloniales, americanistas e historiadores bolivianos*, Biblioteca Boliviana 2, La Paz, Bolivia: Imprenta Artistica, 27–44.

Cobo, Bernabé [1653]. 1979. *History of the Inca Empire*, R. Hamilton (trans. and ed.). Austin: University of Texas Press.

Conklin, W. J. 1991. Tiahuanaco and Huari: Architectural Comparisons and Interpretations. In W. H. Isbell and G. F. McEwan (eds.), *Huari Administrative Structure: Prehistoric Monumental Architecture and State Government*. Washington, D.C.: Dumbarton Oaks Library and Research Collection, 281–92.

Conrad, G. W., and A. A. Demarest. 1984. *Religion and Empire: The Dynamics of Aztec and Inca Expansionism*. New Studies in Archaeology series. Cambridge, England: Cambridge University Press.

Créqui-Monfort, G. de. 1906. Fouilles de la mission scientifique française à Tiahuanaco. Ses recherches archéologiques et ethnographiques en Bolivie, au Chili et dans la République Argentine. *Proceedings Internationaler Amerikanisten Kongress* (Stuttgart) 2, 531–50.

Demarest, A. 1981. *Viracocha: The Nature and Antiquity of the Andean High God*. Monographs of the Peabody Museum 6. Cambridge, Mass.: Peabody Museum Press.

Denevan, W. 1982. Hydraulic agriculture in the American tropics: forms, measures, and recent research. In K. V. Flannery (ed.), *Maya Subsistence: Essays in Honor of Dennis E. Puleston*. New York: Academic Press, 181–203.

Diez de San Miguel, Garci [1567]. 1964. *Visita hecha a la provincia de Chucuito*. Lima, Peru: Casa de la Cultura.

Duviols, P. 1973. Huari y Llacuaz. Agricultores y pastores: un dualismo prehispánico de opposición y complementaridad. *Revista del Museo Nacional* (Lima) 39, 153–87.

Ellwood, R. 1973. *The Feast of Kingship Accession Ceremonies in Ancient Japan*. Tokyo: Sophia University Press.

Erickson, C. 1988. *An Archaeological Investigation of Raised Field Agriculture in the Lake Titicaca Basin of Peru*. Unpublished Ph.D. dissertation, Department of Anthropology, University of Illinois at Urbana.

Fernández, D. 1974. Excavaciones arqueologicas en la Cueva de Huachichocana, Depto. Tumbaya, Provincia Jujuy. *Relaciones de la Sociedad Argentina de Antropología* (Buenos Aires) vol. 8 (new series).

Flores-Ochoa, J. 1983. El cultivo en qocha en la puna sur-andina. In A. Fries (ed.), *Evolución y Tecnica de la Agricultura Andina*. Cusco: Instituto Indígena Interamericana, 45–79.

Garnsey, P. 1988. *Famine and Food Supply in the Graeco-Roman World: Responses to Risk and Crisis*. Cambridge: Cambridge University Press.

Gisbert, T. 1988. *Historia de la Vivienda y los Asentamientos Humanos en Bolivia*. Mexico, D. F.: (Academia Nacional de Ciencias de Bolivia). Instituto Panamericano de Geografía e Historia, Publication no. 431.

Godelier, M. 1978. Infrastructures, societies, and history. *Current Anthropology* 19, 763–71.

Goldstein, P. 1989. *Omo, A Tiwanaku Provincial Center in Moquegua, Peru.*

Unpublished Ph.D. dissertation, Department of Anthropology, The University of Chicago, Chicago.

Graffam, G. 1990. *Raised Fields Without Bureaucracy: An Archaeological Examination of Intensive Wetland Cultivation in the Pampa Koani Zone, Lake Titicaca, Bolivia.* Unpublished Ph.D. dissertation, Department of Anthropology, University of Toronto, Toronto.

Guilett, D. 1987. Terracing and irrigation in the Peruvian highlands. *Current Anthropology* 28(4), 409–30.

Hardman, M. 1979. Jaqi: the linguistic family. *International Journal of American Linguistics* 44, 146–53.

Hardman, M. 1981. Introductory essay. In M. Hardman (ed.), *The Aymara Language in Its Social Context.* Gainesville: University of Florida Social Sciences Monograph 67, 3–17.

Harris, O. 1986. From asymmetry to triangle: symbolic transformations in northern Potosí. In J. Murra, N. Wachtel, and J. Revel (eds.), *Anthropological History of Andean Polities.* Cambridge: Cambridge University Press, 260–79.

Hastings, C., and M. Moseley. 1975. The adobes of Huaca del Sol and Huaca de la Luna. *American Antiquity* 40, 196–203.

Hemming, J. 1970. *The Conquest of the Incas.* New York: Harcourt, Brace, Jovanovich.

Hyslop, J. 1990. *Inca Settlement Planning.* Austin: University of Texas Press.

Idyll, C. 1973. The anchovy crisis. *Scientific American* 228(6), 22–9.

Isbell, B. 1978. *To Defend Ourselves: Ecology and Ritual in an Andean Village.* Austin: University of Texas Institute of Latin American Studies Monographs 47.

Isbell, W. 1983–4. Andean linguistics and culture history: an examination of competing interpretations. *Journal of the Steward Anthropological Society* 15, 241–58.

Jacobs, J. 1970. *The Economy of Cities.* New York: Vintage.

James, D. 1971. Plate tectonic models for the evolution of the central Andes. *Geological Society of America Bulletin* 82, 3325–46.

Kolata, A. 1983. The south Andes. In J. Jennings (ed.), *Ancient South Americans*, San Francisco: W. H. Freeman, 241–85.

Kolata, A. 1986. The agricultural foundations of the Tiwanaku state: a view from the heartland. *American Antiquity* 51, 748–62.

Kolata, A. (ed.). 1989. *Arqueología de Lukurmata,* vol. 2. La Paz, Bolivia: Producciones Puma Punku.

Kolata, A. 1991. The technology and organization of agricultural production in the Tiwanaku state. *Latin American Antiquity* 2, 99–125.

Kolata, A. and C. Ortloff. 1989. Thermal analysis of Tiwanaku raised field systems in the Lake Titicaca basin of Bolivia. *Journal of Archaeological Science* 16, 233–63.

Lamb, H. 1965. Early medieval warm epoch and its sequel. *Journal of Paleogeography, Paleoclimatology and Paleoecology* 1, 13–37.

Lamb, H. 1982. *Climate History and the Modern World.* London and New York: Methuen.

Lansing, S. 1991. *Priests and Programmers: Technologies of Power in the Engineered Landscape of Bali.* Princeton: Princeton University Press.

Lavenu, A. 1981. Origine et évolution néotectonique du lac Titicaca. *Revue d'Hydrobiologie Tropicale* 14, 289–98.

Bibliography 307

Leach, E. 1959. Hydraulic society in Ceylon. *Past and Present* 15, 2–25.

Leyden, B. 1989. Datos polínicos del período Holoceno tardío en el Lago Titicaca, Bolivia: una posible inundación en la Pampa Koani. In A. Kolata (ed.), *Arqueología de Lukurmata*, vol. 2, La Paz, Bolivia: Producciones Puma Punku, 263–74.

Machiavelli, Niccolò [1532]. 1952. *The Prince*, L. Ricci (trans.). New York: Mentor/New American Library of World Literature.

Manzanilla, L., and E. Woodard. 1990. Restos humanos asociados a la pirámide de Akapana (Tiwanaku, Bolivia). *Latin American Antiquity* 1, 133–49.

Matienzo, Juan de [1567]. 1967. *Gobierno del Perú*, vol. 11, G. Lohmann Villena (ed.). Paris and Lima, Peru: Travaux de l'Institut Français d'Etude Andines.

Matos Moctezuma, E. 1987. El simbolismo del Templo Mayor. In E. Boone (ed.), *The Aztec Templo Mayor*. Washington, D.C.: Dumbarton Oaks Research Library and Collection, 185–210.

Mohr-Chávez, K. 1988. The significance of Chiripa in Lake Titicaca basin developments. *Expedition* 30(3), 17–26.

Molina, Cristobal de [1553]. 1916. *Relación de las Fabulas y Ritos de los Incas*. Lima, Peru: San Marti y Cia.

Morris, C., and D. Thompson. 1985. *Huánuco Pampa: An Inca City and Its Hinterland*. London: Thames and Hudson.

Moseley, M. 1975. *The Maritime Foundations of Andean Civilization*. Menlo Park, Calif.: Cummings.

Moseley, M. 1992. *The Incas and Their Ancestors: The Archaeology of Peru*. London: Thames and Hudson.

Moseley, M., R. Feldman, P. Goldstein, and L. Watanabe. 1991. Colonies and conquest: Tiahuanaco and Huari in Moquegua. In W. Isbell and G. McEwan (eds.), *Huari Administrative Structure: Prehistoric Monumental Architecture and State Government*. Washington, D.C.: Dumbarton Oaks Library and Research Collection, 121–40.

Moses, B. 1914. *The Spanish Dependenices in South America*. New York: Harper.

Mujica, E. 1978. Nueva hipótesis sobre el desarollo temprano del altiplano, del Titicaca y de sus areas de interacción. *Arte y Arqueología* (La Paz, Bolivia) 5/6, 285–308.

Mumford, L. 1961. *The City in History: Its Origins, Its Transformations, and Its Prospects*. New York: Harcourt, Brace & World, Inc.

Murra, J. 1968. An Aymara kingdom in 1567. *Ethnohistory* 15(2), 115–51.

Murra, J. 1972. El "control vertical" de un máximo de pisos ecológicos en la economía de las sociedades andinas. In John Murra (ed.), *Visita de la provincia de León de Huánuco*, Ortiz de Zúñiga, Iñigo [1562], 2 vols. Huánuco, Peru: Universidad Nacional Hermilio Valdizen, 427–76.

Nadaillac, M. de [1883]. 1939. La prehistoria de Tihuanacu. In G. Otero (ed.), *Tihuanacu: antología de los principales escritos de los cronistas coloniales, americanistas e historiadores bolivianos*, Biblioteca Boliviana 2. La Paz, Bolivia: Imprenta Artistica, 67–76.

Netherly, P. 1984. The management of late Andean irrigation systems on the north coast of Peru. *American Antiquity* 49, 227–54.

Núñez, L. 1962. Contactos culturales prehispanicos entre la costa y la sub-cordillera andina. *Universidad de Santiago Boletín Informativo* 31, 42–7.

308   *Bibliography*

Núñez, L. 1965. Desarollo cultural prehispanico del norte de Chile. *Revista de Estudios Arqueológicos*, (Antofagasta, Chile) 1, (entire issue).

Núñez, L. 1971. Secuencia y cambio en los asentamientos humanos de la desembocadura del Río Loa en el norte de Chile. *Boletín de la Universidad de Chile* (Santiago) 112, 3–25.

Núñez, L., and T. Dillehay. 1978. *Movilidad Giratoria, Armonía Social y Desarollo en los Andes Meridionales: Patrones de Trafico e Interacción Económica*. Antofagasta, Chile: Universidad del Norte.

Oakland, A. 1987. *Tiwanaku Textile Style from the South Central Andes, Bolivia and North Chile*. Unpublished Ph.D. dissertation, The University of Texas, Austin.

Oakland, A. 1990. Tiwanaku textiles: a view from the provinces. Paper presented at the 30th annual meeting of the Institute of Andean Studies, Berkeley, California.

Oakland, A. 1992. Textiles and ethnicity: Tiwanaku in San Pedro de Atacama, north Chile. *Latin American Antiquity*, 3, 316–340.

Ortloff, C., and A. Kolata. 1989. Hydraulic analysis of Tiwanaku aqueduct structures at Lukurmata and Pajchiri, Bolivia. *Journal of Archaeological Science* 16, 513–35.

Parsons, J. 1968. An estimate of size and population for Middle Horizon Tiahuanaco, Bolivia. *American Antiquity* 33, 243–5.

Platt, T. 1986. Mirrors and maize: the concept of yanantin among the Macha of Bolivia. In J. Murra, N. Wachtel, and J. Revel (eds.), *Anthropological History of Andean Polities*. Cambridge: Cambridge University Press, 228–59.

Polo de Ondegardo, J. [1559]. 1916. De los errores y supersticiones de los Indios, sacadas del tratado y averiguación que hizo el Licenciado Polo. In *Colección de Libros y Documentos Referentes a la Historia del Peru* (Lima) ser. 1, vol. 3, 3–43.

Polo de Ondegardo, J. [1571] 1916. Relación de los fundamentos acerca del notable daño que resulta de no guardar a los indios sus fueros. *Colección de libros y documentos referentes a la historia del Perú*, series I, vol. 3, H. H. Urteaga (ed.). Lima: Sanmartí, 45–188.

Ponce, C. 1961. Informe de labores. *Centro de Investigaciones Arqueológicas en Tiwanaku*, (La Paz, Bolivia), Publicación 1 (entire issue).

Ponce, C. 1969. *Descripción Sumaria del Templete Semisubterraneo*. La Paz, Bolivia: Librería Los Amigos del Libro.

Ponce, C. 1970. *Wankarani y Chiripa y su Relación con Tiwanaku*. La Paz, Bolivia: Academia Nacional de Ciencias, Publicación 25.

Ponce, C. 1971. *Pumapunku*. La Paz, Bolivia: Academia Nacional de Ciencias, Publicación 22.

Ponce, C. 1972. *Tiwanaku: Espacio, Tiempo y Cultura: Ensayo de Sintesis Arqueológica*. La Paz, Bolivia: Academía Nacional de Ciencias, Publicación 30.

Ponce, C. 1980. *Panorama de la Arqueología Boliviana*, 2d. ed. La Paz, Bolivia: Editorial "Juventud."

Posnansky, A. 1914. *Una Metrópoli Prehistórica en la America del Sur*. Berlin: D. Reimer (E. Vohsen).

Posnansky, A. 1945. *Tihuanacu: The Cradle of American Man*, 2 vols. New York: J. J. Augustin.

Pulgar Vidal, J. 1946. *Historia y Geografía del Peru*. Lima: Universidad Nacional de San Marcos.

Reinhard, J. 1987. Chavín y Tiahuanaco. *Boletín de Lima* 50, 29–52.

Rice, D., and P. Rice. 1984. Lessons from the Maya. *Latin American Research Review* 19(3), 7–33.

Rice, D., C. Stanish, and P. Scarr (eds.) 1989. *Ecology, Settlement and History in the Osmore Drainage, Peru*. Oxford: British Archaeological Reports International Series 545(i and ii).

Rivera, M. 1977. *Prehistoric Cultural Chronology of Northern Chile*. Unpublished Ph.D. dissertation, University of Wisconsin, Madison.

Rivera, O. 1978. Quenasfenas: un sitio Chiripa. *Proceedings of La Segunda Reunion de las Jornadas Peruano Bolivianas de Estudio Científico del Altiplano y Sur del Peru*. Internal documents of the Instituto Nacional de Arqueología de Bolivias, La Paz, Bolivia.

Robinson, D. 1964. *Peru in Four Dimensions*. Lima: American Studies Press.

Rostovtzeff, M. 1971. *Rome*. J. D. Duff (trans.), E. Bickerman (ed.). Oxford: Oxford University Press.

Rowe, J. 1946. Inca culture at the time of the Spanish conquest. In J. Steward (ed.), *Handbook of South American Indians*, vol. 2. Washington, D.C.: Bureau of American Ethnology, 183–330.

Rowe, J. 1963. Urban settlements in ancient Peru. *Ñawpa Pacha* 1, 1–27.

Rowe, J. 1982. Inca policies and institutions relating to the cultural unification of the empire. In G. Collier, R. Rosaldo, and J. Wirth (eds.), *The Inca and Aztec States 1400–1800*. New York: Academic Press, 93–118.

Saalman, H. 1968. *Medieval Cities*. New York: George Brazilier.

Saignes, T. 1986. En busca del poblamiento etnico de los Andes Bolivianos (Siglos XV y XVI). *Avances de Investigación* 3. La Paz, Bolivia: Museo Nacional de Etnografía y Folklore (entire issue).

Salomon, F. 1986. Vertical politics on the Inka frontier. In J. Murra, N. Wachtel, and J. Revel (eds.), *Anthropological History of Andean Polities*. Cambridge: Cambridge University Press, 89–117.

Sánchez-Albornoz, N. 1978. *Indios y Tributos en el Alto Peru*. Lima: Instituto de Estudios Peruanos.

Sarmiento de Gamboa, P. [1572]. 1907. *History of the Incas*, C. Markham (trans.). Cambridge: Hakluyt Society, 33–4.

Schaedel, R. 1988. Andean World View: Hierarchy or Reciprocity, Regulation or Control? *Current Anthropology* 29, 768–75.

Servant, M., and J. Fontes. 1978. Les lacs quaternaires des haut plateaux des Andes Boliviennes, premieres interpretations plaeoclimatiques. *Cahiers ORSTOM, Série Geologie* 10, 9–24.

Squier, E. G. 1877. *Peru: Incidents of Travel and Exploration in the Land of the Incas*. New York: Harper Brothers.

Stanish, C. 1991. *Archaeological Survey in the Juli-Pomata region of the Titicaca basin, Peru*. Preliminary report to the National Science Foundation, manuscript on file with the National Science Foundation, Washington, D.C.

Stanish, C. 1992. *Ancient Andean Political Economy*. Austin: University of Texas Press.

Stark, L. 1976. *Historia y Distribución de los Dialectos Quichuas en la Sierra Ecuatoriana*. Ambato, Ecuador: Instituto Inter-Andino de Desarollo.

Stark, L. 1979. History and distribution of Argentinian Quechua. *Abstracts of the 43rd International Congress of Americanists*, Vancouver, Canada.

Sutherland, C. 1991. *Methodological, Stylistic and Functional Ceramic*

Analysis: The Surface Collection at Akapana East, Tiwanaku. Unpublished Master's Thesis, Department of Anthropology, University of Chicago, Chicago.

Tello, J. C. 1942. Origen y desarollo de las civilizaciones prehistoricas andinas. *37 Congreso Internacional de Americanistas, Actas y memorias* 1, 589–720.

Thompson, L., J. Bolzan, H. Brecher, P. Kruss, E. Mosley-Thompson, and K. Jezek. 1982. Geophysical investigations of the tropical Quelccaya ice cap. *Journal of Glaciology* 28(98), 57–68.

Thompson, L., M. Davis, E. Mosley-Thompson, and K.-b. Liu. 1988. Pre-Incan agricultural activity recorded in dust layers in two tropical ice cores. *Nature* 336, 763–5.

Thompson, L., L. Hastenrath, and B. Arnao. 1979. Climate ice core records from the tropical Quelccaya ice cap. *Science* 203, 1240–3.

Thompson, L., and E. Mosley-Thompson. 1987. Evidence of abrupt climatic change during the last 1500 years recorded in ice cores from the tropical Quelccaya ice cap. In W. Berger and L. Labeyrie (eds.), *Abrupt Climatic Change Evidence and Implications*, NATO ASI, Series C, Mathematics and Physical Sciences, vol. 216. Boston: D. Reidel Publishing Company, 99–110.

Thompson, L., and E. Mosley-Thompson. 1989. One-half millennium of tropical climate variability as recorded in the stratigraphy of the Quelccaya ice cap, Peru. In D. H. Peterson (ed.), *Aspects of Climate Variability in the Pacific and Western Americas. Geophysical Union Monograph* 55 (17). Washington, D.C.: American Geophysical Union, 445.

Thompson, L., E. Mosley-Thompson, J. Bolzan, and B. Koci. 1985. A 1500 year record of tropical precipitation records in ice cores from the Quelccaya ice cap, Peru. *Science* 229, 971–3.

Torero, A. 1970. Lingüística e historia social andina. *Anales Científicos* Lima: Universidad Agraria, 8, 231–64.

Torero, A. 1974. *El Quechua y la Historia Social Andina.* Lima: Universidad Ricardo Palma.

Tosi, J., Jr. 1960. Zonas de vida natural en el Perú: memoria explicativa sobre el mapa ecológica del Perú. *Boletín Técnico* (Lima: Instituto Interamericano de Ciencias Agricolas de la OEA, Zona Andina) 5, (entire issue).

Townsend, R. 1979. *State and Cosmos in the Art of Tenochtitlan.* Washington, D.C.: Dumbarton Oaks Library and Research Collection.

Troll, C. 1968. The cordilleras of the tropical Americas Aspects of climate, phytogeographical and agrarian ecology. In C. Troll (ed.), *Geoecology of the mountainous regions of the tropical Americas. Colloquium Geographicum* (Bonn: Ferd Dümmlers Verlag) 9, 15–56.

Valcarcel, L. 1935. Litoesculturas y ceramica de Pukara. *Revista del Museo Nacional* (Lima) 4, 25–8.

Von Däniken, E. 1969. *Chariots of the Gods?* New York: Bantam Books.

Wachtel, N. 1982. The mitimas of the Cochabamba valley: the colonization policy of Huayna Capac. In G. Collier, R. Rosaldo, and J. Wirth (eds.), *The Inca and Aztec States 1400–1800.* New York: Academic Press, 199–235.

Wachtel, N. 1986. Men of the water: the Uru problem (sixteenth and seventeenth centuries). In J. Murra, N. Wachtel, and J. Revel (eds.),

Anthropological History of Andean Polities. Cambridge: Cambridge University Press, 283–310.

Watanabe, L., M. Moseley, and F. Cabieses (eds.). 1990. *Trabajos Arqueológicos en Moquegua, Peru.* Lima: Programa Contisuyo del Museo Peruano de Ciencias de La Salud, Editorial Escuela Nueva.

Weberbauer, A. 1945. *El Mundo Vegetal de los Andes Peruanos.* Lima: Ministerio de Agricultura.

Weil, T. 1974. *Area Handbook for Bolivia.* Washington, D.C.: United States Government Printing Office.

Wheatley, P. 1971. *The Pivot of the Four Quarters: A Preliminary Enquiry into the Origins and Character of the Ancient Chinese City.* Chicago: Aldine.

Wirrmann, D., and L. Oliviera Almeida. 1987. Low Holocene level (7700–3650 years ago) of Lake Titicaca (Bolivia). *Paleogeography, Paleoclimatology and Paleoecology 59,* 315–23.

Wright, A. 1977. The cosmology of the Chinese city. In W. Skinner (ed.), *The City in Late Imperial China.* Palo Alto, Calif.: Stanford University Press.

Zuidema, R. T. 1983. Llama sacrifices and computation: the roots of the Inca calendar in Huari-Tiahuanaco culture. *Acts of the Congress on Ethnoastronomy.* Washington, D.C., in press.

Zuidema, R. T. 1990. *Inca Civilization in Cuzco.* Austin: University of Texas Press.

Index

Abercrombie, T., 215
acllahuasi (house of chosen women), 279
agriculture: and crops in Andes, 51–53, 182–98, 270; and double cropping, 198, 200–201, 204; and fertilizers, 186–87; and heat conservation, 188–90, 295; and irrigation, 183, 189, 216–17, 293; and public construction, 223–28; raised field, 182–98, 214–16, 294; and social organization, 205–31; and surplus crops, 219, 230, 246
Akapana: green gravel of, 109, 111
Akapana complex, 97, 99, 102, 104–29, 249, 302
Alasaa, *see* Arasaya
Albarracín-Jordan, J., 85, 296
Almeida, Oliveira, 43
Almeida, Wirrmann, 43
alpaca, 46, 57, 59, 83, 182, 186, 232
altiplano (Andean high plateau), 15, 19–20, 33, 81, 181, 204; climate and vegetation of, 44–45, 180, 185; and Wankarani, 63
Amazon River, 48, 50–51
Andean high plateau, *see altiplano*
Anderson, I., 289
Andes: highland-lowland relationships, 57–58; and nomadism, 56–57; origins of people, 56–57; physiographic regions of, 40–51; spirituality in, 22
Andesuyo province, 6
aqueducts, 227–28

Arapa site, 248
Arasaya, 24, 100–101
architecture, 3–4, 17–18, 90–93, 105–15, 267
ayllus (family groups), 61–63, 65, 88, 99, 145, 175; and agriculture, 207, 215; and herding, 232
Aymara Indians, 8–10, 12, 30, 100, 237–41, 302; kingdoms (*señoríos*) of, 22–23, 54, 145, 273, 299; spiritual leaders (*yatiri*) of, 19, 49, 119. *See also* Qari; Qusi
Azángaro, Lake, 238

Bali, 216–17
Bandelier, Adolph, 100–101
barrios (neighborhoods), 164, 172, 176
Bastien, J., 215
Bennett, Wendell, 29–30, 63, 104
Berdan, F., 170
Bermann, M., 294, 297
Berthelot, René, 84
Bertonio, Ludovico, 8, 100
Betanzos, Juan de, 6
Binford, M., 285
Bird, R., 34
Bolivia, 11, 13, 15, 16, 58, 181, 302; Pacajes province, 236, 300; Potosí, 11, 301
Bolivian National Institute of Archaeology, *see* INAR
Bouysse-Cassagne, T., 8, 299
Brenner, M., 285
Broda, J., 134, 267
Browman, D., 64, 232–34, 272
Brush, S., 53

Calancha, Antonio de la, 5
calendar, agricultural, 135, 143, 148, 231–32, 247
canals, 224–30, 285, 292
cancha (farm-house enclosure), 61
cardinal directions, *see* Solar path
Castelnau, Francis de, 12
Catari River, 181, 224–25, 292
causeways, 223–28
cemeteries: Chen Chen, 253; Coyo, 275–79; and dedicatory burial, 117–18, 122–24; and offerings, 157–60; shaft-and-chamber, 156, 159–60
censuses (*visitas*), 23
ceramics, *see* pottery
Cerro Baul, 255
Chalon, Pablo, 12
Chavez, Karen, 78, 248
Chavez, Sergio, 78, 248
Chijijawira workshop, 170–72
Chila mountain range, 88–89, 109
Chile, 19, 41, 76
Chimor kingdom, 170
Chipaya Indians, 46, 59
Chiripa: people of, 83–85, 215, 245; pottery of, 63–64, 268; and religion, 65–69, 161
Chiripa complex, 63–70
Chucuito, Lake, *See* Titicaca, Lake
Chucuito province, 239
chullpas (mortuary towers), 145
Chunchukala complex, 97, 104
chunka (decimal household), 212
Cieza de León, Pedro de, 1, 3–5, 21, 97, 104, 187, 211–12
Clement, C., 293–94
climate: and collapse of Tiwanaku, 284–91
Cobo, Bernabé, 7–8, 145–47, 206–9, 234–35
coca, 49–50, 52, 251, 270
Cochabamba Valley, 49–50, 59, 243, 269–71
cochas (sunken gardens), 292–94
Collasuyu, 1, 4, 6, 8, 11, 34, 47
Copacabana peninsula, 63, 78
Cordillera Real, 47, 97, 181
Courty, George, 149
Créqui-Monfort, G. de, 149
crops: maize, 52, 59, 251, 259, 271; potato, 193–94, 198, 200–201; *quinoa* plant, 46, 49, 59, 155, 190, 192, 238
Cuzco, 1, 3–4, 76, 98, 99, 109, 142–47

Demarest, A., 148
Denevan, W., 200
Desaguadero River, 34, 204, 238, 245
Diez de San Miguel, Garci, 22, 27, 239, 273
Dillehay T., 57, 299
drain, subterreanean, 111–15, 129, 134, 155
drought, 285–87, 295
duality, *see* moiety
Duviols, P., 101–2

ecology, 51–55, 148
economy, 51–59, 175–76, 182, 240, 264
Elite, 141, 148–49, 156, 182, 204–6, 231, 281; as divine intermediaries, 161. *See also kurakas*
Ellwood, Robert, 92
environment, 179–80
Erickson, C., 198, 214–16
ethnographics, 32–35

Fernández, D., 46
fishers, 231–40
Flores-Ochoa, J., 292
Fontes, J., 43

Garnsey, P., 205
Gateway of the Sun, *see* sculptures
Godelier, M., 163
Goldstein, P., 252, 256, 259, 263, 268
Graffam, G., 296
Guaman Poma de Ayala: Felipe, 263
Guillet, D., 217, 219

Hardman, M., 34
Hastings, C., 214
Hemming, J., 50
herders, 231–40
huacas (spiritual points of reference), 109, 111, 117, 142, 249
Huakaypata plaza, 109–10
huari (sedentary agriculturalists), 101–2
Huayna Capac, 4, 270–71
hunu (decimal unit), 212
Hyslop, J., 98, 109

iconography: Andean cross, 104–6; ornamentative, 166; religious, 58, 78, 117, 272
Idyll, C., 41

Illimani, Mount, 97
INAR (*Instituto Nacional de Arqueologica de Bolivia*), 30
Inca: decimal system of, 212–13; empire of, 1, 21, 34, 43, 50, 250, 299–300; Illapa deity of, 147; and labor, 206–13; origin of rulers, 4, 10; in Tiwanaku, 121
Isbell, W., 33

Jichuta, 100
Juli-Pomata region, 100, 247, 248

Kalasasaya complex, 30, 78, 97, 104–6, 117, 135, 143–48
kamani (crop guardians), 219, 222
Kantatayita complex, 106
keros, see pottery
Kheri Kala complex, 104, 106
Khonko Wankané, city of, 103, 131, 174
Kolata, Alan, 64, 176, 183, 189, 215, 219, 227, 297
Kot'suñs, see Uru people
kurakas (big men), 62, 76, 100, 207–13, 260–63. See also Elite

labor: as barter, 175; surplus, 205–6; as taxation, 26, 206–9, 251. See also *mit'a*
Lakaya village, 190, 198, 223
Lamb, H., 289–90
language: Aymara, 33, 34, 69, 70, 299; in Collasuyu, 34–35; Jaqi, 34, 67; Pukina, 34–35, 67, 70, 98, 216; Quechua, 10, 33, 34; Tiwanaku, 33–34, 241; Uru-Chipaya, 34, 67, 216
Lansing, S., 216
La Paz, city of, 267
Lauca River, 46
Leach, E., 216
linguistics, 32–35
llacuaz (mobile herding groups), 101–2
llama: bones, 119, 122, 160, 166, 233; caravans, 19, 57–58, 63, 175, 224, 264, 273–75; fetus, 267; figures, 139; uses for, 46–47, 57, 83, 182, 186, 205, 221, 232–37
Lukurmata city, 64, 103, 131, 174, 187, 223, 227, 296
Lupaqa kingdoms, 23–27, 100, 239, 300

Maassa, see Masaya
Machaca, 33, 181, 204
Machiavelli, Niccolo: *The Prince*, 255
mallku, see Qari; Qusi
Manzanilla, L., 118
marriage alliances, 211, 241, 277, 279
Masaya, 24, 100–101
Mathews, J., 85, 296
Matienzo, Juan de, 260–63
Maya civilization, 29, 36–37
minka, see *mit'a*
mit'a (*mit'anni*) (labor service as taxation), 26, 210–11, 214, 223
moat, symbolic meaning of, 90–93, 131
Moctezuma, Matos, 267
Mohr-Chávez, K., 64
moiety, 7, 8, 271; and government, 23–27, 88, 100–102, 129, 218; in labor, 26; and religion, 79–81
Molina, Cristobal de, 6–7, 187
montaña, 40, 48. See also *yungas*
Moquegua Valley, 243, 252, 255–56, 268–69, 294
Moseley, M., 41, 214, 252, 293–94
Moseley-Thompson, E., 286, 289
Moses, B., 300
mounds: burial, 76, 222; house, 221–22; platform, 219–22
Mujica, E., 70, 268
Mumford, L., 88
mummies, 117, 122–24, 145–47, 157
Murra, John, 23, 51, 54, 56, 100

Nadaillac, Marquise de, 13
Nahua race, 13
Netherly, Patricia, 23, 218–19
Núñez, L., 56, 57, 299

Oakland, A., 143, 276–79
Oje city, 103
Omo settlement, 253–69
Ortloff, C., 183, 189, 227
Osmore River, 255–56

Pachayachachic, 5
Pajchiri city, 103, 131, 174, 223, 227, 292
Palace of the Multicolored Rooms, 152–60 passim
paleoecology, 37
Pampa Koani region, 197, 199, 204, 215–30 passim, 292
Paz Zamorra, Jaime, 302

Peru, 1, 19, 34, 41, 58; Chicama, 218; Colca Valley of, 217–18; Huatta district of, 214; Puno, 76, 197
Peruvian Ministry of Agriculture, 197
Polo de Ondegardo, J., 22, 109
Ponce Sangines, Carlos, 30, 59, 61, 100–101, 143, 175
Poopó, Lake, 34, 43–44, 245, 275
Posnansky, Arthur, 13–16, 90, 104, 108–9, 148, 162
pottery, 117, 259, 263, 270; *keros*, 75, 119, 124, 139, 168, 222; Pukara, 78, 268
Pukara culture: art style of, 70–78, 268; early, 59, 245, 248–49
Pukina, 67, 241
Pulgar Vidal, J., 51
Puma Punku, 97, 99, 103, 129–34, 302
Putuni complex, 97, 104, 149–53, 161–64

Qaluyu complex, 70
Qari, 24, 100, 239. *See also* Aymara Indians
Qeremita site, 275
Qolla kingdom, 300
Qoricancha temple, 147
Quelccaya glacier, 285–90, 294
Quimsachata mountain range, 109, 111, 116
quipi stones, 212, 261
Qusi, 24, 100, 239. *See also* Aymara Indians

rainfall, 41, 44, 81, 116, 194, 217, 285–87, 293; and flooding, 111, 199, 224–28
Recuay region, 101–2
Reinhard, J., 109
religion: and ancestor worship, 145, 147; and Tiwanaku, 22, 58–59, 81, 95, 117, 245–46, 249–50, 263; and Wankarani, 62–69
Rice, P., 36
Rice D., 36, 252, 297
ritual: agricultural, 247, 269; and hallucinogens, 139–41, 166, 272
Rivera, M., 76
Rivera, O., 63
Robinson, D., 41
Rostovtzeff, Michael, 282
Rowe, J., 70, 126, 208, 279

Saalman, H., 296
Sacsahuaman, 210

Salar de Coipasa, 44, 238
Salar de Uyuni, 43
Salar Poopó, 43, 238. *See also* Poopó, Lake
Salomon, F., 54
San Pedro de Atacama oasis, 272, 275–79
Sarmiento de Gamboa, Pedro, 6
Schaedel, R., 29
sculptures, 11–13, 17–18, 58, 90, 108, 135–49, 248, 268; *chachapumas*, 126; Gateway of the Sun, 16, 99, 119, 148–49, 248; Yaya-Mama style, 78–81. *See also huacas*
Semi-subterranean Temple complex, 29, 117, 135–43, 249, 268
Servant, M., 43
Solar path: and urban design, 97–98, 143
Spanish conquerers, 1, 10–11, 22, 300–301
Squier, Ephraim, 27–29
staircase: at Putuni, 149–52; symbolism of, 97–98, 117
Stanish, C., 247, 248
stelae: Bennett, 135, 139–42, 149, 249, 268; Ponce, 143–45, 149, 268
suyu (strips of field for farming), 209, 271

Taypikala, 8, 88–90
taypi (place of convergence), 8, 88–89
Tello, Julio, 78
Templo Mayor, 134, 267
textiles, 266–67, 269, 277
Thompson, L., 285–86, 289
Thunupa, 148, 248
Tiahuanaco, 3, 5, 109; ceramic phases of, 29
Tikuna, 100
Titicaca, Lake, 5, 12, 18, 22, 34, 49, 56; basin of, 45–46, 54, 58, 98, 198, 219, 245, 284; early settlement around, 56–59; evolution of, 43–44; and fishing, 238–40; as resource for Chiripa, 69–70; and Solar path, 97
Tiwanaku: and agricultural decline, 283–98; and agriculture, 27, 30, 45, 82, 116, 182–98, 246; architecture of, 58, 99; artisans of, 169–70; ceremonial centers of, 29–30, 98–103; civic-ceremonial core of, 103–4;

decline of, 282–302; expansion of territory, 243–81; four quadrants of, 98–103; geopolitics of, 19, 40, 49–50; kingship in, 92, 98, 284, 298; mythic-history of, 1–20; population of, 199–205; state of, 49–50, 58, 223, 246; urban order of, 84, 91–96. *See also* Taypikala
Tiwanaku, archaeology of, 18–19, 27–32, 58, 78, 89, 121, 178, 252, 269; chronologic period III, 78, 219; chronologic period IV, 78, 132, 204, 219, 222, 247, 275; chronologic period V, 153, 160, 164, 204, 219, 227, 247, 285, 294; Classic civilization, 29, 76, 78, 122, 268
Tiwanaku people: costumes of, 166; and creation myth, 5–10; occupation of, 82–83; precursors of, 59–81; social classes of, 88, 90, 91–92, 160–76
Tiwanaku Valley, 30, 181
Toledo, Francisco de, 238
Torata River, 255
Torero, A., 34
Tosi, J., Jr., 51
Townsend, R., 111
Troll, C., 51
Tropical forest, 40, 50–51

Tuma Tumani ceremonial center, 247
Tumilaca River, 255

Umasuyu, 8, 88–89, 98
Urcosuyu, 8, 88–89, 98
Uru people, 238–41, 245

Valcarcel, L., 73
Viracocha, Contiti, 6–7, 9, 88
Viracocha, Tocapa, 7, 9
Viracocha, Ymay Mama, 7, 9
Von Däniken, E., 17

Wachtel, Nathan, 34, 238–39, 271
Wankarani complex, 59–63, 245
war trophies, 125–26
Watanabe, L., 252
Weberbauer, A., 51
Weil, T., 180
Wheatley, Paul, 84, 88, 98, 111, 142
women, 279
Woodward, E., 118
Wright, A., 84

yanapaqhuna (court retainers), 26, 102
Yayes, town of, 223
yungas area, 48–49, 54, 89, 244–45, 250–72. *See also montaña*

Zuidema, R. T., 98–99, 99, 135, 141, 148